THE LEAGUE OF NATIONS UNION
1918–1945

THE LEAGUE OF NATIONS UNION

1918–1945

by

DONALD S. BIRN

CLARENDON PRESS. OXFORD
1981

Oxford University Press, Walton Street, Oxford OX2 6DP

OXFORD   LONDON   GLASGOW

NEW YORK   TORONTO   MELBOURNE   WELLINGTON

KUALA LUMPUR   SINGAPORE   HONG KONG   TOKYO

DELHI   BOMBAY   CALCUTTA   MADRAS   KARACHI

NAIROBI   DAR ES SALAAM   CAPE TOWN

Published in the United States
by Oxford University Press, New York

British Library Cataloguing in Publication Data

Birn, Donald S
   The League of Nations Union.
   1. League of Nations Union—History
   I. Title
   327'.172'0941   JX1975.L45   80–41064
ISBN 0–19–822650–0

*Typeset by Oxprint Ltd, Oxford
Printed in Great Britain
at the University Press, Oxford
by Eric Buckley
Printer to the University*

Contents

Abbreviations

CAB	Cabinet Office Papers, Public Record Office, London
EC	Executive Committee of the League of Nations Union
GM	Gilbert Murray Papers, Bodleian Library, Oxford
HW	*Headway*
LNU	League of Nations Union Papers, British Library of Political and Economic Science, London
NA	Norman Angell Papers, Ball State University Library, Muncie, Indiana
NLW	Welsh National Council of the League of Nations Union Papers, National Library of Wales, Aberystwyth
RC	Cecil Papers, British Library, London
21YR	'21 Years; LNU 1918/1939', MS

Acknowledgements

The author wishes to express gratitude to the following persons and institutions for permission to use copyright material under their control: The Controller of Her Majesty's Stationery Office (Crown copyright material in the Public Record Office, London); the United Nations Association of Great Britain and Northern Ireland (records of the League of Nations Union); Professor A. K. S. Lambton (papers of Lord Robert Cecil) and Alexander Murray (papers of Gilbert Murray).

Research for this book was made possible by support from the State University of New York Foundation and the Richardson Institute for Peace Research.

Introduction

> If the new effort after world peace fails, as on a cold material calculation of the chances appears most likely, I think that scientific historians, if any survive, will feel a tragic interest in this strange attempt of a past age, so alien from the atmosphere in which they will then be living, to establish a united and peaceful world . . . Even if, like most human efforts, it ends in a confused mixture between success and failure, the efforts of the pioneers will still possess the ordinary degree of interest attaching to such things. Gilbert Murray, *From the League to UN* (London, 1948), 2.

The League of Nations Union started in 1918 with the merger of two societies working for the establishment of a world organization. It became the largest and most influential society in the British peace movement, played an important role in inter-war politics, and launched educational programmes that had a lasting impact on British schools. When the United Nations Organization appeared at the end of World War Two, the Union transformed itself into the United Nations Association. The experience of the LNU raises significant questions about the role of pressure groups in party politics, the influence of public opinion on foreign policy, the formation of 'middle opinion' in the 1930s, the failure of a popular front in Britain and why opposition to the National Government was ineffective. It is also relevant for those with an interest in the comparative study of peace movements and voluntary societies and in the doctrine of collective security.

Despite these claims for attention, the League of Nations Union has received little notice from scholars until recently. This may be explained in part by the difficulties which confronted students of the subject. More likely, it reflects our generation's attitude towards the League of Nations itself. Writers on the inter-war period have generally either ignored the League or downgraded it as unworkable, as an unrealistic extension of liberalism into the arena of international politics. That this attitude should affect their judgement of the LNU is natural, but it does not reckon with the way the Union tried to establish its own cause as distinct from the League. In the late 1930s LNU leaders turned to new solutions which did not involve the League directly, as they sought to promote the idea of collective security through a 'popular front' alliance while relegating to the League the tasks of social and economic development.

Another obstacle to our understanding of the League movement is its conception of public opinion. 'In a democratic age', Lord Robert Cecil wrote in 1919, 'everything depends on public opinion. This means that the public must have an opinion on international affairs, and that its opinion must be right.'[1] This sort of rhetoric left internationalists wide open for attack as 'utopian' in the late 1930s. For, as E. H. Carr could observe in *The Twenty Years' Crisis 1919–1939*, public opinion 'was almost as often wrong-headed as it was impotent'.[2]

If we are to keep Cecil's remarks in perspective we should not interpret them literally. It is a commonplace that police and courts cannot enforce a law unless the law enjoys broad acceptance. Public opinion, in the broadest sense, determines whether the police will be able to enforce the law within any society, and Wilsonian rhetoric about international society can be understood at one level as making an analagous observation. The policeman may need a gun, but when all is working well he does not have to fire it. The LNU never took its faith in opinion so far as to espouse unilateral disarmament, and indeed it wanted to strengthen the 'police'—the League's collective security machinery. But it recognized that in a democracy opinion had to support the use of force.

The LNU's emphasis on the primacy of opinion served a practical purpose, reassuring the public that stronger sanctions might never be needed to keep the peace. Like many other aspects of internationalist dogma it has to be considered in context, as part of the programme of a political movement. The internal dynamics of the LNU help explain its policies as responses to the problems of how to win government support, restrain over-enthusiastic or dissident members, appeal to the loyalty of Conservative sympathizers, finance activities, and gain new recruits. Important tendencies, such as the neutralization of League opinion in domestic politics in the 1920s, are comprehensible when considered in relation to these factors. The process of decision-making within the LNU thus becomes an essential element in this study.

To a great extent the organization reflected the views of one man, Edgar Algernon Robert Cecil, Viscount Cecil of Chelwood. His long-time colleague in the Union, Philip Noel-Baker, said of him that 'no statesman since Mr. Gladstone has had so great a personal following in this country as Lord Cecil had at the time of the Peace Ballot'.[3] Cecil's political career and the Union's course are closely intertwined. His dilemma—how to combine leadership of an opinion bloc with the role of an 'insider' in Westminster— was also the Union's. Cecil worked closely in the LNU with Gilbert Murray, a Professor of Greek at Oxford University. In the context of this study, Murray—a Liberal academic—was very much the politician, constantly searching for the middle ground on any issue to keep people happy. Cecil—the Conservative politician—was more the visionary, less concerned than Murray about the 'wretched machine' they had built to support the League. Murray could write to a friend in 1931 that 'Cecil has been infuriating or frightening his Tory colleagues on the Executive, and I have the work of the world keeping them together . . .'[4]

The League of Nations Union was not created to support Cecil but to popularize the League and the new principles of international relations which came with it. This cause was not controversial—as unilateral nuclear disarmament became a generation later—so it was not easy to characterize what being an LNU member meant. The Union did not gather much information on its own membership, and without data it is not possible to do more than offer a few generalizations about who belonged. Some of these emerge from a 1930 poll of members on 'Public Opinion and the League'. This revealed that Leaguers themselves thought that

the lower middle class, or simply and more generally, the middle class, are the most favourable to the League. On the whole, clergy, teachers and women . . . are held to be favourable, and businessmen unfavourable. A good many replies suggest that the Free Churches are generally favourable, and there appears to be a consensus of opinion that hostility to the League is to be found largely among comfortable persons retired from the Services.[5]

There were a few generalizations about the composition of the membership on which everyone agreed. It had much less support from Conservatives than from Liberals and Labourites. The League cause had more support in England than in Wales or Scotland. The support of the Free Churches had been assumed from the start by LNU organizers; the minister would be the first person they would call on when they arrived in a new town hoping to establish a branch.[6]

Other generalizations of a more subjective sort were often heard. One of the Union's top staff members, troubled by the prospects of gaining more support from the business-oriented Rotary Club in 1934, mused that the 'Union seemed to attract the type of adherent who is a positive anathema to a somewhat hard-boiled businessman and the branch is consequently characterized as soft and unworthy of attention'.[7] Any capsule description of over a million individuals is bound to be inadequate or more revealing of the observer than of his subject. But even so, the LNU's popular image is worth noting. It, more than the chapter and verse of a policy pronouncement, is what a Cabinet minister, newspaper editor or trade union leader probably had in mind when he dealt with the Union .

The LNU appeared to be very much a middle-class do-gooder movement, high-minded and respectable, basically moral in content and attractive to 'liberals' of all parties. It did have pacifist and leftist members who were more in the tradition of radical dissent than of liberal high-mindedness. However, the group as a whole—even where it advocated disarmament or internationalism, which could have been radical causes—was so cautious in its advocacy that it remained thoroughly safe and respectable. In order to remain respectable, to keep in touch with those in power, Union leaders did not follow their analyses through to unpleasant conclusions. While the League cause might have been far-reaching in its implications, and there is truth in A. J. P. Taylor's jibe that 'considered in the abstract, the League was even more revolutionary than socialism', the point is that the LNU kept its discussions so polite and academic that its implications were not reached until it was too late.[8]

Critics of the LNU had categorized it in the 1920s as a bunch of do-gooder pacifists, and when in the 1930s it emerged as a centre of opposition to the National Government's appeasement policies it was difficult to understand. As one student of public opinion put it: 'Lord Cecil demanding firm military action was not, to those who understood and admired him, behaving inconsistently; but to those who disliked him and misunderstood him his conduct seemed queer.'[9] This kind of confusion led to fuzziness in discussing its role later. Were its members just 'cranks'. as Neville Chamberlain described them, men who had been so infuriated by the 1935 Government White Paper proposing rearmament that they were determined to oppose the governments of the day?[10] Were they also to be indicted, along with others in the peace movement, for blocking rearmament and sapping the public's will to fight?

Many historians have been ready to repeat the sweeping indictments of the past uncritically. One writes of the 'consistent opposition of . . . the idealists of the League of Nations Union and other pacifist organizations towards rearmament'.[11] This sort of generalization robs history of a layer of meaning. It blurs the important distinctions between internationalist and pacifist, between Baldwin, who had the power to disarm Britain, and Cecil, who did not. It overlooks the LNU's turn towards rearmament and carries on a debate in the polemical 'Guilty Men' style which has outlived its usefulness. Others have recognized the Union's importance in their studies of particular episodes or themes in the inter-war period, but generalized about the Union or its leaders from an intensive study of only one period, which is risky.[12]

This study will not, perhaps, eliminate all confusion about the League of Nations Union. The group was too big and too involved in matters political, educational, social, and religious to fit into any neat category. If it succeeds, it should at least promote a more critical discussion of the Union's work and place in history.

Chapter I

A New Departure

By the time the League of Nations Union was established in November 1918, the idea of a world peacekeeping organization had already been generally accepted in Britain.[1] The outbreak of World War One had demonstrated to the British public that traditional diplomatic methods could not be trusted to keep the peace. As the struggle dragged to an end the League of Nations emerged as the logical alternative to the 'international anarchy' of the past. New enough to promise solutions, the League approach had become familiar enough through wartime agitation to attract wide support. It brought to world politics some of the same liberal precepts which had stamped the British political experience: a sense of moral purpose, parliamentary procedure, and a faith that differences could be resolved peacefully.

The way was paved for this new approach to international relations by the small groups of intellectuals and politicians who began to meet for discussions soon after the outbreak of war in 1914. G. Lowes Dickinson, a classicist at Cambridge, sparked the creation of one group which met in London to study proposals for preventing future wars. Brushing aside the official explanation of the genesis of the war, that German militarism was the sole cause, Dickinson went on to offer a diagnosis which had great influence on planning for the post-war world in Britain and elsewhere.[2]

He explained the war as the product of an anarchic international system which had no effective machinery to resolve conflicts. His prescription was to end the war with a peace based not on the rights of conquest but on reconciliation and national self-determination. European powers should then form a peace league and allow other states to join it. This would end the international anarchy. Dickinson and his colleagues—dubbed the 'Bryce Group' for Lord Bryce, their most prominent member—distributed a set of proposals based on these ideas in March 1915.[3]

By then, Bryce could report to an American friend that many in Britain were working at schemes for a European or world-wide peace league.[4] Some of them developed plans which were more far-reaching than the Bryce Group's proposals. The Fabian

Society set up an International Agreements Committee to study the peace question in January 1915, and engaged Leonard Woolf to prepare a report on the subject. The Fabian plan, which appeared in July 1915, proposed an international organization with a secretariat and a council which would have responsibiliites in the social and economic field.[5] The Union of Democratic Control was founded by E. D. Morel, Ramsay MacDonald, and others to press for a liberal settlement of the war and an end to secret diplomacy. Several members of the Bryce Group were also on the UDC's Executive Committee and G. Lowes Dickinson co-operated in its propaganda efforts.[6]

The general public heard little about these plans at first. The war not only submerged the issues; it made public discussion of any war aim other than victory difficult. Bryce was especially cautious, impressed by 'the atmosphere of mutual distrust'.[7] When Graham Wallas mentioned a Bryce Group meeting to his wife in October 1914, he added 'Don't mention this to anyone'.[8] The Union of Democratic Control's openly anti-war position brought it under attack from the Conservative press. It was safer for League advocates to remain quiet than to risk the accusation that they were trying to help the enemy or stop the war.

If there was danger in moving too fast, there was also the danger that the opportune moment to win support might slip away. People thought of the war as a crusade, and it seemed important to give that crusade a goal beyond mere victory. So on 3 May 1915 a League of Nations Society was formally constituted in London. Its first appeals for support were appropriately cautious:

There is no question of any 'stop the war' programme, or disarmament, or criticism of foreign policy . . . The Society takes the view that any such Union (of Nations) to be effective must recognize the obligation of mutual support in enforcing the peaceful aims of the Union and defending the members against a wanton aggressor. The society does not however seek to define the degree of obligation which the members of the Union should undertake. That can only be settled according to the number and character of the nations first forming the Union.[9]

By 29 November of that year, when it held its first general meeting, it had 148 members. Its leaders included G. L. Dickinson of the Bryce Group, Sir Willoughby Dickinson, and H. N. Brailsford, Liberal MPs, John Hobson, the Radical economist, Raymond Unwin, writer and social planner and Leonard Woolf, whose own plans for shaping the League had appeared in the July 1915 *New Statesman*. This was to be a propaganda body, working to get public support for the creation of a League of Nations open to all states once the war ended.

The League of Nations Society grew in membership in 1916 but its propaganda remained rather muted. Even within the society there were those who agreed with *The Times* that it was 'inopportune' to press publicly for a League while the war was being fought. Lowes Dickinson grew impatient with this hesitancy and complained to Gilbert Murray in December 1916, about the way established figures (Bryce and others) 'hold their hand because the moment is not ripe [while] the enemy is working to ensure that the moment shall not come at all . . .' [10] The Society kept in close touch with the League to Enforce Peace, its American counterpart, and also with comparable French and Dutch groups.

President Woodrow Wilson first publicly urged that a universal association of nations be set up at a May 1916 meeting of the League to Enforce Peace. His support for the idea, particularly after American entry into the war in 1917, established the League as the chief war aim and helped the cause in Britain immensely. The work of building public support became less suspect. Books and pamphlets on the League appeared frequently in 1917, and some public meetings were held. Now major political figures like Lord Grey, who had been Foreign Secretary when the war began, saw the League idea as a way to encourage wartime co-operation with the United States. When the League of Nations Society organized a public meeting in Westminster on 24 May 1917, it could present Lord Bryce, General Smuts, the Archbishop of Canterbury, and other big-name speakers to the crowd.[11]

The response to this activity in Whitehall was uneven. Most officials had no sense that a revolution was brewing in the conduct of international relations. However, one Minister, Lord Robert Cecil, took the League idea very much to heart. He urged the creation of a world organization in late 1916 and was able to get an official body set up to examine his proposal and other plans for a future League. This was the Phillimore Committee, which reported in March 1918 in favour of establishing international machinery based on a conference among the Allies.

This was a very different thing from the League of Nations Society's plan for a league of all nations, victors and vanquished alike. The question of what kind of League to set up was now a matter of heated debate. In *Disloyalty: the Blight of Pacifism*, published in 1918, Harold Owen explains that when a pacifist says he wants a League which includes Germany, 'he wants the League to be a bath of whitewash for the Hun'.[12] The way out would be to establish an organization without Germany, based on the Allied alliance, which could of course be done before the peace. A suitably chastened Germany could be included later.

This German issue, and the feeling that went with it that the League of Nations Society had become too pacifist, split the society. Two coalition Liberal MPs, Charles McCurdy and Major David Davies, led the movement for the formation of a league of allies before the end of the war. Davies had tried in 1917 (along with others involved in the magazine *New Europe*) to organize a society to arouse interest in foreign affairs. Its aim had been 'to drive a middle policy between the jingoes and the pacifists'.[13] Davies now pleaded for support from Society members and then in June 1918 convened a meeting at his office to establish a new body, the League of Free Nations Association. Gilbert Murray (who was elected Chairman), H. G. Wells, the eminent writer, J. H. Thomas, the Labour politician, and journalists J. A. Spender and J. L. Garvin were among those who joined this new group. Its letter-head stressed that it was 'representative of the public life of this country' and 'in no sense a pacifist or defeatist organization'. With Davies's enthusiasm and considerable financial backing the new association got off to a running start. It was not attempting to get away from the League of Nations Society so much as to bring the Society with it. From the start it made overtures to the parent body. First, it suggested in a private letter to Willoughby Dickinson that the two societies co-operate.[14]

The leaders of the League of Nations Society were put on the defensive. Its most active parliamentary members, Willoughby Dickinson and Aneurin Williams, had to proclaim that their group was not pacifist. They tried hard to recruit Conservatives, but found it difficult to shift their programme to the right.[15] G. Lowes Dickinson, who sat on a committee to advise the Labour Party on international questions, knew how hard it would be to maintain left-wing support if the Society started to advocate the early formation of a League by the Allies. The Labour movement had been divided on its response to the war. Now most leading Labourites, or at least most who did not back the Lloyd George Coalition, agreed that the League idea might be tainted by the establishment of what was almost a new anti-German alliance.[16] Yet the Society's leaders realized that amalgamating with the League of Free Nations Association might have to be risked anyway. The movement was too small to be divided—the Society had about 1,400 members in mid-1918. Moreover, as G. Lowes Dickinson had to admit, 'the other association knows how to carry on propaganda, and we do not'.[17]

On the other side, the League of Free Nations Association was ready for amalgamation, if on the right terms. So it was easy enough to get joint talks started, only weeks after the new group was established. By 26 July Murray, C. A. McCurdy and other representatives of the two societies formulated a statement on the League on which both could agree. It said that a complete league could not be established until the war was over, but that the Allies 'should take every possible step to show the practicality of putting into effect the idea of a League of Nations and with this object should formulate and if possible agree upon the terms of a scheme under which a League should be formed'. This interim organization among the Allies should not be called a 'League of Nations'; it was to be only a provisional framework of the true League, which must await the end of the war.[18]

The question of when a League should be established was thus settled quite easily. However, this issue had only been a reflection of a more fundamental division in the League movement. Its original sponsors, who had made their commitment early in the war and were attracted by the idea of a peace without victors, disagreed with the newcomers who saw themselves as more politically astute and practical. To David Davies, people like G. Lowes Dickinson and Leonard Woolf were liabilities, linked in the public mind with 'peace by negotiation'. Given the hardening of public attitudes in Britain in the months before the 'Khaki Elections' of December 1918, it is easy to understand Davies's concern with keeping the League idea alive, even while the public clamoured to hang the Kaiser. Many Society members in turn regarded the 'League Now' people as jingoes out to wreck the League idea. With these suspicions to overcome, it took weeks of negotiations and a push from the outside to bring the two groups together.

The push came from Lord Grey, who was ready by 1918 to end his two-year absence from public life in order to promote the League cause. He had attended a League of Free Nations Association meeting in July and agreed to write a pamphlet on the idea of a world organization.[19] The LFNA badly wanted Grey to assume its presidency, as the one respected figure who could make the League a national cause. Grey announced that he would lead the League movement only if it were united; it was absurd to have competing societies. The leaders of the two groups pushed on with the details of amalgamation.

Meanwhile, they co-sponsored a very successful meeting in London on 10 October 1918, which Grey addressed. It was a moving occasion, and Grey's simple words made a strong impression on those in the hall.[20] The name 'League of Nations Union' was chosen for this new society dedicated 'to promote the formation of a World League of Free Peoples for the securing of international justice, mutual defence and permanent peace'.[21] That title had been proposed for the League of Nations Society in 1915; now it symbolized the merger. Members of Parliament responded on 24 October by forming a parliamentary LNU group which Lord Selborne, Cecil's brother-in-law, was invited to head. On 9 November the amalgamation was complete. the League of Nations Society had 2,230 members at this time, the LFNA 987. Yet the smaller, better-financed group appeared to be annexing its parent, with Murray becoming the LNU's Chairman and the LFNA's salaried administrator staying on to run the LNU.[22]

Total membership rose to 3,841 by the end of 1918, as organizers moved around the country drumming up support. The Union could now appeal to the public 'We have won the war . . . But shall we reap as the harvest of our victory, a permanent and lasting peace?'[23] By joining this new organization, citizens could show the politicians and diplomats what kind of settlement they wanted. It was to be based on a 'League of Free Peoples', with its members bound:

1. To submit all disputes arising between themselves to methods of peaceful settlement.
2. To suppress jointly, by the use of all the means at their disposal, any attempt by any state to disturb the peace of the world by acts of war.
3. To create a Supreme Court, and to respect and enforce its decision.
4. To establish a permanent council which shall provide for the development of international law, for the settlement of differences not suitable for submission to the Supreme Court, for the supervision and control of armaments, and for joint action in matters of common concern.
5. To admit to the League all peoples able and willing to give effective guarantees of their loyal intention to observe its covenants, and thus to bring about such a world organization as will guarantee the freedom of nations; act as Trustee and guardian of uncivilized races and unprotected territories; and maintain international order; and thus finally liberate mankind from the curse of war.[24]

With the British League movement unified, Davies travelled to the continent, conferring with delegates of the French and Italian societies backing the League idea. The leaders of these societies took it for granted that they should try to formulate policies jointly. They held an Inter-Allied Societies Conference in Paris in January 1919, under the presidency of Leon Bourgeois, the former Premier of France. Representatives from Britain, France, the United States, Italy, Belgium, Serbia, Romania, and China agreed on a seven-point programme, which was virtually identical to the LNU programme adopted two months earlier, except for the addition of points urging armaments limitation and the renunciation of secret treaties. A deputation headed by Bourgeois presented these proposals to the 'Big Four' at the Paris Peace Conference. The LNU was well pleased with the way informal wartime contacts with other societies were blossoming. It had added cause for satisfaction when the Covenant was adopted in April, for it too corresponded broadly with the Union's programme.

This experience strengthened the conviction of British Leaguers that it was possible to organize public opinion to play a significant role in determining foreign policy. When the Covenant came under attack from the left for establishing a league of governments instead of a 'league of peoples', LNU leaders had an answer at hand. For if the delegates at Geneva, the seat of the League, were government officials, they would still carry out the wishes of their people as propounded by the various voluntary societies in their own countries. The role of the League society was thus pivotal.

This theory assumed that the voluntary societies would be independent of their foreign offices. In its contacts with other groups during the war, the League of Nations Society had tried to respect this ideal. When he was trying to organize a conference with French and Italian society leaders in August 1918, Willoughby Dickinson said he was 'convinced that if we leave it to Governments to develop policy we shall make no progress'.[25] The League movement would have to take the lead and expect governments to follow.

In early 1919 there had been traces of prickliness in the Union's relations with the Foreign Ofice. In March Eustace Percy explained to Arthur Steel-Maitland, a Conservative MP active in the LNU, his hesitancy about approaching the Union openly to muster support from the draft Covenant, because he was in the Foreign Office. When he had sounded out a leader of the Union, Percy gathered that 'they were very much afraid of being "got at" and wished to keep themselves free from any suspicion of government influence'. In what turned out to be an excessive display of caution, Percy asked Maitland to 'work' the Union from the inside instead.[26] The LNU was in fact timid in taking initiatives independently of Whitehall in the early post-war years.

It was an open secret that most societies abroad fell even further short of the ideal of independent leadership of opinion. LNU officials could poke fun at those societies which were little more than tools of their governments. One pointed to the Hungarian society, which had 'two wonderful rooms given them by the government overlooking the river at Budapest' and jibed that 'of course they may find it more difficult to say plainly what they think of the Hungarian Government than we should to criticize the British government'.[27]

In various ways the Union tried to generate more co-operation between League societies. It helped maintain an inter-allied society office in Paris during 1919. It started a *Review of the British and Foreign Press* which was sent to French, American, and Italian groups, in the hope that they might reciprocate with reviews of their own newspapers.[28] It also encouraged the idea that a permanent organization of voluntary societies should be established to formulate a joint programme for the future. In the context of events in 1919, this internationalist focus was useful in making the Union's independence from the government more credible in the eyes of the left. With Ramsay MacDonald and others levelling criticisms at the peace settlement which the Union supported, this was important. The LNU was invited too, but did not attend, the Berne Conference of the Second International in January 1919, which included representatives from Germany and neutral countries. Critical leftists who had been there could speak with a kind of authority the Union lacked.

This situation provided another reason for the Union to push for the creation of a permanent international non-governmental group committed to the League of Nations. When a Conference of Associated Societies convened in Brussels from 1 to 3 December 1919, with over 100 delegates from sixteen countries in attendance, such an organization was launched. The LNU delegation, headed by Davies and Willoughby Dickinson, returned home rather crestfallen with the way things had worked out. For one thing, the Union failed in its effort to base the new 'society of societies' at Geneva, the seat of the League. Instead, the numerous representatives of French and Belgian peace groups at the meeting—in addition to their League society delegates, the French and Belgian sent many from other groups as well—saw to it that it should be based in Brussels. The absence of American and Scandinavian representatives also marred the occasion for the Union delegates, who tried to insist that no final conclusion or organizational rules be reached until these absentees were consulted. Even more irksome was the failure of most other delegates to agree to the LNU's idea of their mission. The British wanted to get down to the nuts-and-bolts business of shaping a programme and encouraging the development of large and active societies around the world. Instead they complained that 'much labour was devoted to the declaration of abstract principles and to propositions solely within the purview of the League of Nations'.[29]

These were indications of the kind of problems that were to dog the efforts of the group, the International Federation of League of Nations Societies, for years to come. Not that the British never got their way. Cecil was eventually to head the group, it did finally move to Geneva, and the LNU's success did give it a leading role in the Federation. However, the Federation never gave substance to the ideal of international co-operation in forging world public opinion. It was, like the League itself, always too wary of offending governments to promote a coherent policy. The member societies were generally not able to mobilize opinion effectively at home or to influence decision-making in their own governments. The success which the Inter-Allied Societies Conference enjoyed in 1919 was misleading then. Voluntary societies helped make the Covenant become a reality, to be sure. But their manifestoes and deputations counted only because they fitted in well with the plans of the League's official sponsors.

President Wilson was of course the most prominent of these. Wilson left his British followers uneasy, though, chiefly because he did not appear very interested in their views. Bryce tried unsuccessfully to persuade the President to convene an informal preliminary meeting to develop Anglo-American League plans.[30] LNU leaders managed to see Wilson during his visit to England in December 1918. Murray met him at Buckingham Palace and a deputation headed by Grey and Asquith (the former Prime Minister and now an LNU Vice-President) conferred with him at the American Embassy. The President was encouraging, although he left Murray uneasy when he boasted about how obstinate he could be.[31] Grey tried to follow up by writing to Colonel House, Wilson's aide, reassuring him that the British public supported the League. Grey was alert to the difficulties which a treaty incorporating the League might face in the US Senate, but he egged the President on to try for the 'most concrete form of a League of Nations and the most far-reaching that can be produced at the Peace Conference'.[32]

LNU leaders remained uneasy about their American champion during the Peace Conference. Wilson had espoused open diplomacy, but now he met Clemenceau and Lloyd George behind closed doors. In January 1919 the Union's new organ, *The League of Nations Journal*, tried to sound hopeful about the President's leadership, but had to confess that 'we are still ignorant of the exact nature and scope of President Wilson's proposals . . .'[33] League supporters trusted Wilson's intentions but feared that he was managing his case badly.

Cecil, the League's first official sponsor, became the LNU's link to the proceedings in Paris. Cecil resigned as Minister of Blockade at the end of 1918, but said that he was still a supporter of the Lloyd George Government except on the single issue which led to his resignation—the disestablishment of the church in Wales. His rather puzzling resignation and excessive zeal for the League set him off from his ministerial colleagues. He was still the obvious choice for the British section of the League of Nations Commission in Paris. Cecil set up an advisory committee headed by Lord Phillimore to keep him in touch with League supporters while he worked on the Covenant. Murray, Willoughby Dickinson, Davies, and Alfred Zimmern were included and kept the LNU in touch with the work in Paris. Union leaders found it easy to support Cecil. Their proposals were very similar to his except for a few points to do with the functions of a League Assembly and Court of Justice.[34]

The Lloyd George Government had no coherent strategy governing its attitude towards the creation of a League. The Foreign Office-sponsored Phillimore Committee had come out in favour of sanctions, but its report was never adopted as official policy. Collective security was the subject of dispute in Whitehall. Sir Eyre Crowe, senior permanent official in the Foreign Office, had responded to Cecil's first proposals for a League in 1916 with a stinging critique of the idea. How, he argued, could nations be expected to observe a boycott or any other sanction for collective enforcement if they had to risk exposing themselves to attack by powerful neighbours?[35] By the time of the Peace Conference, most officials had accepted the need for a League, but they disagreed over what kind was needed.[36]

Cecil was drifting away from the centre of power in Lloyd

George's shifting coalition, but he was still able to press his case for a strong League effectively. He could count on the support of the LNU and the important opinion bloc it represented. What contributed more to his success was the Prime Minister's desire to placate the United States. Lloyd George hoped to use British responsiveness on the League issue to trade off for American co-operation in areas he considered really vital.

Cecil played on this desire to win over the Americans at a critical point in the negotiations of the League of Nations Commission. Negotiations on an Anglo-American draft Covenant were well under way by the end of January 1919, when Lloyd George came forward with suggestions for a League of a very limited sort. The plan reflected Whitehall's scepticism about joint resistance to aggression. It would in effect have made the League a device to facilitate continuing consultations among the powers. Cecil was able to argue that negotiations were so advanced that he could not reverse himself and advocate the new proposals without hurting Britain's relations with the United States. He in effect brought Britain into agreement with a 'Wilsonian' League.[37]

It was a narrow victory which left Whitehall unconvinced. The Admiralty had spelled out its reasons for opposing the Covenant in December and saw no reason to reverse its opinion.[38] The service departments managed the strategic problems posed by the League simply: they ignored them. The Foreign Office could not go that far, but it minimized the importance of the Covenant or carped at the intrusions on its prerogatives characteristic of the Lloyd George administration, with the League treated as one new affliction among many. Crowe would speak of the way Article 16 of the Covenant—the key commitment to collective security—had been 'lightheartedly adopted' in Paris. Cecil had to admit that the Covenant had been put through 'by rather unusually rapid procedure', but held that Article 16 had grown out of the Phillimore Committee's recommendations and full discussion in the Cabinet.[39]

Cecil had to work against this background of official indifference or hostility in the early post-war years. He fended off extreme proposals, such as the French plan for an international military force, which almost certainly would have undone his fragile triumph. His caution, his willingness to champion a Covenant which fell short of their hopes, angered many of the most dedicated supporters of the League ideal. As news of the peace settlement reached England it only confirmed the doubts many had had about the secretive proceedings in Paris. The Covenant, the fruit of their years of working and dreaming, was linked to a controversial and unpopular peace treaty.

A strong feeling emerged on the British left that the settlement was not only unjust but impossible to enforce. Philip Snowden, a leading Labourite and pacifist opponent of the war, described it in harsh but not unusual terms. 'The treaty should satisfy brigands, imperialists and militarists. . . . It is not a peace treaty, but a declaration of another war.'[40] The League of Nations was flawed because it was part of that peace settlement. Its most obvious weakness was the exclusion of Germany and the Soviet Union; on this and other grounds the Covenant would have to be changed. The statement issued by the Trades Union Congress in 1919 said that the League could succeed only if it could be transformed into a real 'league of peoples'.[41] Only some Labourites who had supported the war became immediate supporters of the League. J. R. Clynes, the Parliamentary Labour Party's spokesman in the debate on the peace settlement, was most active on behalf of the League of Nations Union.

The response from the predominantly Liberal and socialist intellectuals and politicians who led the League movement was no less severe at first. Murray, Woolf, H. G. Wells, and seventeen other LNU notables published an open letter on 24 May 1919 that illustrated their thinking. They asked the Allies to reconsider the proposed peace terms before trying to enforce them on Germany. The treaty, they said, belied the spirit of Wilson's Fourteen Points of peace and amounted to 'a breach of faith with a beaten enemy'. The League was being transformed into an Allied alliance to hold Germany by force in an inferior position.[42] Leonard Hobhouse said 'if I had been Wilson I had rather put a bullet through my head than signed those terms'.[43] Bryce typified most Liberals in supporting the establishment of a League while remaining critical of the rest of the settlement. He could 'remember few cases in history where negotiations might have done so much good, and have done so much evil'.[44]

The LNU, which had encouraged the public to adopt high League ideals, found itself in the embarrassing position of having to defend the Covenant against critics who found that the reality fell too far short of those ideals. A few who had worked with the League of Nations Society went into open opposition. H. G. Wells began to rail against the 'sham world parliament' and criticized those who abandoned the 'original demands and promises of

Crewe House and the League of Nations Union'.[45] G. Lowes Dickinson, disappointed at the way his brainchild had come to life, resigned from the LNU Executive, where he felt his taint of 'pacifism' had relegated him to a minor role. Yet he remained ready to lecture in support of the League.[46]

Within a League movement based on the left, Cecil appeared to be an over-cautious politician. He looked quite different to those in power whose support he knew was essential to the League enterprise. To them, he was a maverick, less an active party politician than a crusader for his cause. This did not mean that he was out of political contention in 1919, for normal electoral politics had long been suspended and a politician who was bidding for a non-party base of support could not be lightly dismissed. Cecil agreed to become Chairman of the LNU (with Murray stepping down to Vice-Chairman), launching a campaign to win support for the League which might also benefit his career.

At his first public appearance as a Union leader, on 13 July 1919, in London, Cecil charted a moderate course for the League movement. He called for the admission of Germany and the Soviet Union to the League. Yet, typically, he added that there should be 'some guarantee' that Germany would enter 'as a genuine friend of the League idea . . . We have a right to ask that the new Germany should go through a certain novitiate . . .'[47] While he urged that the League become a 'league of peoples' and not of governments, he did not use that slogan in quite the same way as a Ramsay MacDonald or a member of the traditional peace movement. Cecil's concern was to win support for the covenant, not to revise it. If the peace settlement was not one on which the League could be built, 'then we should ask the League to change it'.[48] When the LNU was invited to a conference on the League in Brussels, Cecil directed the response to indicate that if the conference 'is to consider ways of arousing and sustaining public interest in the League, the Union would gladly be represented, but if it is called with the object of considering possible changes in the Covenant, [these] ought not to be considered until the provisions of the Covenant shall have been put to some extent to the test of experience'.[49]

The LNU did not pit itself against all revisions of the Covenant. At first, it seemed to make revision the main reason for its continuing existence. Its Special Committee on Reorganization reported in 1919 that since the Covenant did not carry into effect the full ideals for which the Union had been established, this was the prime task of the Union.[50] Articles in the LNU's journal, *The Covenant*, suggested the creation of a standing commission to advise on questions relating to Covenant revision. One of these emphasized that League societies had to do more than interpret and popularize the League; they had to bring the needs of the people to the League and encourage the process of amendment of the Covenant.[51]

These two aims were not reconciled in practice. For if the League were to be popularized, it could not be subjected to root-and-branch criticism. Cecil impressed on other Union leaders how narrowly they had succeeded in getting the Covenant through and how impractical it was to demand more right away. The *League of Nations Journal* of September 1919 set what was to become the characteristic LNU approach towards revisionism. With the League under fire, there was 'danger that the public may become convinced that the Covenant is indeed unworkable, and relapse into indifference or pessimism'.[52] The new arrangement should be given a fair chance before revision was considered. Carping criticism could only do harm. 'To complain of the flaws in the Treaty and the imperfections of the Covenant is merely to complain that the work we have to do has not been done for us.'[53]

The LNU emphasized the virtues of the Covenant. Other societies, notably the Union of Democratic Control, could be left with the tasks of preaching on the defects of the Versailles Treaty and the League. The UDC wanted the new organization to function as a kind of world parliament with popularly elected representatives, and not as a conclave for diplomats. Yet even Arthur Ponsonby, an early supporter of the League idea and a leader of the UDC, had to admit that the LNU 'may be able to do some good work with jingoes and moderates'.[54] From the left, the LNU looked increasingly like a mission to the Conservatives.

This mission required an emphasis on the way the League could keep the peace without interfering with national sovereignty. It was doubly difficult, because it meant not only that those in power had to be assured that Britain's international commitments would not be too burdensome, but also that Britain had a solemn binding commitment to the Covenant. Eric Drummond, the Secretary-General of the League on Cecil's recommendation, tried to win Conservative support with the same appeal. The League, he wrote to Balfour, gave Britain the best means to realize her traditional objectives in Europe: peace and the prevention of the dominance of any one power. Moreover the Covenant gave Britain a voice in

Europe without great entanglements, for 'the obligations under the Covenant, when they come to be examined, are extremely light'.[55]

Cecil had taken from his experience in Conservative politics and Government an awareness that the old attitudes towards foreign relations, the old suspicions, could not be legislated out of existence by a more perfect Covenant. For him, a patient effort to educate public opinion provided the key to change. Hence his comment that 'in a democratic age everything depends on public opinion . . . ' [56] This reliance on the efficacy of public opinion reassured Conservatives. With public opinion somehow doing the job of enforcing the Covenant, there was less cause to worry about the possible obligation to use force.

The LNU played a vital part in this scheme. It had been started to create a League, but now it had other work to do, building mass support for the world body and making sure that the Government used it properly. There was no real debate in 1919 over whether or how the LNU should continue to function. The business of organizing committees, establishing branches and raising funds hardly seemed to require any justification by now. The only question was how far these activities on behalf of the League should go and who would pay for them. Their emphasis on public opinion may have led Union leaders to a cautious view of how far the Covenant should go—for it should not outrun opinion as to what was reasonable—but it left the way open for an ambitious assessment of the role of the LNU itself.

In these crucial early years, the Union's course was set by a few key leaders: Cecil, Grey, and Murray, principally. In the public mind, the organization became indissolubly linked with their names. The rank-and-file membership, growing rapidly and constantly in flux, was hard to place. But every newspaper reader, every politician, had his own image of Cecil. The son of a Prime Minister and bearer of one of the greatest names in British politics, Cecil had an image ready for him even before he became a vigorous wartime leader as Parliamentary Under-Secretary for Foreign Affairs and Minister of Blockade. His resignation on a religious issue and his mildly progressive views were perhaps considered eccentric, but Cecils were known for their eccentricity so this did not jar the image.

Grey, who had in effect created the LNU by insisting on the amalgamation of two rival societies, had a greater reputation than Cecil at the end of the war. Yet, although he was only two years older (born in 1862), his public career seemed almost at an end just when Cecil's was becoming most active. His steadily increasing blindness, already evident while he was Foreign Secretary, restricted him. His role as President of the LNU, from 1918 until his death in 1933, was therefore not an active one. Nor was he very active politically. He held on to the Liberal leadership in the Lords (against Lloyd Georgite opposition) only until 1924. His opinions were highly valued by those who were in day-to-day control, but he was rarely present at the meetings, deputations, and other activities at Union offices in London.

Gilbert Murray, Vice-Chairman and then from 1923 to 1938 the Chairman of the LNU Executive Committee, was at first glance an odd companion for Cecil and Grey. Probably the best known classicist of his generation, he held a Regius Professorship at Oxford University. Born in Australia in 1866 of Irish descent, Murray came to England as a boy; like Cecil and Grey he studied at Oxford. His marriage to Lady Mary Howard, daughter of the Earl of Carlisle, brought him close to the orbit of some Whig grandees, but his academic duties left him little time for politics at first. He was an active member of the Liberal Party, however, and with the war became particularly concerned with international affairs. In 1915 he published a book defending Grey's foreign policy against criticism by what he called 'pro-Germans'.[57] It prompted a rejoinder from Bertrand Russell which labelled Murray's book 'an elaborate defence of Grey' done 'under the tutelage of the Foreign Office'.[58] Murray soon had his problems with Whitehall. His approval of the Lansdowne letter (and a peace short of victory) and criticism of the imperialist extremism of the War Cabinet led Balfour, the Foreign Secretary, to ask for the return of a letter of commendation he had earlier given Murray. Criticized in some newspapers for 'pacifism' and even 'Bolshevism', Murray protested that his views were simply those of 'the average non-ministerial Liberal'.[59]

After the war, Murray plunged into work in support of the League. He followed in Cecil's footsteps by accepting an appointment to represent South Africa as a delegate to Geneva from 1921 to 1923. He also became active in the League-sponsored Committee on Intellectual Co-operation in 1922, and followed Henri Bergson as President of that body for eight years. And he took on the demanding post of LNU Chairman, coming down twice weekly from Oxford to London to attend meetings and supervise the work at headquarters. His Oxford friend and colleague H. A. L. Fisher called it 'almost a public scandal' that Europe's foremost Greek scholar should be spending so much of time on the Union.[60] He skilfully played the role of moderator and arbiter at Grosvenor Crescent, the Union's headquarters, answering countless letters and resolving staffing and financial problems.

As Chairman of an Executive Committee which brought together people of different parties and viewpoints, Murray tried to subdue his own political viewpoint and emphasize the need to keep the organization going. His working relationship with Cecil was remarkably close; he stepped down as Chairman in Cecil's favour in 1919, and was quite willing to do it again in 1923, when Cecil again left the Government.[61] There were differences between the two men: Murray was an agnostic, Cecil an intensely devout Christian; Murray was as cool as Cecil was intense. But their identity of outlook was great.[62] Murray could truthfully write to Cecil in 1938 that they had worked together without a single difference over the years. 'Of course', he said, 'on political matters I naturally tended to accept your guidance but I never had the feeling of yielding against my judgement.'[63]

It seemed obvious to Cecil, Grey, and Murray that the job at hand was to organize public opinion and not get lost in doctrinal discussions on international affairs. If enough people joined the LNU then its leaders would speak with authority, and opinion could be translated into action. It was hoped that members would be well-informed and ready to work actively in their branch, but they would not be required to do anything beyond paying their dues. They would show on the membership rolls in any case, and that alone would have its effect.

From the start, Union recruitment appeals reflected this no-nonsense emphasis on rapid growth. *The League* printed suggestions on 'How to get new members'.

Whether a man approves of the League of Nations or whether he does not, he should support the League of Nations Union for rectifying the ignorance of the Electorate.

Tell someone who says the League is utopian, that we can at least build a good foundation for future generations to build on. Then there is the man who says that people are so tired of war that peace would be kept for a generation or so without the League of Nations . . . The answer to him is that the League is the best means of guiding the world gradually out of the industrial chaos into which it is falling . . .

Then there is the man who says: 'Oh, the League would be vastly improved if such-and-such an Article were amended, or such-and-such an Article were added.' To him you should point out that, as an individual, his idea can never gain world-wide attention; whereas the Union acts as a sort of clearing house for ideas regarding the League . . .

The commonsense way of getting new members is to keep off academic controversy, and to establish points of agreement . . .[64]

The appeal might vary a bit from year to year and from place to place, but the emphasis on getting new members and using them to demonstrate strength was constant.

The biggest restraint on this appeal was lack of money. In early 1919 Union leaders debated expansion of their work based on a nation-wide appeal for funds. Davies, the chief backer of the organization who had provided it with offices in Westminster, was willing to offer a further £10,000 if the Executive would launch a big fund-raising campaign.[65] He envisaged a £1,000,000 fund which could support the LNU permanently, and advanced many proposals towards this end, including a three-week campaign to be initiated by the Prime Minister and the sale of badges for a 'League of Nations Day'.

Davies's ambitious plans worried others on the Executive. Willoughby Dickinson, former head of the League of Nations Society, was particularly sceptical. He recalled how Davies had promised the Society money if it expanded. Then Davies resigned and the Society was left to flounder financially.[66] The LNU's work in early 1919 cost about £3,000 a month, while receipts ran at £100. Murray agreed with Dickinson that Davies's scheme was too ambitious. He thought a big campaign would bring in £30,000–£40,000 at most, so the Union's current expenses were too high. After the peace, the Union might have to be scaled down to a much smaller society. Murray and Dickinson started examining their individual financial liability in the event of some sort of collapse.[67] Dickinson mused on the Union's dilemma in having to confess that it could get only one man in England to finance it, but he was in no position to block Davies, and planning for a big campaign went ahead.[68]

Fund-raising was the Union's central concern in these months. Indeed, it occupied so much of the Executive's time and attention that it helps to explain why other fundamental questions about how to run the organization were not explored in more depth. The £1,000,000 campaign was delayed until October, when Parliament was to open, and LNU expenses were trimmed in the meantime.[69] Even so, the level of expenditure continued to run high in 1919, presumably because a generous endowment fund would soon be paying the bills. The campaign opened at Mansion

House on 13 October 1919, and a costly flurry of activity began, with pamphlets broadcast freely and agents travelling round the country. The response was disappointing and the LNU's problems mounted. By May 1920 news of these problems reached Geneva, where Eric Drummond received reports from his staff that the LNU might collapse within a month.[70] Drummond was moved enough by this misleading news to write to Cecil urging him to continue the Union's work for the good of the League.[71]

The Union tried to make its appeal as broad as possible against this background of financial exigency. Accordingly, it played up the notion that it was at the centre of the political spectrum. Its journal said in a January 1920 editorial that there were three schools of thought in Britain—traditionalists, revolutionary socialists, and those who put their trust in the League of Nations. It played up the dilemma of the reasonable Leaguer caught between extremists. Traditionalists would associate him with socialists, while socialists would dismiss him as another sort of capitalist-militarist.[72] One trouble with this sort of neat grouping was that people managed, then as now, to hold many conflicting opinions at once.

In order to define its centrist position the LNU moved away from its wartime antecedents towards the right. It tried to sell the League to the public as, in effect, the best insurance policy the Empire could ever buy. 'We have a small army and a vast Empire . . . It is immensely important to us to preserve our *status quo* by the peaceful methods of arbitration and international co-operation rather than by the maintenance of armies and navies which a return to the Balance of Power would force upon us.'[73] The potential rivalry between Empire and League for the loyalty of Englishmen, a rivalry which the Beaverbrook press discussed often, made the LNU all the more determined to show that no conflict need exist.

The Mandate System set up under the Covenant not only brought territory to Britain; it was a mechanism for improvement. The Union wanted to administer the 'backward races' for their own benefit, with their rights protected and their economic interests advanced. When politicians fell into the wrong kind of rhetoric about empire, as Lloyd George did before the Commons in discussing Britain's right to be in Mesopotamia in March 1920, the LNU complained. We should not claim a right to be anywhere, the Union's journal scolded. 'It is, according to the Covenant, the wishes of the inhabitants that is the principal consideration in selection of a mandatory.' Lloyd George, who had referred to Mesopotamian oil deposits, was reminded that 'mandatory Powers are not empowered by the Covenant to exploit resources of a territory in their own interest'.[74] For some, mandates might be means of exploiting old colonies under new names. At Grosvenor Crescent, they were seen as one of the best features of the noble experiment.

The centrist strategy kept the LNU from moving too far to the right. It even shed some right-wing heretics, members who also supported the Entente Peoples' Alliance, a society aimed at the perpetual maintenance of the wartime alliance. There was considerable overlap between the two groups, so a merger at first seemed natural. The Union's General Secretary opened talks on the subject in February 1919, and then worked out a plan for the society to join the LNU as its 'Entente Alliance Branch'. But the anti-German focus of the group worried most Union leaders. The LNU was, after all, committed to the admission of Germany to the League at the earliest possible moment and it could not compromise on this. The merger failed and some disgruntled members resigned.[75]

This effort to define a middle position in politics and appeal to the public had considerable success. People wanted to know that their wartime sacrifices had not been wasted, so they supported the League as the one tangible gain of the war. Liberals were the readiest converts, and they joined the front ranks of the LNU in such numbers that even Cecil began to rail against their dominance. Moderate Labourites saw no conflict between support for the League and interest in the Soviet 'experiment'. They looked forward to the day when a Labour Government would use the League, not as a tool of the old diplomacy, but as a new way to peace.[76] Conservatives began to heap praise on the League too, but their ambitions for it were more restricted than those of Labourites. They saw it as an extension of conventional diplomacy. The LNU was bringing together people who might disagree about everything except the importance of the League. It grew from 3,217 members when it started in November 1918 to 60,000 by the end of 1920.

The Union's membership figures, although impressive, were well below the goals set by its leaders. At the end of 1922 members were told that 'the best New Year's resolution we can make is to increase our membership to a million within the next twelve months . . . with our success will come the only possible guarantee of world peace'.[77] This was the sort of optimistic goal typical of the LNU's early years; it took ten years more for membership to total 1,000,000. But the problems of mass membership were there from the start, because the LNU tried to please everybody and allow for divergent views of what British League policies should be.

In the immediate aftermath of World War One it was easy to gloss over divergent views on the use of force or the purpose of the League. Pacifists could swallow their doubts about the Covenant and join the Union. The League did, after all, offer a pacific approach to world problems, and if some of its supporters talked about sanctions, the whole issue was a rather detached one. With no threat to peace, why argue about what might never be? The Peace Society, an old-line religiously oriented group, could thus say in one breath that the peace treaty was 'a betrayal of the ideals in the spirit of which the War was presumably fought' but that the League was 'a landmark on the road to world peace'.[78] The peace movement brought forward many visions of the League in the 1920s. If the League of the Peace Treaty, the 'League of Victors' which excluded Germany, the League which demanded sacrifices to enforce peace, if these Leagues were despised or forgotten, then there were other Leagues to talk about.

The LNU encouraged pacifists to join even if they had doubts about its policies. In branches where there were few pacifists the few might still be the most active members. This helped put a 'pacifist' label on the Union. The ambiguity of the word 'pacifism' confused the situation further. In the 1920s it broadened in popular usage to include all who worked against war, whether or not they countenanced the use of force. Non-resisters who combined social action with a total rejection of violence and Conservative Leaguers were lumped together by the press or politicians as 'pacifists'. The LNU tried to keep its distance from pure pacifist organizations and activities, but the distinction was lost on the public. Neville Chamberlain was able to lament in 1938 that his job was made more difficult by 'the League of Nations Union and other war-like pacifists'.[79]

The difficulty with a recruitment strategy of trying to make the Covenant appeal to everybody became clear when LNU leaders tried to translate their numbers into influence. They faced a very difficult sort of opposition from politicians who claimed to be League supporters too. Union leaders had left the definition of support so vague that it could be used against them. With everyone 'pro-League', there was no way to insist that the path of true internationalism lay in pursuing LNU policies.

More basically, politicians could neutralize League opinion because the League was not a sufficiently important issue to override party loyalties or force significant shifts in political alignments. Bryce complained in 1921 that the League was not really in the front rank of issues. 'The Governments are chilly, the Army and Navy, the Civil Service and Society are either cold or contemptuous. The masses do not really care, being overpowered by Labour and Socialism.'[80] Cecil too was unhappy with the way the Government failed to assume the kind of initiatives he wanted. He worked to remove the Lloyd George Government and replace it with a new coalition under Grey that would give the League the kind of support it needed. 'It is no use for us to set up a League of Nations which if it means anything must mean a new departure in international relations and yet go on with a foreign policy in other respects founded on the old nationalistic and militaristic assumptions.'[81]

Clearly the biggest difficulty with the LNU model of translating opinion into action was that it depended on what happened in Geneva. Hopeful talk about the future could not conceal the obvious shortcomings of the League, an organization with limited powers and dependent on sovereign states that could not be transformed overnight into dedicated members of a world community. Moreover, the international movement which supposedly stood behind the League was slow to develop. Other League societies had some influence, but none were as large as the LNU. The Union's assignment was manifold then. It had to make the Covenant central to British foreign policy and use Britain's key position to strengthen the League. It also had to encourage voluntary societies in other countries. The Covenant was only the foundation of the League edifice; the real work of building an organization still remained.

Chapter II

The Early 1920s

World War One had aroused an interest in international affairs that was hard to sustain in peacetime. The issue in the 1920s was not whether or not to support the League, but how best to use it in furthering national interests. Few people seemed concerned. Even if the LNU did mobilize opinion, more potential problems remained, for foreign policy was the traditional preserve of a small élite, jealous of its prerogatives and conservative in its values. Lloyd George's presence at 10 Downing Street showed that this élite could be challenged. Yet he remained sceptical about the League's possibilities and LNU leaders viewed him as an obstacle. Great campaigns, related to the anti-slavery and corn law movements, had forced changes in policy in the past. But now no foreign policy issue had strong moral appeal or was so immediate in its consequences that it could hope for anything like the same impact. Furthermore, League supporters were unwilling to risk a direct bid for voter support or to challenge the political party system.

That system remained in a state of flux at the end of the war, with a predominantly Conservative coalition in power, the Liberals divided and Labour moving into the position of chief opposition party. LNU leaders took it for granted that they would work within that system, which had proved its resilience in an era of war and revolution. Yet how? One possibility might have been to affiliate with a political party and work within it to realize objectives. Most Union members were Liberals or Labourites and the foreign policy programmes of their parties were broadly in line with the aims of the LNU. Alternatively, the LNU might have tried to define a role as a pressure group, nominally non-partisan, but ready to throw its support to the party most nearly supporting its programme. Such pressure groups have something with which to promise and threaten.

The LNU had been established as a non-party organization of a different type, one more familiar to the American political scene. Its principles dictated that it steer clear of direct involvement in electoral politics. Leadership positions in the Union were carefully distributed to politicians of all three parties, although not in proportion to their strength nationally. Liberals, the most natural Leaguers, had more than their share of seats on the Executive Committee. At least in theory, the Union would be able to exert influence through friends in office, regardless of who was in power. Yet, equally, it had to be very circumspect in criticizing any government. Balanced from within and cautious about giving offence without, the LNU had chosen a tricky role to play on the political stage.

It is striking that there was so little discussion at the start of how the LNU might best function. That it should include people from all parties and that its leaders should try to exert influence quietly from the inside was not surprising. Some important Conservatives, Balfour and Austen Chamberlain, both Foreign Secretaries, did appear to be friendly, and Cecil was Conservative. Adopting a more overtly political line would have meant, in practice, opposing the Conservatives and tossing away these sources of support. The other parties hoped to profit from League opinion, but they did not want the LNU Executive Committee usurping their decision-making powers. Especially after politics returned to normal in 1922, they wanted the LNU neutralized. The Union gradually did become more active in politics, but in its first years it was hamstrung by restrictions it had set on its own behaviour. So it was often passive while the years of opportunity for the League became years of opportunities lost or denied.

The first targets of the LNU's attention were the problems left unsolved by the Peace Conference, the status of Germany most pressing among them. The question of how to maintain security against a resurgent Germany preoccupied the French and determined their relations with Britain and their position at Geneva. At the Peace Conference, Cecil had opposed what he regarded as a French effort to turn the League into an anti-German alliance. He worried that the Covenant might be labelled a new 'Holy Alliance' if the French had their way, and tried to steer the League away from the effort to enforce reparations payments. He wanted Germany disarmed, but thought that could be the price of her admission to the League. Cecil tried to strike a balance here; if he linked the League too closely to enforcement of the treaty on Germany he would weaken its appeal in Britain. Yet if he tried to dissociate the organization from these problems entirely it would make the League seem less important. The Supreme Council, the continuation of the wartime alliance, continued to meet frequently from 1920 to 1923, and was perceived as a rival to the new world body. Cecil did not want to give it more business at the League's expense. The LNU wanted the Supreme Council abolished, for 'all ententes are superfluous but the one all-embracing League'.[1]

As Britain's relations with France deteriorated and Germany's absence from Geneva cost the League more and more popular support, LNU leaders saw that they could not simply endorse the Government's policies and hope for the best. The question of German admission, complicated by Germany's insistence on being in the League Council as well as the Assembly, was caught up in a tangle of interrelated problems and not solved until 1926. Well before that, however, it served notice to LNU leaders that they would have to speak out or risk impotence. Cecil edged in this direction with anti-coalition schemes which did not escape the Prime Minister's notice.[2] The Union still directed only the mildest reproaches towards Whitehall. It urged that Germany be admitted and that the League be used more and to better effect, but it was reluctant to challenge those—Curzon at the Foreign Office or Balfour in Geneva—who did not share its perspective.

Germany's admission was important because it raised fundamental questions about the League. American admission was not as vital in the eyes of LNU leaders. Important though it was in determining the outcome of the Geneva experiment, the refusal of the United States Senate to ratify the Peace Treaty and join the League did not loom very large in Britain. For one thing, it was not clear for some time whether the Americans might not join after all. Then, too, America's entry was not a political issue as was Germany's. Some Conservatives used the absence of the United States as their excuse for downgrading or opposing the League, but most League supporters suspected they would have been hostile in any case.

In a way this was strange. The League idea had been for Grey and for Bryce, whose name was almost inseparable from the Anglo-American connection, a way to encourage co-operation with the United States. Other LNU leaders were just as firm in their advocacy of close ties with Washington, if only because the success of the League might hinge on it.[3] The lead article of the first issue of the *League of Nations Journal* had described Wilson's visit to Britain as reuniting the 'Anglo-Saxon race'.[4] Cecil had worked hard at the Peace Conference to ensure that the budding Anglo-American naval rivalry did not damage prospects for the League, while Grey worried about the opposition Wilson faced at home during the conference. Both LNU leaders wanted Wilson to be more flexible, reasoning that no part of the Covenant was worth as much as American participation in the League.[5]

Even before Grey went to the United States on a diplomatic mission in September 1919, he had concluded that it would be unwise to campaign openly for American entry into the League. Such an action would be apt to stimulate the opposition. This view became a precept governing the Union's handling of the question of American entry: never plead or appear too anxious. It was actually only a new form of the familiar guideline for Britain's handling of the 'special relationship' with the United States. This policy was in line with the advice to the LNU from the League to Enforce Peace, its American counterpart. The important thing was to make the League successful and avoid creating any impression that American membership was indispensable.[6]

So Grosvenor Crescent played down the American entry question. Its comments were usually optimistic. When the Senate rejected the Treaty of Versailles, LNU members were told that since 'the American people are whole-heartedly in favour of the League of Nations . . . there is no reason to suppose that America will continue to hold herself aloof from it'.[7] Harding's election then 'cleared the way for the entry of the United States into the League of Nations'.[8] Even in 1923, when Cecil made a speaking tour in the United States as a guest of the Foreign Policy Association, *Headway*, the LNU journal, commented on the enthusiasm of his audiences and concluded that without doubt 'opinion is moving'.[9]

While the attitude of Union leaders towards the United States was optimistic and positive, it was hardly that towards the Soviet Union. Cecil, when interviewed during the Peace Conference, took a 'very despairing view' of the situation in Russia. Bolshevism would never come to terms with the old social order; it 'was impossible as a basis of society and nothing could be built on it . . .'[10] Bryce was intensely hostile, sharing in full measure the fears of the British upper classes about the 'contagion of Bolshevism'.[11] Yet they never thought as did Americans Nicholas Murray Butler and Elihu Root, that the League might serve as a temporary western alliance against the Soviets.[12] Instead, they tried to remain fair despite their hostility, and they wanted the Soviets in the League.

Cecil and the LNU even emerged in the unlikely guise of champions of the Soviet Union in 1920 during the Russo-Polish War. For the LNU, the war presented a case to test whether the British Government really intended to base its foreign policy on the League. When it looked as if war might erupt, the Union urged that the League issue strong warnings to both sides and then appoint a commission to investigate the situation in Eastern Europe. The Allies adopted the suggestion, enabling the Union to think that it had scored a triumph. The Soviets, however, were wary of League involvement and refused to co-operate with the investigation.

By May 1920 British policy towards the conflict became a major issue. The Government, although still sending consignments of arms to Poland under an agreement made the previous October, hoped to avoid further involvement.[13] The re-establishment of trade relations with the USSR was important to Lloyd George, and in any case the Polish offensive was going well. Cecil failed in a new effort to have Britain summon the League Council to deal with the war. He conceded that League intervention at that time might favour the Bolsheviks, but this was not the main consideration. The paramount question for him was whether the Government was in earnest about using the League as the essential organ of international relations. The LNU backed Cecil fully and helped him put pressure on the Government.[14]

The debate on the Russo-Polish War was Parliament's first far-reaching discussion of the role of the League in British foreign policy. The Labour Party, led by J. R. Clynes, an active LNU supporter, and the Liberals led by Sir Donald Maclean joined Cecil in an appeal for an activist League policy. They faced Conservative opponents whose scepticism about the League was cloaked in rhetoric of concern for the new organization. Bonar Law, the Conservative leader, obliquely praised Cecil's enthusiasm for the League but observed 'that there are others who take as keen an interest'. Yet they 'take a different view, and think that, if you were to try to get the League of Nations mixed up with the settlement of this war, neutrals would not come into it, and you would damn it as an effective instrument'.[15] This debate was the forerunner of many in which 'the opponents of the League never appeared on the platform', as Duff Cooper later put it.[16] A reasoned discussion of how to use the League could never develop, and the confusion over British policy towards Geneva remained.

In this episode in 1920 the Union defined a clear position that 'unless the League is prepared to deal with all disputes leading or likely to lead to war, it will have failed in its primary purpose'. It also criticized the unfair way that the League had been pushed into investigating the Soviet attack on Persia, while avoiding a similar response to the Polish attack on the Soviets.[17] The LNU did not follow this declaration with a forceful campaign directed at British policy in Geneva. Instead, with selective optimism, it heaped praise on the League for its little triumphs. The public was not told of the difficulties to be overcome if the League was to be prepared for a real crisis.

The League's first year was not without accomplishment, as the Union hastened to point out. Cecil wrote in a 'birthday' letter for *Headway* that 'much has been done. A dangerous dispute between Sweden and Finland has been put in a fair way to settlement; hostilities between Poland and Lithuania have been arrested; an International Court of Justice has been established . . . The 1st Assembly . . . was a magnificent success. So far the machinery and organization of the League, whenever tested, have proved adequate.'[18] The League had to have successes for the Union to succeed, so LNU literature celebrated League achievements which were modest, measured against the crises of the post-war world.

If sceptics still doubted whether the hidden hand of public opinion or 'the League spirit' would suffice to keep the peace if a dispute were to arise between big powers, the Union reassured them by describing the settlement of a 1922 episode in which France had claimed the right to draft into her army British citizens living in Tunis and Morocco. Once a deadlock had been reached in the dispute, 'under the pre-war system of international relations, Great Britain's next step would have been something approaching an ultimatum . . . But, fortunately, the world is better equipped for such an emergency now than it was in 1914. Great Britain and France both turned to the League of Nations . . .'[19]

The most important lesson the LNU drew from these episodes was that the League succeeded because it practised open diplomacy. By contrast with its 'rivals', the Supreme Allied Council and the Conference of Ambassadors, the League offered 'the only successful method of counteracting the poison of the old secret diplomacy'.[20] Union publications explored the precise meaning of the new diplomacy in practice, and some Leaguers advocated a maximalist position, 'that every dispute between nations shall be discussed openly. That every complaint laid by one nation against another shall be laid openly, that no treaty or agreement shall be signed or even proposed without the open sanction of the People's representatives. . . .'[21]

The first of Wilson's fourteen points, 'open covenants openly arrived at', proved in some ways the most elusive. Union leaders tried to take the lead in the crusade for openness, which was central to the British left's view of foreign policy-making. E. D. Morel had won praise for proposing, at the 1921 Annual Conference of the Labour Party, that all treaties should not only be published but that governments should have to seek approval for them before ratification.[22] Cecil was convinced of the value of keeping diplomatic proceedings public; he lauded the League Council's decision to issue comprehensive summaries of its discussions followed by the complete *Procès verbaux* of its debates (while keeping its meetings private). However the LNU did not pursue its demand for openness systematically, by laying out explicit guidelines for the conduct of diplomacy, as Morel and his Union of Democratic Control did. It was too hesitant about offending those in power to tackle the issue forthrightly.

The Union shied away from other proposals designed to weaken the hold of the old diplomacy. It did not go along with the idea that the three British representatives to the Assembly in Geneva should be chosen in a special national election. This sort of scheme, LNU leaders feared, would divorce the delegation entirely from the government of the day. It wanted one representative to be a Minister, preferably of Cabinet rank, reporting to an Interdepartmental Standing Committee of League Affairs. Under Lloyd George's administration, the League was a Cabinet responsibility. The appointment of unsympathetic delegates to Geneva, notably Viscount Esher, the long-time member of the Committee of Imperial Defence, in 1922, stimulated the LNU's efforts to change this arrangement. When the management of League affairs did change after Lloyd George left office, it was not in the way the Union wanted. The Foreign Secretary was given authority for the League and he chose to work through the Foreign Office's Western Department rather than through a separate League department.

The LNU wanted the two non-ministerial British delegates to Geneva to be appointees approved by Parliament, somehow representing public opinion at large, rather than the Government. When delegates were appointed to Geneva who were not from the party in power (G. N. Barnes in 1920, Willoughby Dickinson in 1923, and Murray in 1924), the LNU applauded but kept asking for more. It suggested that one of the delegates or alternates appointed each year should be a woman, and one a 'wage-earner'.

However, it did not press hard for these changes.

The Union was, if anything , more conservative in responding to proposals to alter the functions of the League itself. The first League Assembly considered a number of proposals for Covenant revision, including one independent inititative by G. N. Barnes to develop an international League force. LNU leaders stayed away from serious consideration of these changes. They might ruminate about the future, as Murray did in 1921. 'When we have a complete League of Nations and are really co-operating we shall have to consider a joint limitation of population and all sorts of strange things.'[23] But they opposed change now. Cecil even defended Article 10 of the Covenant, which he had initially opposed, when it came under attack in Geneva. Critics said that this article, which bound League members to 'undertake to respect and preserve as against external aggression the territorial integrity and existing political independence of all members of the League', was a perpetual guarantee of existing borders. Cecil said it was misunderstood and was not a prop for the status quo at all. It was not, he insisted, an obstacle to peaceful change or even internal revolt.[24]

During the League's first year of business the LNU was cautious on most issues. It kept its own suggestions modest and resisted the more extreme proposals of others. It waited for the Government's lead, and if no lead was forthcoming it held its silence. On one issue it saw the need to act. This was disarmament, the first order of business for the 1920 Assembly. The Versailles Treaty provided for German disarmament as a prelude to world disarmament. Article 8 of the Covenant called for the reduction of national armaments to the lowest point consistent with national safety and specified that the Council should formulate plans for such reduction. It also said that the private manufacture of armaments was 'open to grave objection' for which the Council should suggest remedies, and called for a full exchange of information about the scale of these armaments among members of the League. This treaty obligation to disarm was backed in Britain by popular sentiment. It was for liberal opinion the linchpin of the whole new era in international relations.

There had been little public discussion of armaments as a separate issue during the war, and the first British governmental plans for a League did not include disarmament.[25] It emerged as a minor issue in the elections of 1918, but grew during the Peace

Conference into a major focus of concern in Britain. By September 1919 Viscount Esher could argue that it was the most critical demand the Prime Minister would have to face. For 'all other questions whether of labour or finance are subordinate to the moral shock of finding that the League of Nations does not mean reduction of armaments . . .' 'The Prime Minister', Esher said, 'will have to choose between the risks of a disarmed nation and internal revolution. He will have to carry the League of Nations to its logical conclusion.'[26]

During the first League session, Whitehall did not give a lead towards disarmament. Britain was cutting its arms expenditures for reasons of economy, but it did not advance any coherent plan for international cut-backs or controls. Whitehall joined the Quai d'Orsay in rejecting a small power proposal to freeze arms budgets for two years. LNU leaders were anxious to show that controlled international disarmament was practicable. They wanted to stay in the forefront of the important movement of opinion on this issue and counter the arguments of those who said that only direct disarmament, unilateral if need be, could work.

The LNU established an Arms Limitation Committee which began meeting in February 1921 under the chairmanship of General J. E. B. Seely, and including Maxwell Garnett, the Union's General Secretary, Oswald Mosley, its most dynamic parliamentary member, J. M. Keynes, the economist, and Archibald Hurd, who had written on naval affairs. This committee first sent out a questionnaire which it wanted the League Secretariat to distribute to member nations. It asked what armaments they would need for 'preserving order at home, for preserving order in colonies and overseas dependencies and for protecting those territories from invasion by civilized neighbours (but not from aggression by hostile uncivilized states): and protecting the country and its overseas dependencies from external aggression by rival states and for the enforcement by common action of international obligations'. Since the Versailles Treaty had imposed severe arms limitations on Germany, with the understanding that she would thence have only enough to preserve order at home, there was a vague force for moderation implied by the first question. States would presumably find it hard to argue that they needed more to maintain domestic order than Germany did.[27]

In the aftermath of the war, disarmament was a subject fraught with emotional overtones, a difficult subject to discuss in a cool, rational way. Yet the LNU began to define a middle position between the uninformed and simplistic pleas for disarmament from political platforms and pulpits and the technically correct apologias of the experts. There was nothing particularly remarkable about the proposals which the Union put forward on the subject in 1921, and indeed they looked excessively cautious to many in the peace movement. However, this effort to bring together military experts, scientists, economists, and politicians produced a worthwhile set of recommendations. They were oriented towards arms limitations and control rather than 'disarmament' (a word the Covenant never used) and helped put the discussion of the subject on a practical level.

The Arms Limitation Committee anticipated its critics by broadcasting its view that any substantial reduction in armaments to a proposed scale would have to await the complete execution of the Peace Treaty, the resolution of matters in the Soviet Union, and the inclusion of all major powers in the League. The Committee also agreed that it was impracticable to expect to be able to restrict the kind or degree of scientific progress in developing new weapons systems, for this required an international control commission, armed with powers of inspection and prohibition, which self-governing states would not tolerate. The League could start by issuing a code of conduct in war, prohibiting certain methods of destruction and specifying the standard of treatment of prisoners of war. It could also try to promote freer scientific intercourse by requiring members to register all discoveries applicable to war. While the Committee went along with the LNU's opposition to a League international army, it said the Council could create land, sea and air police forces to control or protect specific territories and work gradually towards the establishment of an international League police force.[28]

One committee member, Archibald Hurd, objected to the section of the LNU report which said that the British Navy should adopt a 'one power standard' (that is, that it build up to the level of the largest single navy in the world, dropping its traditional 'two power standard'). The report urged Britain, at the forthcoming Washington Naval Conference, to announce what it considered the appropriate level of armament which the various navies should maintain. Hurd also took exception to a memo in the appendix of the report that suggested that the composition of navies could be changed, because highly armed cruisers of less than 8,000 tons could do any work on the high seas without constituting an offensive threat to others. This point reflected one perspective in inter-war naval thought, that the day of the big battleship was over, and that navies should rely on smaller ships. On such points, as on the use of submarines, there was continuing controversy. The report turned out to be almost prophetic in its references to the upcoming naval conference. The United States, and not Britain, submitted the sort of proposals the LNU wanted on the number of capital ships allowed each power.

Before the Washington Conference brought Whitehall into agreement with this approach at the end of 1921, this section of the report was considered extreme. The rest of the report was well received; LNU proposals on armies and air forces were incorporated into the League Assembly's report on the limitation of armaments in October. The Secretary-General saw to it that all member nations got a copy of the entire report. Encouraged by this experience, the Union proffered more advice on disarmament to Whitehall. It urged that the League Council give the matter extra urgency by considering it under Article 11. That is, instead of simply acting to fulfil Article 8 which called for arms limitation, Britain was supposed to ask that it be considered under an article dealing with war or the threat of war.[29]

The main stage of progress on armaments limitation in the coming months was not be in Geneva, but in Washington. The Union had welcomed President Harding's invitation to the conference and urged the acceptance of a one power naval standard between Britain and the United States, coupled to an agreement with Japan. The conference had a more menacing aspect, however, as many Britons speculated that Harding might use the meeting either to alter the League or to set up some new Association of Nations. The very fact that this highly publicized conclave was taking place outside of League auspices could be an ominous sign. *Headway* reassured its readers, as the conference began in November, that 'Washington is not a rival, but a complement to Geneva . . . Without the League the Washington Conference would lose half its significance. . . .'[30]

As the conference progressed, a more worried tone crept into the pages of *Headway*. One columnist reminded readers that naval disarmament was a peripheral concern, of interest chiefly to three states. Land armies were the main problem and it was not clear that success at Washington would make military disarmament any easier.[31] The LNU ended by applauding the Washington treaties for sticking so closely to the line which the Union's report had advised. But Cecil was more impressed by the dangers than the achievements of Washington. He knew how illusory this 'triumph' might prove if it were not followed by military disarmament. Indeed he said in one speech that 'if all the maritime powers were to disarm, or very drastically limit their armaments, I am not at all sure that they would not increase the danger of war rather than decrease it . . .' [32]

Before the Washington Conference ended, more of Lloyd George's conference diplomacy began to unfold. At Cannes, in January 1922, France and Britain made one more attempt to complete a bilateral defensive treaty which had been mooted since the Peace Conference. The effort was a disaster which helped push Premier Briand out of office. It confirmed Cecil's fears about the shortcomings of Lloyd George's foreign policy. He did not like the French treaty idea to begin with, for it might make co-operation between Germany and the West difficult. The alternative, he argued, to these piecemeal conferences and groupings of powers, was a general obligation not only to France but to Europe. The League could be the means to this; it should be the keystone of British policy.

The Washington Conference had been the first step in Lloyd George's initiative to achieve world recovery. The second step, taken at Cannes, had failed badly and it was thereafter unclear whether much could be achieved at his next conference in Genoa. This effort at European pacification began in April 1922 with over thirty nations invited. It implied reconciliation with the Soviet Union, and hence gave rise to strong opposition in Britain, even from within the Cabinet, where Winston Churchill adamantly opposed recognition of the USSR. The implications of Genoa for the League were at first not clear. At one point League supporters hoped that the League Secretariat would manage the conference. But Lloyd George, probably assuming (wrongly) that the United States might become involved if it were kept clear of the League, rejected this idea. From the LNU's viewpoint there was less justification for this venture than there had been for Washington. Before the conference it declared that 'the future of peace of Europe and the safety of France would be better secured by maintaining, supporting, strengthening and developing the existing League of Nations rather than by forming new alliances confined to limited groups of powers'. [33]

The Rapallo agreement of 1922, by which Germany recognized the Soviet regime, settled pre-war debts and set up trade relations with the USSR, took away what little chance for success the Genoa

Conference might have had and it staggered to an end in May. Surveying the wreckage, the Union could only find a vindication of its views. Rapallo, it warned, might easily develop into a full-blooded alliance if the Allies persisted in their old policy, and if 'they keep Germany and Russia out of the League, out of the general streams of trade, out, in short, of the life of the world'.[34]

In the course of these events in 1922 the LNU began to redefine its role. With the League ignored and overshadowed, it felt it could no longer wait for the Government to act. The Union's non-party status prevented open opposition to Government policy, but now the Union tried to establish positive goals which it considered desirable. Cecil won over the LNU General Council to the idea of setting forward 'a definite constructive political policy' consistent with LNU principles. Instead of just telling the public how the League began and what it had accomplished, the Union was now ready to give its opinion on what the League ought to become. The General Council began to implement this new more activist policy at once with a series of recommendations. It asked the Government to 'formally lay it down that the League is the keystone of its foreign policy and so inform all its representatives abroad'. Whitehall should make it policy to include Germany, the Soviet Union, and the United States in the League. The Prime Minister or the Foreign Secretary should attend important meetings of the League Council; moreover, a League Minister should be appointed to the Cabinet.[35] This policy was an improvement; the Government's positive response to most of the recommendations showed that it was worth while to take the lead in matters affecting the League.

Some Conservatives railed at the idea of the Union playing any substantive role in foreign policy-making. Balfour in particular, as British delegate to the League and an Honorary President of the LNU, tried to restrict its scope. He complained to his cousin Cecil that since the Union could wield electoral power he was now wary about lending his name to policies with which he might disagree.[36] Balfour argued that the LNU was giving the League the wrong kind of support. 'What between the idiots who think [the League] inherently foolish if not wicked, and the idiots who think it should be a cure for all international and many national ills, it never has behind it the sort of public opinion required to give it stability and strength.'[37] Many at Grosvenor Crescent suspected that if they followed Balfour's advice they would be unable to do or say anything at all. How could you, as one put it, run an organization which was supposed to put the League in the forefront of your foreign policy and then limit it to offering harmless advice on International Copyright?[38]

A few League activists found the new Union policy still too constraining. Oswald Mosley, who threw himself into Union work with his customary dynamism in the early 1920s and was LNU Parliamentary Secretary, wanted the Union to be able to criticize the Government when necessary. If the Union's reluctance to do this was based on its fear of losing Conservative supporters, then Mosley argued that it would lose the support of its best adherents in order to placate people who would never support a real League policy. Similarly, Violet Bonham Carter, Asquith's daughter and a leading Liberal, said that the 'drugged unanimity' which the LNU maintained to avoid giving offence was not going to arouse enthusiasm for the League. She preferred to speak for the League on Liberal Party platforms rather than restrict herself by speaking for the LNU.[39]

Using its new freedom, the Union tackled disarmament and security issues more aggressively. With prodding from Cecil, the Executive sent Lloyd George a letter critical of the proposed Anglo-French Pact.[40] It criticized the pact as a 'partial arrangement' which might 'bring back the old system of hostile groups of European powers piling up competitive armaments against one another'. The LNU asked the Government to aim instead for a general defensive scheme 'which might be regional in its application, open to all States Members of the League together with the three leading states at present . . . outside it'. It should be based on the conception 'that if states, particularly Continental states, are to be asked to reduce materially their land armaments, it is necessary to give them in exchange some effective security against invastion'.[41] Here was the linkage between disarmament and security which Cecil was to develop into Assembly Resolution 14 later in 1922 and then into the Draft Treaty of Mutual Assistance. Here too was a sign of the LNU's willingness to meet the French half-way on the key issue of using the League to enforce the peace.

In 1919 Cecil set himself and the Union in direct opposition to French notions of using the League in this way. Even before he became Chairman, the LNU was cool to the idea of an international army and insistent that the Covenant already provided the essentials of security if it were used properly. The Union included some, like Davies, who espoused international organized force, but it had been wary of even more limited use of the League in the enforcement of security.[42]

The letter to Lloyd George and the support for the Draft Treaty of Mutual Assistance which followed it were signs of the Union's willingness to change, to address the kinds of problems the French insisted had to be dealt with before disarmament could begin. Instead of wishing away these objections and continuing to talk about public opinion as a panacea, the LNU's leaders backed Cecil in his quest to make the Covenant work. By February 1922 it was becoming apparent that they were not going to get far with disarmament unless they were willing to move in this direction.

The Washington Naval Conference aroused hopes that a direct approach to disarmament might work in Geneva. Esher, British member of the Temporary Mixed Commission of the League, submitted proposals for the reduction of land armaments which tried to apply the same methods used in Washington. He wanted the size of standing armies in peacetime restricted on a numerical basis, with the restrictions fixed by ratio. Esher based his plan on standing armies because, he said, only they could be used decisively in the early stages of a war. This very questionable assumption, and his plan's failure to consider reserves, budgets, material, and other vital matters, lost him support. The League rejected his plan, concluding that it was almost impossible to arrive at a common measure of comparison for peacetime armies.[43]

The Esher plan's failure grew in part from a misreading of the Washington experience. Disarmament had not really been 'direct' there at all; only the agreement of the powers on a pact regulating the situation in the Pacific area made the Five Power Naval Treaty possible. Then, too, naval disarmament did not present the same technical problems as land disarmament. The Naval Treaty had not provided for inspection, for instance. But most significantly, Washington had only been able to limit certain classes of vessels. If there was to be a holiday in battleship construction, the Washington powers could still strengthen their navies in other ways.

The French, both in Washington, where they ruled out disarmament except on battleships, and in Geneva, where they opposed the Esher plan, made it clear that they wanted a well-organized system to guarantee their security. Premier Poincaré was no Leaguer, but he was forced to look to the League almost by default. He had set so many conditions to French participation in a pact with Britain that hopes for such a pact were fading even before the Genoa Conference. In Britain there were some (Eyre Crowe, Austen Chamberlain) who were willing to consider the idea of going beyond a limited pact with France to a more extensive alliance. But even the 'Francophiles' were not going far enough to please the French, and they were restrained from going further by fears of entanglement in the web of alliance diplomacy.

The way was open for another approach and Cecil took it. As Rapporteur of the League's Third Committee in 1921, he had pushed through a resolution recommending that a disarmament plan should be drawn up in the form of a treaty or other precise document. In 1922, while representing not Britain but South Africa in the Assembly, Cecil stayed in close touch with the British member of the Council, H. A. L. Fisher. Fisher urged him to develop a disarmament plan in the Temporary Mixed Commission but did not tell him how to do it.[44] Cecil conferred with the Frenchmen on the commission (including René Viviani, the former Premier) and they were able to hammer out the main lines of an agreement. It called for a new Treaty of Mutual Guarantee which would bind signatories to reduce armaments according to an agreed plan. If they did this, they would be assured of help from other signatories on the same continent in the event of an attack.

This was a retreat from the ideal of the world-wide League in its emphasis on continents as the units for security. But this 'continentalism' was a reasonable response to the League's failure to attract the universal support which its founders envisaged. The League Council—which under the plan would have gained in authority—had the power to decide what constituted aggression and what the sanctions should be in each situation, so decision-making was still kept in Geneva. It was an ingenious effort to achieve general disarmament while keeping obligations reasonably specific and local. The LNU was easily persuaded to go along with this kind of continental collective security plan. On 16 March 1922 it approved a draft disarmament treaty plan along the lines Cecil advised. It specified the procedure in case of attack or menace (the Secretary-General of the League to be informed; he would summon the Council which by a three-quarters majority can direct permanent military commission or a committee thereof to submit plans for assisting the victim). Such plans would bind the contracting powers in their own continent. Reduction of armaments would proceed as specified in the treaty.[45]

Cecil tried to win Whitehall's backing for this scheme, but

without success. He pleaded with Maurice Hankey, the Secretary to the Cabinet, that he should at least be kept informed of what the Government was thinking about it.[46] In May 1923 Cecil was brought into the Baldwin Cabinet as Lord Privy Seal with responsibility for League affairs, but this did not signify any change of heart towards his plan. For one thing, the Draft Treaty raised the unpleasant prospect that one part of the British Commonwealth might be involved in a League 'war' while other were not. Or even worse, that the Commonwealth would try to act in unison, involving Britain in every region's disputes. Canada rejected the scheme, and Dominion opinion was generally cool to it. The Chanak Crisis[47] of September 1922 left Whitehall particularly wary about offending the Dominions, so there was a formidable objection on this count. The Draft Treaty also faced unanimous opposition from the service departments, which were wary of the commitments it might impose and doubtful about the assistance it could provide.[48]

The French and their allies did support the plan, but this was not an unmixed blessing in the eyes of the British public. Conservatives berated it as risky. Pacifists disliked its emphasis on enforcing peace. Leftists—noting Moscow's rejection of the treaty—feared that the Soviet Union might be scared away from the League altogether if it were accepted. Berlin's opposition was more muted, but the Union of Democratic Control and others argued that it was anti-German. Some LNU members also objected to the continental focus of the scheme. Oswald Mosley took this line of attack at a June 1924 Council meeting where a modified version of the scheme was still being debated. Regional alliances, he said, were a return to the methods of balance of power politics.[49]

In the face of these objections, the LNU leadership campaigned vigorously for the adoption of the Treaty of Mutual Assistance throughout 1923. All other issues were played down to muster support for it. Hence, when the French occupied the Ruhr as a 'productive guarantee' for German reparations payments in January, the Union response was hesitant. Under Cecil's guidance, the LNU gave top priority to winning French acceptance of the Draft Treaty and was unwilling to antagonize France over reparations until the questions of security and disarmament, and of Germany's admission to the League, were settled. Union branches were warned that a strong movement of British public opinion might antagonize the French and jeopardize a solution.

The Executive Committee chose to ignore the resolutions of its German Sub-Committee, which under the historian G. P. Gooch's chairmanship pressed for active intervention by the League. On 15 January 1923, the sub-committee had urged that Britain raise the Ruhr issue for discussion by the League Council, that the Permanent Court of International Justice should investigate the legality of the French move, and that other League societies should be asked to press their governments to get the question brought before the League Council.[50]

Instead, the Union leadership tried to contain British opinion. The February *Headway* said that it would not be wise to press the Government to take any initiative and that it was already too late to raise the question of the legality of French occupation. France should be allowed to see for herself that her plan could not work.[51] Memos to the branches and to Union speakers stressed the links between the reparations questions, security, and disarmament, and justified Britain's refusal to bring the issue to the Council. They conceded only that if another power should introduce it, Britain should not hinder the discussions.[52] The Executive Committee warned its delegates to the International Federation Council that they should not take part in any moves to force action on the Ruhr on the French Government.[53]

This kind of high strategy was not easy to sell to the left or even to the Union rank and file. By early February Murray saw this and began to express his doubts. He pleaded with Cecil not to discourage protest meetings which allowed Union members to vent their feelings over the situation. If not, then the LNU might appear to be part of a conspiracy which had disarmed Germany and then allowed it to be invaded. The charges which the UDC and others levelled against the League as a tool of the French had to be answered.[54] Inquiries poured in to Grosvenor Crescent from the branches asking why nothing was being done until on 22 February the Executive began to respond. It asked that the whole complex of reparations problems be brought before the League Council but that the timing for such a request should be decided by the Government. It also agreed to hold a public meeting on the Ruhr, but then cancelled its plans after a few days.[55]

In March *Headway* continued to urge restraint on Union members, and predicted that the French would soon see the error of their ways. ('It is because we desire above all things to secure intervention by the League that we refrain from pressing for it at the moment . . .')[56] The German Sub-Committee, after trying repeatedly to force action on the Executive, resigned *en masse*. The mass letter of resignation referred to the Union's earlier failure to take the sub-committee's advice on war guilt, the Silesian question, the Saar Valley and reparations. It singled out Cecil for particular criticism.[57]

Finally, in April, the Union began to offer some solace to its restive members. In an editorial headed 'The League must Act'. *Headway* called for 'decisive action' to end the 'intolerable' Ruhr situation. The Executive Committee followed this with a plan for 'The League and the Ruhr' on 3 May. France and Germany should be given security in such a pact as the Treaty of Mutual Assistance and Germany should be admitted to the League and the Council. German territory should be evacuated and an international commission (which included Americans) should be set up to determine Germany's capacity to pay, and then to propose a settlement of reparations and allied debts. Britain should now refer the Ruhr matter to the Council and act generously in regard to the debts owed to her by France. She should also agree that the restoration of the devastated areas in France and Belgium was the first charge on any reparations payments by Germany.[58] These were the LNU's guidelines for the coming months. They proved reasonable enough to keep the July General Council meeting harmonious. Cecil, by then in the Cabinet, was on hand to explain Government policy. Union leaders now contradicted some of their judgements on the crisis; Murray said it posed the League with 'the greatest danger in its history'.[59]

When the Ruhr crisis took a new turn in October, with the collapse of Germany's passive resistance to French occupation, the LNU proposed convening a conference to find the way out. Philip Noel-Baker, who was emerging as the LNU's most dedicated Labourite leader, hoped such a conference would isolate France.[60] Others were less sanguine about the chances of success for such a reparations conference. The solution eventually reached, with the Dawes Plan, left Union opinion satisfied. The LNU had not, in any case, campaigned actively on the Ruhr. Its overriding concern in 1923–4 was the achievement of a security plan which would 'put teeth' into the Covenant and permit disarmament. Other issues were played down, other demands quieted, so that the Draft Treaty of Mutual Assistance could be given the proper support.

Cecil's presence in the Government was the other key determinant of LNU policy in this period. He was the acknowledged leader of League opinion and his old colleagues at Grosvenor Crescent were reluctant to criticize him (or often, by extension, British foreign policy). Murray, who succeeded him as Chairman, worked to keep LNU policy in line with Cecil's views. When this did not suffice, Cecil was capable of threatening resignation from the Union to get his way.[61]

Cecil's appointment worked effectively, as Prime Minister Baldwin no doubt hoped it would, in restraining the League movement. It did not yield results for the LNU because Cecil's position in the Cabinet was weak. Because of his insistence that his first duty was to the League (and that was handled by the Foreign Office), Cecil was given office without a department.[62] Lord Curzon, the Foreign Secretary, denied him a room at the Foreign Office and full access to Foreign Office files. He chided Cecil for taking independent initiatives and supposedly poaching on areas unrelated to the League.[63] Cecil's position as a Conservative free trader in the Commons was also becoming difficult, so when Baldwin called a General Election late in 1923 Cecil asked for and received a peerage. He rejected an offer to join the Liberals and did not seem very interested in the speculation that he might be considered for the Foreign Office by a Labour Government. As he saw it, his devotion to a non-party cause, the League, could not be reconciled with the acceptance of party office.[64]

Cecil was in Geneva representing Britain when the Corfu incident occurred in August 1923. After Italy seized Corfu, Greece brought the matter before the League Council, thus presenting the League with one of its first major trials. Cecil advised Baldwin to use the League to 'bring the Italians to reason', and Britain initially encouraged a solution to the dispute through the League.[65] The LNU Executive followed Cecil's lead and urged Whitehall to do everything possible 'to secure that the League shall not hesitate to enforce the Covenant in the present critical instance . . .'[66]

The British position soon began to soften, as other voices urged restraint on Baldwin. Even Cecil, under fire in the press (the *Daily Mail* called him a warmonger), began to advise Whitehall to take a flexible position. On 5 September he suggested a formula which would have allowed the Conference of Ambassadors to supervise settlement of the dispute, albeit on lines laid down by the council. This compromise preserved some of the League's prestige, while bending in Italy's direction on the main point.[67] Before a solution emerged at the end of September, with the Conference of

Ambassadors ordering the Italians to evacuate Corfu and the Greeks to pay them very heavy reparations, the crisis proved an unwelcome trial for the League. Mussolini showered it with denunciations and threats of resignation. Smaller nations complained that the Covenant was not being applied because Italy was a big power. Public opinion had been aroused over Mussolini's behaviour, but the crisis showed how unrealistic it was to imagine that opinion could coerce a law-breaker or enforce the Covenant.

Many Union members were bitterly disappointed with the League and the Government over Corfu. Mosley spoke in his memoirs of the League being 'wrecked' by it.[68] Baldwin was alert to the possibility that the LNU might not give Cecil a warm welcome on his return from Geneva in October. He discouraged Cecil from attempting to talk about Corfu on the 'comparatively narrow platform' of the Union, and suggested that he present his report elsewhere.[69] The LNU passed a resolution deploring the regrettable action of the Conference of Ambassadors in the dispute and suggesting that the conference be kept from any further extension of its duties. It said that in future cases where the League and the conference overlapped in jurisdiction Britain should recognise the League as the superior authority.[70] In order to reassure disenchanted supporters the Union issued a pamphlet, 'Did the League Fail?' This tried to show that Italy's quick withdrawal from Corfu represented a success in disguise for the League, which had taught Italy a lesson. The Italians would 'be less likely to challenge the League in the future'.[71]

If there were lessons in the Corfu experience, the Union did not learn them. It kept saying that it would all be easy and that there was nothing wrong with the League system. It continued to stress the importance of public opinion as a sanction. Cecil, with his proposals for a Treaty of Mutual Assistance, was still trying to build up the collective security machinery of the League. However, it is understandable that many in the LNU would wonder that force was really essential to keep the peace. The problems of the thirties did not have to be solved in the twenties, but there had to be an awareness created that collective security might not work and that force was as much a factor in international relations as ever.

Instead, in some Union branches, the notion that public opinion obviated the need to use the sanctions machinery of the League was allowed to flourish. If Union leaders overlooked the way their case was twisted or misunderstood, then a stream of branch resolutions should have reminded them. The Altrincham branch asked in 1923 for an inquiry into the value of Article 16, 'with a view to suggesting either its amendment or excision from the Covenant' because 'the power of public opinion is a more effective sanction and one less liable to abuse, than the threat of military or economic weapons'.[72] Some LNU leaders either half sympathized with this line of thinking, like Murray who later described Article 16 as 'unfortunate',[73] or, like Cecil, they seemed surprised that this sort of thinking was encouraged by their remarks. Cecil wrote Murray in 1936, after 'reading an utterance of mine in 1923, in which I seem to have relied almost entirely on public opinion and ignored the necessity of backing it up by material action'.[74]

The LNU had taken some initiatives in the early 1920s and had ventured to offer advice to the Government. It remained a determinedly uncontroversial organization which had done almost as much to contain League opinion as to activate it. The course suggested by Mosley had been rejected. That is, the LNU was not to be a critical and activist group commanding the allegiance of a small core of devoted League supporters. Instead, it traded off this possibility for mass support. Inoffensive, blessed by all parties, it could have a popular appeal much wider than any other group in the peace movement. Politicians of all parties were quite willing to climb on the bandwagon once it was obvious that the ride was free—that joining the LNU did not require one to *do* anything. By 1921 the LNU Parliamentary Committee included 330 MPs supposedly working to further the objectives of the League.[75] By 1924 the *National Review* could observe that 'the League of Nations has become the common obsession of all Front Benches and no Prime Minister's speech is considered complete without some reference to "King Charles' Head" '.[76] With everyone for it it did not count. Party leaders had defused the League as a political issue.

The LNU's 'bore from within' strategy could not work in this context. Even with Cecil in the Baldwin Cabinet, it had not yielded dividends. Popular enthusiasm for the League idea remained alive in Britain, but it obscured differences of opinion as to what the League was or what it should become: a collective security club enforcing the peace or a forum for encouraging peace without the use of force, a world state in embryo, or a tool for diplomats to use in advancing the interests of their governments. The LNU, itself prey to this confusion, gave an uncertain lead to the British people on these questions. Many Union members grew frustrated because no distinctive League approach to world affairs emerged, no open diplomacy, and no world disarmament.

Chapter III

Suggestion is not Opposition: the Mid-1920s

Ramsay MacDonald's accession as head of the first Labour Government in 1924 opened up new possibilities for the League movement. *Headway* greeted the election which brought MacDonald into office with a show of enthusiasm. There had never been, it said, a Parliament more firmly pledged to support the League.[1] In some ways things did improve; the Prime Minister attended the 5th Assembly in Geneva, for instance. There was little reason to applaud the substance of his League policy, especially in the critical area of disarmament and security. Indeed, the LNU's relation with the first Labour Government soon became acrimonious.

Part of the explanation for this was MacDonald himself. Since he had taken leadership of the Parliamentary Labour Party in 1922, MacDonald made it clear that he not only had reservations about the Covenant, but also about its most prominent supporters. Where his predecessor, J. R. Clynes, had worked closely with the LNU, MacDonald wanted none of it. He blew up a petty slight—his name had been omitted from a list of leaders on the Union's Labour Committee—into a feud with Grosvenor Crescent.[2] At one point he warned the public that they might become 'the mere catspaws of the League's devotees', especially if they allowed the League to hinder co-operation with the United States.[3] When he became Prime Minister in 1924 he declined to become the Union's Honorary President, as all other Premiers had been. He instructed his secretary not even to 'bring to his notice any letter containing any mention of the League of Nations Union'.[4]

Apart from his personal feelings about LNU leaders, MacDonald also had understandable political reasons for avoiding close affiliation with them. If the Union was nominally non-partisan, it was an open secret that its leadership was predominantly Liberal in the 1920s. Even Cecil could agree with critics that *Headway* was 'little better than a Liberal propagandist publication'.[5] The League of Nations had become the pet cause of a liberalism in decline, and some Labourites were wary that co-operation with the LNU might compromise their authority and independence. The fact that their supporters cared more about the Covenant than Conservatives only made the LNU more threatening to Labour politicians than to their opposite numbers on the Conservative benches.

LNU leaders knew they had a problem in 1924. Murray told Cecil that he was sitting 'tight and being extra friendly to Labour people when the opportunity offers'.[6] He jibed that this meant that any 'criticism of Russian policy' at an LNU meeting had to be 'guarded ... moderate ... and better prefaced by an apology'.[7] More importantly, their experience with the Labour Government in 1924 helped push Union leaders into broadening their conception of the League. They gradually accepted the notion that the League could have some bearing on the problems of economic and social change which concerned Labourites. The League cause had made some headway in the early 1920s in overcoming hostility to the League as part of an unjust peace settlement. This had complicated the work of LNU organizers with local Labour groups, especially in industrial areas such as South Wales. At first, the LNU, in the words of one Labour leader, 'wouldn't be touched with the end of a barge pole'.[8]

If overt hostility to the League had declined on the left, it was not yet clear to Labourites that the League had much positive to offer. The LNU did not help matters here, presenting a picture of the League as a purely political and legal body. Union literature might point to economic conditions as a cause of unrest in central Europe or elsewhere, but it prescribed nothing stronger than a revival of trade to remedy these conditions. Domestic economic problems were handled with the care one would expect from an organization trying to win over the right to a left-wing cause. Union leaders knew that many of their followers were in fact Labourites, but this gave them all the more reason to show restraint by example. Cecil had (in common with some other progressive Tories in the post-war period) identified himself with profit-sharing and 'co-partnership in industry' schemes for reforming capitalism. He was not anxious for the LNU to address itself to economic problems, for he knew that most Conservatives were wary of suggestions in this area.

The Union made a few gestures in the direction of Labour. In the list of questions for parliamentary candidates which it prepared in 1921 for by-election use, one asked: 'Would you agree to any draft convention agreed upon by the International Labour

Conference established by the Treaty of Versailles (or, alternatively, do you agree that every draft convention agreed upon by the Treaty of Versailles should be submitted to the House of Commons)?'[9]

Even this was too much for Cecil's brother, Hugh, who warned that there was no point in putting such questions to candidates unless the Union was trying to throw its support to the Labour Party.[10] The LNU kept its question about the International Labour Office, but missed other opportunities to strengthen its standing with Labourites.

When the Government refused to submit the Washington Maternity and Eight Hours Convention and a League recommendation on unemployment to the House of Commons in 1921 and Union branches throughout the country bombarded Grosvenor Crescent with angry resolutions, Union leaders ducked the central issue. They went along with rank-and-file opinion in urging submission of the convention to the Commons, but only on the grounds that Parliament was the only competent authority to accept or reject them. As to the merits of the conventions themselves, they did 'not enter into the question'.[11]

In 1924, with Labour in power, the LNU switched course. It began to publicize the work of the International Labour Organization and show how it could help win concrete gains for British workers. The Washington Hours Convention, the agreement of the International Labour Conference establishing an eight-hour day and a forty-eight-hour week, was well suited to this purpose. The Union dropped its initial non-committal attitude and came out for ratification 'in the interest of British industry, and in order to promote more humane conditions of labour'.[12] When in 1929 the second Labour Government announced that it was ready to move for ratification, the Union talked about it (prematurely) as a triumph.

The Industrial Advisory Committee of the LNU included six employers as well as six trade union representatives (three of them selected by the Trades Union Congress), two nominees of the Co-operative Union and six members of the Executive Committee. While it tried to win support for the League from businessmen's organizations, its main function was to act as a bridge to the Labour movement and publicize the work of the ILO. Its chief activity from March 1924 on was to organize an annual conference on some subject under consideration by the ILO. The first of these, held at the London School of Economics (as most were) was on unemployment. Speakers chosen to represent a wide range of viewpoints (J. M. Keynes, Lady Astor, Pethick-Lawrence, and others) considered various components of the problem: international trade, provision of work for the unemployed, unemployment insurance, migration, and so on. The next such conference, in November 1925, was on social insurance. After each, the LNU distributed a volume on the work of the conference to those with some expertise on the subject.

After the General Strike, on 13 May 1926, Murray broadcast an address entitled 'Towards Industrial Peace' which suggested that the League might serve the needs of British industry in another way—as an example. Murray left no doubt about his sentiments during the strike ('an utterly false step') but praised the TUC leaders' 'big and generous action' in calling it off. He started with the assumption that mistrust was the heart of the problem in industry and proposed that League methods could help affect a cure. Before trouble started, the opposing parties should sit down and work things out together, just as nations did at Geneva.[13] This theme, and the incompatibility of class war at home with peace in international life, dominated LNU presentations in the economic area for years to come.

Even as the LNU adopted some programmes to improve its standing on the left, it shied away from others. Its cautious attitude towards co-operation with other peace groups, for instance, antagonized the leftist supporters of these groups. While many LNU members were anxious to help in the Women's Peace Pilgrimage or the Peace Sunday activities of the Peace Society, Grosvenor Crescent often discouraged them. In 1927, after reviewing the issue of co-operation, the Executive said that 'by identifying the Union with supposed fanatics, extremists, cranks, and Bolsheviks, [it] has offended valuable members and put off other support which it hoped to win'. It pointed to the problems which had arisen when a Union branch had joined on equal terms with other local peace groups in some activity and then found itself outvoted, 'following in the wake of persons who are actually hostile to the League'. It suggested that the LNU pay closer attention to local conditions and the degree of control it should have before extending its co-operation.[14] The General Council followed this with a resolution welcoming co-operation with bodies working for peace and international friendship 'provided always that in each case the Branch should be satisfied that the outcome of that activity increases public support for the League of Nations'.[15]

The Union leadership's vigorously pro-imperial posture gave another sign to the left that the LNU was a doubtful quantity. Imperialism had lost much of its lustre as an ideal by the 1920s, at least for most leftists. In the Union rank and file there were many signs of a critical attitude towards imperial abuses. Mosley's outspokenness on Ireland won him the sympathy of many members. Branch meetings raised embarrassing questions, as the Chelsea LNU did in 1923 when it asked whether South Africa was still entitled to be a mandate holder after its fierce repression of Bondelswart's Rebellion.[16]

Union leaders discouraged such gestures. Grey steered away from the Irish issue, which he feared might be 'death to the LNU'. Members were reminded that the League could not interfere in the domestic affairs of a Member State unless invited to do so by that State.[17] More than that, members were constantly reminded of the virtues of the imperial system.

Headway cautioned readers in 1924 that 'the worst service any supporter of the League could do his cause would be to challenge Mr. Austen Chamberlain or even the Duke of Northumberland or the Earl of Birkenhead when they dwell on the value to mankind of that great experiment in international government known as the British Empire'.[18] 'The British Empire' it said in 1926 'is the best League of Nations.'[19] For those who did not see it that way, like those Indian students 'bitten deeply' by 'the national virus', the prescription might be some Geneva elixir. Under the heading 'Progress in India' *Headway* praised the efforts of a British professor at Madras Christian College who was setting up India's first LNU Junior Branch to overcome the nationalist 'bias'.[20]

The Mandates Commission provided the model of high-minded imperial administration which the LNU held up as an ideal. 'Abuses in mandated territories', the LNU *News Sheet* reported in 1927, 'are now almost non-existent. The commissioners' is not an easy task, but they fulfil it nobly'.[21] The Union opposed efforts by the British Government in 1926 to restrict the power of the commission to conduct investigations in mandated territories.[22] It proposed in 1929 that the mandate system be extended automatically into any territory which was transferred from one colonial power to another. In addition it encouraged all States to send reports on all their colonial possessions to the commission.[23]

On several issues, then, the LNU was out of sympathy with most Labourites. Certainly in 1924, when the Labour Government was formed, the Union was in a weak position *vis-à-vis* a hostile Prime Minister. Cecil and his supporters still hoped that the Draft Treaty of Mutual Assistance, their main objective, might stand a chance for British acceptance. MacDonald had not given them any grounds for such hope in 1923; his comments on the scheme had sometimes been vague, but never favourable. He had said that there had to be a more complete political settlement before disarmament could work, and he stuck to his point of view in office.[24] The Union urged him to appoint a Royal Commission or committee of inquiry to study the issue and report in time for the 5th Assembly in September 1924.[25] MacDonald instead proposed to refer the matter to the Committee on Imperial Defence, which left the LNU unhappy. It guessed what the attitude of the service members of the CID was, and knew that Hankey, its Secretary and moving force, was hostile.[26] The Union appealed again to the Prime Minister for a special committee, or, that failing, that he enlarge the CID with more civilians and make its discussions of the Draft Treaty public.

The Union set up a committee of its own to revise the Draft Treaty so as to eliminate some objections to it. The committee, consisting of Cecil, Murray, Mosley, and John Waller Hills, the LNU's Conservative Vice-Chairman, did polish it up but without altering the major contours of the scheme. None of this impressed MacDonald, who in a meeting on 19 June with Cecil tipped his hand against the scheme, citing the opposition of the Dominions.[27] Britain's note of rejection to the League Council followed on 5 July ending all hope for the treaty.

The rejection was coupled with a proposal to convene a world conference on armaments, including countries not in the League, in order to discuss all available plans, including the Draft Treaty. this vague suggestion was brushed aside by Cecil, despite its implication that the Draft Treaty might be considered again. Cecil instead tried to rebut the objections to the treaty in the Government note: that it would not really lead to disarmament because its guarantees against aggression were ineffective and that it required too much of the member nations.[28] The LNU sent a memorandum to the Prime Minister signed by 124 members of all parties, expressing anxiety that the British rejection might be interpreted as meaning that Britain was ready to withdraw the responsibility for dealing with disarmament from the League or that it had rejected the principle of linking security with disarmament.[29]

This repeated knocking at a door which had been slammed was

not entirely without logic or result. It was designed to salvage at least something from the wreck of the Draft Treaty. The principles embodied in the treaty had important Labour supporters; Arthur Henderson, for instance, although without much leverage on foreign policy in the summer of 1924, was sympathetic to the Union's case. Moreover, MacDonald's statements were vague enough to give rise to the hope that the question was still up in the air. Shortly after he sent in the 5 July note of rejection, the Prime Minister spoke in the Commons, agreeing with a speech by Asquith which backed the principles in the Draft Treaty.[30]

At first, the strategy yielded no results. Lord Parmoor, head of the British delegation to Geneva, made an opening statement to the 5th Assembly in September which seemed more emphatic in its opposition to collective security than anything MacDonald had said. Murray, also on the delegation, wrote to Cecil that it was 'pure pacifism' which made things more difficult.[31] Parmoor's pacifism, and the wariness of continental commitments which came with it, of course made the task of other non-pacifist opponents of collective security easier. Hankey thought MacDonald had dished the Draft Treaty 'splendidly' at this stage.[32] However, the debate within the Labour Government on the issues raised by the Draft Treaty had not ended yet. Within a couple of weeks Murray saw the tide turning in Geneva, and the delegation moving from opposition to the treaty 'step by step . . . into a very similar treaty'. This new treaty, which emerged as the Geneva Protocol, a plan based on compulsory arbitration, seemed to Murray 'rather milder and less definite than the TMA because the present French are far more reasonable than the late French'.[33]

Cecil did not view the Protocol as an adequate replacement for his Draft Treaty. It was vague where its predecessor had been specific. However, its emergence was a victory for the Union cause which gave reason to hope that a solution to the disarmament–security deadlock might be possible. The LNU quickly endorsed the approach of the Protocol (officially the 'Protocol for the Pacific Settlement of International Disputes') and congratulated the 5th Assembly for 'the great advance towards permanent peace achieved by the general recognition that arbitration, security and disarmament go hand in hand'.[34] The Executive urged the Government to form a special committee representing all sections of British and Dominion opinion to examine and endorse the Protocol proposal. Where the Draft Treaty had limped along without attracting much support from

Conservatives or Labourites, this new plan was off to a good start.

Headway proclaimed in November that 'nothing that has happened in the past month, or for many months and years before that, can compare in importance with the approval by a unanimous vote of the Assembly on the Protocol . . . Unlike the Treaty of Mutual Assistance whose place it has taken as the approved way of approach to the eternal problem of reduction of armaments, the Protocol has attracted immediate attention in this country.'[35] The compulsory arbitration idea was bringing Labour opinion round from a rather fuzzy pacifist isolationism towards a position closer to the Union's. It was clearly very popular in the LNU rank and file, if only for that reason.

Arbitration, a concept which had figured so importantly in the pre-war peace movement, presented something of a political challenge to Union leaders. The League Assembly of 1924 placed it alongside security and disarmament in the triad of objectives needed to secure peace. The LNU had no problem in campaigning for the so-called Optional Clause, by which nations agreed to submit disputes of a judicial character to the permanent Court of International Justice. However, with Conservatives and Liberals doubtful about the principle of arbitration, Union leaders hesitated about pressing it further.

In the continuing discussions on the subject in the 1920s, Cecil seemed fearful that arbitration might divert attention from disarmament and security rather than provide access to them. He was generally unhappy with Labour's performance at the League; Drummond confirmed his suspicions that Britain was managing her case badly.[36] Disappointed to be out of office, he still was restrained in discussing MacDonald. If Labour was doing badly, he said, it was because the Prime Minister was too dependent on bureaucrats for advice. They were really to blame.[37]

By the end of 1924 divisions within the LNU on arbitration were evident. In the brief election questionnaire the Union distributed for the General Election, the two questions on the Protocol were kept accordingly non-committal. *Headway* ran an article, 'The Case Against the Protocol', by 'A particularly competent Dominion authority' which argued that the British Empire could not commit itself to backing the status quo in Europe. A new mechanism without sanctions had to be developed.[38] In any case, Conservatives opposed the Protocol in the elections, and their victory dimmed its prospects.

Cecil was brought into this second Baldwin Government as

Chancellor of the Duchy of Lancaster with the League portfolio. Two Conservatives who had also been early League supporters, Steel-Maitland and Eustace Percy, were also in the Cabinet. Cecil was not seen as a political threat by Chamberlain, the new Foreign Secretary, as he might have been seen by Curzon. Yet Chamberlain opposed his appointment and was still jealous of his reputation in League matters.[39] When Cecil was to be appointed to a League Committee on Opium, Chamberlain could say that if Cecil were in Geneva 'they will treat him as our foreign minister in all that affects or may affect the League and will constantly treat any stray expression that he lets drop as an authoritative expression of our views'.[40]

Cecil wrote to Chamberlain in support of the Protocol, but his efforts were perfunctory.[41] The LNU tried more earnestly to forestall its rejection, urging Baldwin to convene a conference with Dominion leaders to iron out a policy and propose whatever reservations or conditions were needed to get agreement.[42] Chamberlain backed Crowe and his other officials in opposing further commitments to the League. His reply to Cecil mentioned the alternative to the Protocol which Crowe was promoting, a tripartite defensive pact with Belgium and France.[43] The Government went through the motions of consulting the Dominion governments and did not reject the Protocol immediately. But by the beginning of 1925 it was a foregone conclusion that the Protocol could only, as one Foreign Office memorandum put it, either die a death of inanition or come up at Geneva to be shelved.[44]

Despite many bad omens, the LNU kept campaigning for the Protocol, which by January had attracted the signatures of seventeen nations. *Headway* talked as if Britain's options were still open although the situation was quite different from what it had been the previous summer when the Union had campaigned for the Draft Treaty after it had been rejected. A limited regional arrangement to quell France's fears was too much for some members of the Baldwin Cabinet (Amery, Churchill, and Birkenhead), and a general League security agreement was out of the question. The essence of the Protocol, along with compulsory arbitration, was the commitment to impose sanctions against any aggressor. This had no important Conservative supporters.

Chamberlain told the League on 12 March 1925 that Britain would not sign the Protocol. He criticized specific features of it: its restrictions on preparations for war and its insistence that an aggressor must pay money for the cost of his aggression. He also cited his objections to a sanctionist League of any sort and went on to suggest an approach which was markedly different from that of the Protocol, a limited defensive arrangement to meet special needs. A European security arrangement between France and Germany, with Britain and Italy as guarantors, was developed along these lines and signed at Locarno the following October.[45]

Grosvenor Crescent's response to this shift in Government policy was interesting. The Executive reaffirmed its support for the Protocol even after it was laid to rest. It insisted that 'comparatively slight' amendment 'should suffice to meet any valid British objections'.[46] At the same time it agreed that while a Franco-German treaty was no substitute for the Protocol it was acceptable. However, if such a pact were not framed as 'a first step towards something like the Protocol' then small states might interpret it as a sign that a Great Power Concert of Europe was being revived.[47] Chamberlain had clearly indicated that his new proposal was meant as a substitute for the Protocol. The LNU did not challenge him directly, but appeared to misunderstand what he was doing. Drummond sounded out Cecil about this 'impractical policy', which had raised doubts in official circles.[48]

The LNU's action was not entirely absurd, even if it did not sway hearts or minds in the Baldwin Cabinet. For one thing, Conservative objections had been less to the particular mechanism of the Protocol than to the very idea of strengthening the Covenant. The Union could not simply concede on this. Then, too, LNU leaders knew that they would disappoint two important wings of League opinion if they gave up on the Protocol too easily. Many Labourites had been weaned away from their earlier reluctance to support the League by compulsory arbitration. MacDonald seemed to grow more eloquent in support of the Covenant now that he was out of office,[49] and the Union did well to encourage this Labour support. On the other side, Davies and his followers saw this as a critical juncture for the principle of collective defence, and wanted a vigorous campaign for the Protocol. The Executive took a middle course, agreeing that the principles of the Protocol deserved support even though the Protocol had now been judged unacceptable by the Government. Beyond these internal considerations, Murray saw a more basic purpose served by this insistence on a security pact. As he told Cecil in May, 'the great snag before us in League of Nations work is the intense reluctance of the British people to undertake any binding engagement'.[50]

The LNU thus launched an intensified campaign in support of the principles of arbitration, security, and disarmament in May. It sent deputations to 10 Downing Street, conducted mass meetings and collected petitions in order to keep the demand for a Protocol with suitable reservations alive.[51] It prudently added that some new plan for all-round reduction and limitation of armaments through security and arbitration would be equally acceptable. Cecil chaired a Union meeting on 25 June and encouraged these objectives, even though they were not those of his Government. He did include a note in the programme notice to the effect that he was not bound to LNU policy in any way![52]

Chamberlain did not consider himself an opponent of the League. He did not view his plan for a Franco-German pact as a way of scuttling the League, but of supplementing it where it was weakest; he was in fact quite ready to tell Briand that the 'pivotal idea' of his Locarno treaties was that there would be recourse to the League whenever trouble arose.[53] But his exasperation with the LNU and its demands for far-reaching commitment to the League began to seeth at this stage. He threatened to resign from the Union in June because of the continuing campaign for the Protocol,[54] and rejected an invitation from the Birmingham LNU with an angry rejoinder that he did not want to advance support for the Protocol. Chamberlain also showered Cecil and Murray with complaints about the LNU; he objected particularly to a circular, 'Arbitration or War', which used his own remarks and Baldwin's out of context. Grosvenor Crescent disclaimed responsibility for the circular.[55]

Cecil was restive in office and often at odds with his colleagues. On the Protocol and Locarno, progressive League supporters were increasingly unhappy with the Government and the Union. Cecil supported Locarno and defended it against critics who felt it subverted the League idea. It was a rearguard action, defending the Government from LNU critics, and he did not enjoy it. His hold on the Union slipped, and Murray had to restrain him from over-reacting when an article in *Headway* criticized Britain's role at the 1925 League Assembly. The offending article did not represent official LNU policy, and Murray could explain it away as the most harmless way to give vent to the many grievances building up in the movement.[56]

The LNU leadership defended the Locarno Pact against its isolationist and internationalist critics as a cautious step in the direction of establishing that general security which the Treaty of Mutual Assistance and the Protocol had tried for earlier. They added the proviso to their statements that 'of course we should like the Government to go further'.[57] Noel-Baker thought that Locarno was similar enough to the Draft Treaty (without its disarmament clauses) to represent a Union victory.[58] Chamberlain's rhetoric about Locarno being 'only a beginning' encouraged the assumption that other better agreements would now follow. When the Executive welcomed the conclusion of the Locarno Pact on 22 October 1925, it added pointedly that it was rejoicing because the final protocol of Locarno stated that once the treaties were in force disarmament could proceed under the Covenant.[59]

The expectation that Chamberlain would go on to strengthen the League and achieve disarmament did not last long. During 1926, in dealing with Germany's admission to the League Council, which was to follow the Locarno settlement, Chamberlain left Union opinion sorely disillusioned. He retreated into the worst habits of the old diplomacy, and seemed ready to play along with the French manœuvres to bring Poland into the Council along with Germany. Even before the Germans applied formally for League admission in February, Grosvenor Crescent suspected that their application might be in for trouble. An LNU representative, Gerald Spicer, visited the Foreign Office to convey the 'great apprehension in Union circles' at the prospect that Poland might win a permanent seat on the Council along with Germany. He argued that this could weaken or destroy the League. Whitehall continued to go along with the French on the issue, and Spicer's visit only alerted officials to the need to neutralize opinion on it.[60] Chamberlain explained to Murray and Hills why he backed the Polish and Spanish claims to permanent membership on the Council. He seems to have impressed them with his case, for they presented it to the Executive without mentioning that they had heard it from the Foreign Secretary. However, the Executive refused to consider the claims of other powers until the promises given to Germany were fulfilled.[61]

The German admission question began to dominate the Union's relations with Whitehall. Here the League and the LNU could not be shunted aside, for the composition of the League was the issue. There were Union members who supported the Polish and Spanish claims to the Council. Chamberlain's explanation, that bringing Poland in along with Germany might encourage these neighbours to co-operate, attracted some support. Drummond encouraged this approach, so it would not be fair to call the debate one between pro- and anti-Leaguers. As far back as 1922 an LNU sub-committee had come out for Spanish admission to permanent membership 'in view of her pre-eminent position among the Spanish speaking nations', while the Executive had withheld judgement on the issue.[62] Most League supporters did not want to dilute the significance of German admission by coupling it to other cases. The issue had taken on significance as a sign that the painful years of post-war settlement were over and that the League was not established.

Chamberlain's policy had no serious opposition in the Cabinet. Hardliners like Churchill who had had their doubts about Locarno saw support for Poland as a realistic move.[63] Cecil was very cautious in his opposition. He told Chamberlain that the Poles were a kind of 'orientalized Irish' who made unreasonable demands, but respected whoever stood up to them. He tried to brandish the force of 'League opinion;'[64] Chamberlain was not impressed. Cecil's sense of grievance grew; he complained about the way Chamberlain constantly resorted to private conversations when open diplomacy was called for. Exasperated, he tendered his resignation, but then quickly withdrew it when friends assured him that the issues were not clear enough to make sense to the public. *Headway*, following Cecil's lead, called for the League to get 'back to publicity' in June, and said that secret meetings encouraged intransigence and blackmail.[65]

The LNU gradually gained respect for its case in Whitehall. A tone of disdain had rarely been absent when the Chamberlain Foreign Office had discussed League opinion in the past. One memorandum on the 1925 Greco-Bulgarian dispute recommended that the matter be buried, but warned that the Bulgarians 'and our League enthusiasts will insist on its being repeatedly exhumed. They will talk of "the prestige of the League being at stake" '.[66] However, in the midst of the campaign on German admission, with the LNU circulating petitions against the 'sudden and unconsidered change in the fundamental constitution of the Council'.[67] Chamberlain was put on the defensive. He had to produce his instructions in a Commons debate before going to Geneva in order to reassure opinion that he did not intend to prevent or delay Germany's entry. Foreign Office references to the LNU were now much less casual. William Tyrrell wrote to Chamberlain in Geneva that 'after the three week League of Nations Union debauch, people here are beginning to rub their eyes and to ask themselves whether they have not been carried too far in their zeal for the League and whether it was desirable to send you out tied hand and foot to Germany'. Even the Geneva correspondent of *The Times* had been captured by the League enthusiasts, Tyrrell complained.[68]

The Union was delighted with its success in deflecting Chamberlain's course. 'It is hard to resist the conclusion', *Headway* said, 'that in this case public opinion very largely did its work. The general declaration of the will of the country was abundantly justified and produced the result it was intended to produce'.[69] *Headway* revelled in the hostile *Daily Mail*'s charge that the Front Benches in Parliament were now at the disposal of a 'mischievous clique of international busibodies'.[70] The compromise settlement which brought Germany into the League at the end of 1926 (with Council membership raised from 10 to 14, Germany made a permanent member, and what amounted to semi-permanent status created for intermediate powers) was an anti-climax after these triumphs in March. The Union felt powerful enough to look to the future with renewed optimism. Cecil told Murray that League affairs were going well in Britain and that the opposition was silenced. 'I have no doubt that any Government that really set itself in opposition to the League would be immediately turned out.'[71]

Chamberlain, bitter about the experience, took the tone of the 'realistic' League advocate in discussing it. 'If the League is killed,' he said, 'it will be by the enthusiasts who will not recognize realities.'[72] The Foreign Secretary argued that though he 'gushed less' he knew the League had influence and dealt with it accordingly. It was 'as a hard fact' and not only or mainly because of British public opinion that he took account of the League.[73] Indeed, he said that 'if anything could frustrate my efforts . . . to increase the authority and strength of the League, it would be the consistent wrongheadedness of the *secretariat* of the League of Nations Union. They have not a grain of judgment and have never once been right.'[74]

League supporters had grounds for optimism at the end of 1926. The League, with Germany as a member, was widely regarded as a centre of world diplomacy. The Union could bask in its reflected glory, with an impressive total of 600,000 members and branches in almost every large town in England and Wales. As one post-war problem after another was settled, and Europe entered its 'Age of Locarno', the British public could feel reassured about international affairs. The measured pronouncements of the LNU did nothing to disturb this popular mood.

The Locarno treaties remained in favour with League opinion; second thoughts came only much later. By the mid-thirties it was part of the common wisdom that Locarno was a special arrangement which had undercut the League. But in 1927 *Headway* was still lauding the Locarno treaties and calling for an 'Ocean Locarno' from the powers at the Geneva Naval Conference.[75] Locarno was never as warmly supported by rank-and-file Union opinion as the Protocol, but there was no real opposition to it within the LNU in the twenties.

However, the assumption which had won Locarno its backing in the Union—that it would lead to better things—quickly proved false. Chamberlain was not at all ready to champion the causes of disarmament and arbitration which the Union supported. He tipped his hand in a few well-publicized statements. At a 1927 Council he said that the League might expect to have less work to do now that the greater difficulties in Europe were settled.[76] At the opening of the 1928 Assembly he said that while Britain would honour its obligations to the League it would incur no new ones.[77] This kind of comment flew in the face of a key assumption of the LNU: that the League, whatver its shortcomings, could become something better. Chamberlain's 'realistic' support of the existing League would not suffice if he closed the doors to progress.

The optimism of LNU leaders had certainly been excessive if they thought they could do much about this. They kept spelling out recommendations for general simultaneous reduction of international armaments, but to little effect. The specific proposals they had ready in the summer of 1926 called for a halt in all increases on armaments and then a uniform percentage reduction (on expenditures, manpower, or some combination of the two) which would apply world wide until limits set under Article 8 of the Covenant were reached. If universal agreement did not prove feasible, then the LNU said that regional agreements would still be worth while.[78]

It was only reasonable in 1926 to recognize that a regional arms pact might be the best one could hope for. But this scaling down of expectations from the LNU report of five years earlier was still marked. In 1921 the Union placated backers of an international police force by advocating League forces to protect certain territories. In 1926 such advocacy seemed pointless, and the division within the movement on this question widened. Davies entered a minority report in which he put the case for an international force. The sections of the LNU report which dealt with the use of chemicals and gases, and of a code of conduct in warfare generally, also revealed the more sombre outlook in 1926. The Union moved away from advocacy of regulations because it knew that they could not be enforced. Only in naval disarmament, where there had been progress, could the report speak in specific terms. It called for the Washington limit of 35,000 tons on battleships to be reduced to the 10,000-ton limit (with 6,000 for cruisers) set for Germany at Versailles.[79]

In Geneva the preparatory commission for a disarmament conference began to meet in May 1926 with the United States (although not the Soviet Union at first) represented. It was hard for even the most dedicated Leaguer to expect much relief from that quarter, as the commission entered into its almost interminable discussions. In these talks, and in the Geneva Conference between Britain, the United States, and Japan, which met in the summer of 1927 in an effort to extend the Washington naval agreements, the British Government was shown to be very far from sharing the Union's perspective.

Cecil, as a member of that Government, had to champion a case he disliked at Geneva. His position was not simply that Britain should cut back further on armaments; certain reductions, such as the ones which Britain had made unilaterally in keeping with her expectation that no war was expected for ten years, could be dangerous. He had criticized the Washington naval agreements from this perspective, that the wrong kind of disarmament was worse than none. Baldwin had used unilateral reductions of the sort Cecil opposed to satisfy the budget-cutting impulse of Conservatives, and therefore Cecil was unable to win support in his party for comprehensive disarmament. He was on the defensive within the Baldwin Cabinet as an unrealistic crusader for a cause. Tom Jones's *Whitehall Diary* records that the Cabinet found him 'sometimes remote from reality'.[81]

Cecil complained to Baldwin about the case he had to argue at the preparatory commission in Geneva against limiting military aircraft and air reserves. He came close to resigning in April 1927, insisting that unless he had room to bargain 'it would be better for someone else to take my place here'.[82] When Britain turned from the deadlocked commission to naval talks in the summer, Cecil was again caught in a difficult situation. As a principal delegate to this conference Cecil had to block American proposals to limit

British cruiser strength. He accepted the rationale for the British case against parity with the United States in cruisers, that Britain needed more because of her longer sea-lanes.[83] However, the main thrust of the British case was to treat the United States as a potential adversary—which he felt was foolish—and to look at the Navy (and not the League or collective security) as the bulwark of Britain's defence.

There was indeed an element of unreality in the British attitude towards the United States. In the aftermath of the Washington Conference, in the decade between the termination of the Anglo-Japanese Alliance and the Manchurian crisis, the really problematic factor was the future role of Japan in East Asia. Seen from this perspective, the sparring over navies between Britain and the United States does appear almost silly. Yet, when Cecil tried to cut through the morass of technical disputes to improve Anglo-American relations and make some headway on arms limitation he got nowhere. Cecil knew he was outgunned in the Cabinet on most League issues, but even he grew alarmed at the gap between the Cabinet and himself over the limited arms control measures proposed at Geneva.

Apart from these broader questions of policy, there were more specific factors moving Cecil towards resignation from office. The Geneva Conference was making the Government look so inept that it gave Cecil a good opportunity to resign and unfurl his disarmament banner. The Cabinet had changed its initial plans and authorized full parity with the United States early in the conference. Then it reversed itself again in July by approving a parliamentary statement (by Balfour) that had the effect of limiting its concession by insisting that no long-term precedent was created by it. Cecil felt that Balfour's statement undercut him as a delegate. He offered to resign, at first 'on some health pretext or the like'.[84]

Then, in a letter of 9 August 1927 to Baldwin, he resigned on grounds more far-reaching and potentially dangerous to the Government. The letter proclaimed arms limitation the most important question of the day and listed many past issues—the Draft Treaty, the unconditional rejection of the Protocol, the ministerial declaration against compulsory arbitration, the partial failure of the League Preparatory Commission—where Cecil had been overruled.[85] With recriminations growing daily over the Geneva Conference, this kind of resignation could not be ignored. Chamberlain tried to dissuade Cecil, not out of resignation so much as out of the kind of resignation which might upset the public. 'By censuring your own Government', he argued, 'you by implication justify the Americans; you play straight into the hands of Big Navy Steel Trust gang; you provoke an international controversy . . .'[86] In response to this pressure, Cecil kept weakening his resignation letter—the fifth edition of it finally appeared in the press—so while his resignation was 'political' it had lost its fire. He was conciliatory enough, constantly insisting that no one had treated him badly, to lead his colleagues to wonder whether he even meant his resignation to stick.[87]

This resignation inevitably raised the issue of the LNU's political position. Cecil, co-President along with Grey, wanted to bring his case for disarmament to the public. Some friends urged him to make his resignation the start of an electoral campaign, but he was reluctant to abandon the Conservative Party. He chose instead to avoid party politics as such and start an 'educational' campaign on disarmament through the LNU, his speeches and writings. This would stress the need for an arbitration and security system as the prerequisite to disarmament by international agreement. It would return to first principles by emphasizing that the League had not been created as a convenience for diplomats, but as a way to rid mankind of the threat of war. Cecil sent a statement on his resignation to the Union membership explaining that he had taken the step 'to get full freedom to advocate disarmament'.[88]

LNU leaders knew that the adoption of Cecil's campaign might put them on a collision course with the Government which could split the Union. Hills, the most active Conservative on the Executive at the time, agreed with Cecil and Murray that the risk was worth taking. They would avoid making disarmament a party issue as far as possible but knew that they would look like the Free Trade Union trying to hang on to its Conservative supporters.[89] Duff Cooper, another Conservative on the Executive, was more hesitant and argued that the LNU should be careful not to censure the Government and antagonize its friends in office. In this number he counted Chamberlain, who, he said, needed all the help he could get against Churchill, Birkenhead, and the rest.[90] Murray hoped that he could keep Conservative support by emphasizing that the real cleavage was not on party lines, that Chamberlain and even Baldwin were closer to the LNU than to the Churchill faction on some issues. Moreover, Murray argued, much of the Liberal press had been anti-League and might be ranged with Churchillites, Beaverbrook, and socialists like

Wedgewood in the 'opposition'.[91]

Murray seemed to relish the opportunity to move the LNU into a more openly critical position. It allowed him to stay with the tide of League opinion without crossing Cecil. Personally, he agreed with Grey that arbitration had to be emphasized more and he jibed at Cecil's Conservative 'friends' who were 'frightened' of the idea. But he was, as usual, ready to follow Cecil's lead. In this case he accomplished it by emphasizing disarmament over arbitration and security in the League 'triad'.[92] Murray launched the Union drive to back Cecil with a sweeping letter to *The Times* on 2 September denouncing the way the Government had handled League issues. He berated it for using the League only 'occasionally when the old methods for one reason or another have broken down'.[93]

Cecil's resignation did not worry Whitehall at first; Chamberlain thought it left the Government stronger, if anything.[94] Nevertheless the Foreign Office did try to play its old game of neutralizing League opinion, after Grey had given a rather non-committal speech on the resignation. An official, Walford Selby, wrote a fifteen-page letter to Grey on 3 September, complimenting him on his sound judgement in avoiding premature criticism of the Government. Selby deplored the way Cecil, and those in agreement with him, were attacking Chamberlain's policies and implying that unless they had their way all hope was lost for the League.[95] Grey's response showed that while he may have been out of touch with Cecil and Murray his views were no less forceful than theirs. He insisted that public opinion had to be educated and encouraged, and that the Government should then push on as far as opinion allowed towards arbitration and disarmament.[96]

Labour opinion seemed quite favourable to Cecil's resignation and the Union campaign. The Liberals, however, had been divided on the arbitration and security questions, so the LNU's efforts centred on them. Murray worked through Herbert Samuel, keeping him informed on the Union's line because 'it might be useful . . . in shaping Liberal policy'. He told Samuel that while Cecil intended to state his case in a non-party way, it was likely to become a political issue in the LNU anyway. Murray mentioned that he himself had made common cause with MacDonald on supporting the principles of the Protocol, and urged Liberals to do the same.[97] When this tack failed, Murray warned Samuel that Liberals were allowing their reservations about the Protocol to confine them to a position opposing the 'tremendous movement of opinion' on the question.

Murray also tried to draw Samuel into a meeting with Henderson, Cecil, and perhaps Grey.[98] Despite Lloyd George's objections to the idea, Murray still hoped to get leading Liberals to issue a strong statement on disarmament and arbitration. If Liberals did not do this, he told Samuel, their party would risk sending the League movement's half-million liberally inclined voters into the arms of Labour.[99] Samuel did meet with Grey and Murray, but to no effect. Grey used the occasion to push his argument against further arms limitation talks; Samuel was hesitant about committing himself because this might serve to show that the Liberal leadership was divided. Cecil observed that one difficulty in getting the Liberals to support disarmament was that armaments firms and hence 'a certain capitalist element' influenced them just as it influenced Conservatives.[100]

Union leaders tried to get as much publicity as possible for their campaign. Noel-Baker pressed friendly writers to concentrate their fire on disarmament. He hoped to get beyond the usual League circles and to enlist the services of Sir Frederick Whyte and the 'Round Table' people.[101] Murray and Noel-Baker conferred on how to get the *New Statesman* into line.[102] C. P. Scott was anxious to put the *Manchester Guardian* at the service of the campaign, and met Cecil on 8 September to find out his plans.[103] The *Guardian* followed with letters by Murray and MacDonald critical of Chamberlain's League policy and supporting the principles of the Protocol.[104] *The Times*'s coverage was, by contrast, unsympathetic to the Union.

At a special meeting of the General Council in late October 1927 the LNU spelled out its objectives. It was now risking a great deal, asking its Conservative members to stay with it in what was clearly an anti-Government campaign. It tried to minimize internal divisions by keeping the less controversial goal of disarmament in the forefront, ahead of arbitration and security. The Council stressed 'that the general reduction and limitation of armaments by international agreement before it is too late is essential to the maintenance of permanent peace, the fulfilment of our international obligations and the achievement of national economy'.[105]

This solicitousness kept really dedicated Union Conservatives like Hills behind the campaign, but that was not enough. In the many committees and branches of the Union serious trouble was brewing. Captain G. D. Fanshaw, an MP, led protests in the Finance Committee against a special appeal for funds to help the disarmament campaign. After all, he argued, the campaign might run counter to Government policy and do real harm.[106] LNU staff members were unenthusiastic about the campaign because it might prove too divisive; even Mrs Edgar Dugdale, one of Cecil's relatives and head of the Intelligence Section at Grosvenor Crescent, was raising problems for the Disarmament Campaign Committee.[107] By November Cecil had to egg a now hesitant Murray on, warning him that if the campaign was having harsh consequences for the Union, the consequences would be worse if it were dropped.[108] Cecil tried to meet Conservative opposition head-on by arguing that the party would suffer if people got the impression that one could not be a loyal Conservative and League supporter at the same time.[109]

Conservatives now redoubled their efforts to push the LNU back into line. First Lord of the Admiralty Bridgeman, who had been a delegate to the Geneva Conference with Cecil, made hard-hitting speeches in which he tried to undercut those Conservatives who supported the disarmament campaign. At Welshpool on 9 December Bridgeman lashed out at the Liberal Party, which he accused of trying to make the LNU a sort of Liberal caucus serving its own purposes.[110] By the time of the Union's General Council in December, Cecil was forced on the defensive. He had to protest that he never intended to use the campaign to belittle, destroy, or injure the Government.[111]

Even as its campaign faltered at the beginning of 1928, the LNU began to enunciate positions that were significant in the context of its past relation with the Government. In 1925, during a long-running debate with the Foreign Office on whether British delegations to Geneva should be purely governmental or should represent different strands of opinion, Hills had enunciated Grosvenor Crescent's view of its position *vis-à*-vis the Government:

[Non-party organizations] should always try to act with the government of the day. They should search for reasons for support and should never take up a carping attitude. If they have to differ they should try first the method of private suggestion. Suggestion is not opposition. If suggestion fails they should again consider whether the point at issue is so vital that a body consisting of all parties must oppose the government which some of them support politically. This is a very last resort; and in the case of the Union has never arisen.[112]

Now Murray spelled out the LNU's right to disagree in what was almost a declaration of independence, when compared to Hills's statement: 'If there is to be any public interest at all in the League, people must be free to form and express however respectfully, their

own opinions . . . Yet . . . this degree of publicity is alien to the
diplomatic tradition and consequently irritating. . . .'[113]

On a number of vital issues—disarmament, British signature to
the 'Optional Clause' which would pledge it to adhere to decisions
of the Permanent Court of International Justice, and collective
security through the League—the Union had differed sharply
with the Government. Now Murray was announcing that it was
dangerous to pretend that those differences did not exist. The
public tone remained polite; Cecil thought privately it was still too
polite. He now wondered if he had been wise to turn to the LNU as
his vehicle after his resignation. The restrictions of a Union platform were forcing him to act more moderately than he felt. What
Cecil felt was that a change of Government was needed, even if the
alternative was another Lloyd George administration![114]

LNU leaders kept their public statements as scrupulously non-
partisan as they could. Cecil issued an almost apologetic explanation in March 1928 of what steps the Union took to ensure that
there was no party bias in its programme and literature. He
admitted that 'it may be true that Liberal and Labour politicians
are in fact attacking the Government over armaments, and using
some or all of the same arguments as those used by the Union', but
he said nothing could be done about that.[115]

On the substantive disarmament issue the LNU did not back
down. Union leaders knew that they had bent over backwards to
keep their words inoffensive to Conservatives. Surely they could
not be expected to say nothing at all. When *Headway* returned to
the subject in May 1928, it showed the determination not to be
cowed of one who had been silent too long: 'If Wilberforce and
Clarkson had thrown up the sponge because, to begin with, the
Government was against them, how long would it have taken to
abolish slavery? If Shaftesbury had dropped his agitation against
factory abuses because he could not convince the Government in
ten minutes, how long would it have taken to get the Factory Acts
passed?'[116]

Chapter IV

The Late 1920s to the Early 1930s

The disarmament campaign which the LNU launched in 1927 was a disappointment. The public did not respond and the Union found itself isolated. Despite its brave words about independence, Grosvenor Crescent still hesitated before criticizing Whitehall. In October 1928 *Headway* lamely pledged that LNU activities 'will be characterized by that abstraction from party politics which the Union has solidly sustained through a full year of criticism, misunderstanding and heartburning'.[1] The Union could still count on at least a show of friendliness from the Prime Minister; Baldwin was quite willing to speak at its tenth birthday meeting at the end of the year. However, the events following Cecil's resignation underlined the continuing dilemma of the LNU in politics. The Conservatives were not about to be divided against themselves; they would react quickly to curb the Union when it moved into any dangerous electoral territory. They would use the LNU's desire to remain on good terms with them fully, complaining and threatening resignation whenever necessary.

As the Union looked forward to its tenth birthday meeting, its leaders had good reason to question their assumptions. They had built up the largest and best organized League movement in the world. Yet their impact on the conduct of foreign affairs was slight. Whitehall gave them a polite audience and then ignored their advice. They had no trouble attracting supporters, but serious problems were developing within the Union organization. Murray mused that 'if we are silent we incur very heavy losses on the left. People are already leaving us to join the Council for the Prevention of War, which has been very active during the last two months. If we speak, there is danger of splitting the Union'.[2]

If the name of the Peace Pledge Union or some other group were substituted for that of the Council for the Prevention of War, Murray might have been voicing identical fears at almost any time during the next decade. Berated from one side for being overzealous and from the other for being impotent, the LNU was hemmed in by its non-party status. In the 1930s, when the League was in decline and LNU membership sank with it, there were new questions raised about whether the Union had been organized on the right basis after all. Had it been right to emphasize size as a criterion of success or influence? To avoid spelling out for members the perhaps unpleasant consequences if the League were challenged? To gloss over weaknesses in the structure of the League which might prove fatal?

Within the LNU in the late 1920s, members were increasingly raising questions about the way things were organized. The idea of having politicians and other public figures running the organization was bound to cause some hard feelings among rank-and-file members. A high-powered central organization, using up most of the Union's funds, could be justified by results. When the 'names' could not produce results, then it was natural for some members to question priorities, to ask whether more should not be spent on branch activities and less on London. F. G. Penman, a Branch Secretary who was on the Executive in 1927, suggested that the internal administration of the Union be turned over to a sub-committee. His main complaint was that there was a wide gap between the branches and the Executive; few members of the Executive knew or cared much about what was going on in the branches of the organization they administered. Since most of them lived in London they were not in contact with members from around the country, and they never heard reports from the Regional Organizers or LNU staff speakers who did travel.[3]

The Union had moved towards decentralization in the early 1920s. At the General Council's 1922 meeting special privileges were accorded to the Welsh National Council, which was self-supporting and ready to sponsor its own campaigns and collections. Then in 1923 the Council backed the principle of decentralization 'both to the forming of the policy of the Union and to carrying out that policy so far as it affected the work of the local organizations of the Union'.[4]

This proved difficult to put into practice. Consultative committees listened to complaints from around the country and decided that the solution was the creation of district councils, regional offices to act as headquarters in miniature on a county or local level. They would provide more accessible leadership than did Grosvenor Crescent. By 1928 many County Federations with paid staff had been established, but only three district councils had been willing to take on the administrative work for their area: distributing *Headway*, keeping records, fund-raising, and so forth. With administrative decentralization proving costly, the

Executive recommended that it might be stopped. It urged instead that more 'Federal' councils be created, with a larger base than the district councils and, it hoped, a better financial base. Regional representatives on the Grosvenor Crescent payroll would also try to provide the branches with more help.[5] However, neither this, nor the adoption of a new system of postal ballots for thirty members of the Executive Committee, solved the problem. Ordinary members of the LNU did not like the way things were going and wanted their say. Their mood was angry enough to make a challenge for leadership of the Union appear feasible before very long.

If there had been anything remarkable about the LNU's internal affairs in the 1920s it was that there was so little friction. To put it into another perspective: why were the rank-and- file members so ready to follow the Executive Committee? The tactics of quiet persuasion which seemed so natural to politicians in the corridors of power must have been viewed with suspicion by many Union members. They may have been conservative by comparison with others in the peace movement, but they were still predominantly of the left. Yet they acquiesced as their leaders kept trying for support from Whitehall with polite non-partisan methods. They accepted token concessions from governments time and again without protesting. There were, to be sure, attempts to push the policy of the Union in one direction or another. The LNU, with its large membership and propaganda machinery, was a natural target for take-over attempts. But the LNU's experience with them only underlines the loyalty or apathy of its rank-and-file members. On some issues tempers ran high within the LNU and there was agitation. But a sustained challenge had not developed in the 1920s.

The way the Union was organized helps explain this. Its very size made it difficult for any group of discontented members to muster support. The General Council, which held final responsibility for Union policy under the Royal Charter granted in 1925, was unwieldy. It met only twice a year, bringing together delegates from the branch organizations. Even though most eligible delegates did not attend, there were still almost a thousand delegates at some meetings. Hence it was difficult for the Council to accomplish anything and real power passed to its Executive Committee.

This group of about fifty met once every two weeks in London to make major policy decisions and supervise the staff of over one hundred at Grosvenor Crescent. The composition of the Executive Committee changed from year to year, but it usually had the same balance between politicians and professors, trade unionists and businessmen, retired soldiers and sailors. Although Executive Committee members elected by postal ballot could not be 'pegged' occupationally by the committee, co-opted members were. So vacancies could occur for a trade unionist or (in July 1939) for a Conservative MP who was a supporter of Prime Minister Chamberlain *and* of the League of Nations. The names of certain regulars recurred from year to year. David Davies and the Revd Gwilym Davies from Wales; Willoughby, later Lord Dickinson; Sir John Power, the Conservative MP; H. S. Syrett, a solicitor who had been Private Secretary to Lloyd George at the Ministry of Munitions; and of course officers and leaders of the Union such as Hills and Noel-Baker. Many regulars were women: Katherine Courtney, who had been President of the British Women's International League, and Mrs Dugdale, Balfour's niece who had been in the LNU Intelligence Section, were both regulars after 1928. The near absence in this group of Conservatives, or in any case of Conservatives of some standing not in Cecil's family, was apparent. There was much talk about the need to balance the Executive, but few willing Conservative volunteers.

Some rising politicians, the young Mosley or Duff Cooper, for instance, were willing to invest the time and effort required to be active in the LNU. It required dedication for them to stay the course. Accordingly, the Executive got most of its members from the fringes of the political power structure. By contrast, the *Honorary* Officers of the Union were the prime ministers, party leaders and other major political figures—but they were usually no more than window dressing.[6]

The Executive Committee could take advantage of the fact that rank-and-file opinion, as it emerged from Council meetings, was very diverse. There were so many shades of opinion represented within the Union that one cancelled out the other. For every leftist student demanding a clearer stand, there was an older Conservative who felt the LNU had taken too many stands already. Those members who did have strong feelings on an issue faced overwhelming obstacles in getting the organization to respond. It was easier to resign and work through another group, or to ignore national Union policy and work at a local level within a Union branch.

Tensions had built up in the late 1920s, sometimes taking the form of a jurisdictional dispute between the Executive and the Council, sometimes of the country's resentment of London. A Re-organization Sub-committee studying these problems in 1930 reported that headquarters was too aloof. Instead of providing friendly counsel or a stimulus, the branches saw it pressing for more money or sending over-complicated direction for action. The sub-committee advised several changes and urged Executive Committee members to attend Council meetings, and Federal and county committee meetings as well.[7]

At the beginning of 1931 several members led by Lieut.-Gen. Sir Alexander Hamilton Gordon circulated a long printed memorandum to branches in an effort to create support for major changes in the organization. The 'Gordonites' had tried to get the address lists of Branch Secretaries from Grosvenor Crescent but were turned down, so they could not get quite the effect they had hoped for. The Executive tried to settle the challenge through private meetings with the rebels, but they were rebuffed in turn.[8] The 'Gordonites' argued that the Union's failures were due to unsuitable ways of conducting business. They said that the Council was too big for serious debate and could do no more than ratify the Executive's decisions. Yet the Executive did not really represent LNU opinion.

The Gordon Movement's Conservative political emphasis was clear. Captain A. Pelham-Burn, one its leaders, was especially critical of the way Cecil, albeit in his private capacity, had urged voters in 1929 to vote for pro-League candidates.[9] Pelham-Burn and the other insurgents wanted to limit the LNU's political role so that its leaders could not make dangerous appeals to Conservative voters. They emphasized the need for the Union to confine itself to educating the electorate and 'coordinating' public opinion. This meant taking a less partisan line at meetings and carefully avoiding commitment to advanced views. Above all, it meant leaving foreign policy to the Foreign Office.

This political focus was not all what most Leaguers wanted. They were impatient with polite non-partisanship and anxious for results. The 'Gordonites' could promise increased membership but little else. It was never, therefore, a plausible challenge to the Union leadership. However, because its political message was interlaced with pleas for organizational reform, for a decentralization of power at the expense of the Executive, it struck a responsive chord for many members.[10] Council members seized on the criticisms of the LNU's internal management in the

Gordon Memorandum, specifically the delay in forming county councils and the lopsided use of funds. They wanted more spent on organizers and less on publications by the central office.

The Gordonite challenge did not lead to any massive overhaul of the LNU. It was one aspect of a continuing movement towards reorganization which achieved some success in 1931. The General Council was trimmed down to make it more workable by allowing for one representative for each 300 members. The newly constituted Council which began meeting in December 1931 was not only more manageable in size, but also more representative than its predecessors, with delegates invited from almost every county. The postal ballot for the Executive Committee was also modified in this wave of reform. In addition to a general list, it also had a regional list of thirteen candidates, so that Wales–Monmouthshire region, Scotland, and the eleven administrative regions of England the Union had created each were guaranteed a representative on the Executive Committee. Each of these regional candidates had to have worked in a branch, district, regional, or national council in his own area. The Council also set up a Regions Committee to consult with the Executive and keep in touch with grass roots sentiment.[11]

These changes satisfied the demand for reorganization. The re-vamped Council was quick to take stands on policy, so that the same sort of Conservative complaints which had previously been directed against the Executive (committing itself to controversial stands, etc.) were thereafter directed at the Council as well. When the Council supported a controversial proposal for an international air force in 1934, it was Cecil's turn to protest against 'the doctrine that anything the Council passes becomes an article of faith for members of the Union'.[12]

The dissastisfaction of Conservatives prompted a few other changes in 1931. Sir John Power initiated discussions with the Conservative central office on how to make the LNU more acceptable to the party. The chief difficulty, as Power saw it, was that it was too easy for a local branch organization to fall under the control of leftists. The remedy, he hoped, was the establishment of county or 'federal' councils to keep errant branches in line.[13]

The LNU leadership, battered by the 'Gordonite Revolt', did not resist this quiet effort by Conservative insiders. Conservatives had influence out of proportion to their numbers for another reason as well. The Union's ambitions outran its income, and its most important outside contributors were Conservative businessmen. In 1930 the contribution of the branches to he. quarters produced only a bit more than half of the total of £42,126. income.[14] With its membership fees kept low to facilitate recruitment, the LNU was kept very dependent on outside contributors.[15]

Colonel H. F. T. Fisher, who had been the LNU's General Secretary in its early years and thereafter headed its Appeals Department, was able to play on this situation with considerable success from the Conservative viewpoint. At times his department appeared to be the tail wagging the LNU dog. Certainly in 1931 he helped push for the creation of more federal councils and for the other changes which he hoped would reduce the influence of 'extremists'. If Fisher imagined that these schemes would win the LNU the support of leading Conservatives he was soon disappointed. Nevertheless, Fisher kept using the leverage of his office. In 1932 he reported that 'whilst there are literally hundreds of potential donors whom I could call upon, I do not feel I can honourably do so until there is some definite assurance that the right type of County Secretary will be appointed. I say this in the interests both of the Union and of the donors themselves.'[16]

The problems of the League movement overseas had also become evident by the late 1920s. Drummond was moved to write to Cecil in 1928, pleading with him to reorganize the International Federation of League of Nations Associations which 'seemed to lead to dissention more than union'.[17] The Federation had grown steadily since it started in Brussels in 1921 with only twenty member societies. Under the guidance of the Frenchman Theodore Ruyssen it had attracted forty members by the end of the decade. Some of these groups were large; the French League society had more than 120,000 members in 600 branches by the end of 1927, roughly a fourth of the LNU's total at that time.

However, the International Federation was in many ways a liability to the League instead of a source of strength. *Headway* noted in 1928 that little could be expected of the Federation's annual congresses, with some societies 'so weak as to be almost negligible' and with the 'national point of view not infrequently overshadow[ing] the international'.[18] These congresses met each year and formulated resolutions which it presented to the President of the League Assembly and printed in the League *Official Journal*. The whole enterprise had a quasi-official stamp which lessened its credibility as the voice of League opinion.

League officials were alert to this problem from the start. The head of the League's Information Section in London told Cecil in 1923 that something had to be done to establish in the public mind that the movement was independent and not simply a branch of the League.[19]

Cecil was not sure what to do when Drummond urged him to get the Federation into shape. He felt that it spent too much time on policy and too little on propaganda. League societies were useful chiefly for what they could do in their own countries, he told Drummond, and they should be discouraged from communicating directly to Geneva. As for co-operation between societies, the prospect which League supporters had once found so promising. Cecil was not sanguine. Only in a few situations, where they could exchange information or the like, did Cecil see the need for representatives of different societies to consult one another.[20]

This was a very limited conception of what League societies could do in concert, but a realistic one. Conceivably the LNU could have done more in co-operation with a few strong sister societies, notably the French, but there were problems even here. On some key issues which arose at Federation meetings in the next couple of years, British and French societies were at odds. The French, for instance, championed Foreign Secretary Briand's proposals for a European Federal Union in 1930. The LNU saw this plan as a threat to the League and to the British Empire, and was willing to consider it only if it were placed first on the agenda of the League Assembly where its chances were slim.[21] Extensive co-operation with the French was to come only in 1939/40, when war was on and the old controversies no longer mattered.

Unable to do much about the failings of the international League movement, LNU leaders developed a rationale which made it seem less vital. They stressed that it was *British* opinion and *British* leadership which really counted in the world. Salvador de Madariaga, who headed the Disarmament Section of the League Secretariat and then represented Spain on the Council, reflected on the bewilderment of Cecil, Murray, H. A. L. Fisher, and the other British 'civic monks' when they arrived in Geneva and discovered that the world was full of foreigners. To envisage how things should work, they found, was every different from making them work. This was especially true when foreigners had the irritating habit of rejecting your sound advice![22] Hence they redoubled their emphasis on the importance of Britain. *Headway* commiserated in 1928 that 'most of the readers of these pages would agree that if there happened to be fifty Great Britains or fifty nations with the same tolerance, far-sightedness, generosity and statesmanship as characterises our own country, everything would be much better than it is . . .'.[23]

British internationalists berated their countrymen for being insular, yet in this assumption of superiority lay an insularity as great as any they condemned. There might have been a redeeming feature in this emphasis on the disparity between British and foreign opinion or behaviour. If the arguments about the inadequacies of others were pushed a step further they might have led to real questioning of internationalism's first principles on the nature of world public opinion and its potential effect on the League. Instead it remained for Conservatives to bring home the lesson that others felt differently about the League and might not appreciate British motives or suggestions. During the Ethiopian crisis Chamberlain told Murray that neither 'in France, Germany nor Italy does anyone believe that our motives are disinterested . . . or that the real cause of the British attitude is loyalty to the League in and for itself'. That 'should teach us not to count on that motive prevailing in the nations which deny it to us'.[24]

In 1928, as the disarmament campaign waned, public attention in British League circles returned to the subject of arbitration. The 9th Assembly of the League had prepared a number of model treaties for dealing with disputes which did not come under the international court's jurisdiction. Adopted by the Assembly in 1928, the 'General Act' for the Peaceful Settlement of Disputes grouped together an ambitious package of conciliation and arbitration proposals. Whitehall was initially cool to these arbitration proposals. Government spokesmen said that they were premature, that since public opinion provided the ultimate sanction for arbitration, it would be wise to wait for opinion to develop further before taking on this new commitment.

Cecil too remained hesitant about arbitration, particularly about the proposals then current to invite the United States into an all-inclusive arbitration treaty. 'All-in' arbitration, which has been defined as a pact of perpetual friendship under a different name,[25] might, he suggested, be seen as a British trap in Washington and result in damage to Anglo-American relations.[26] Most LNU members wanted their organization more firmly committed to arbitration; pressure for British signature of the 'Optional Clause' did not satisfy them. The Union sponsored a scholarly conference on arbitration in June 1928 which reached no particular consensus, but at least showed that the Union supported the idea. By the end of the year the LNU urged study of the Assembly's 'General Act' as the basis for a general and all-inclusive arbitration treaty.[27]

Advocacy of 'all-in' arbitration had by then become entangled with that for the outlawry of war which in turn helped generate the Pact of Paris signed in August 1928. The 'outlawry' idea (the more proper word 'renunciation' was used in formal discussion) had developed considerable support in the United States and from the LNU perspective it was seen as a way of encouraging American co-operation in world affairs. Salmon O. Levinson, the Chicago businessman who had launched 'outlawry' with an article in the *New Republic* in 1918, had met Cecil in 1923 and asked for his support. Cecil spoke approvingly of outlawry, but it was clear that he thought of it less as a well worked out proposal than as a way to win more public support for the League.[28]

Outlawry did not arouse much enthusiasm in the Union at first. Its American proponents clearly had little use for the League and the Permanent Court for International Justice. Yet *Headway* still was willing to concede in 1923 that outlawry justified itself 'if its only result is to awaken American public opinion to a sense of its responsibility.'[29] Only when Briand proposed in April 1927 that France and the United States conclude a treaty outlawing war between their two countries did Union leaders begin to take the topic seriously.

Then they wanted to harmonize the outlawry proposals with the Covenant, and capture the high moral tone of the idea of renouncing war so as to harness it to the causes of disarmament and collective enforcement. The LNU Secretariat prepared a draft treaty which tried to achieve these goals. It said that aggressive war was an international crime and pledged signatories not to resort to war except in self-defence or 'action in pursuance of Article 16 of the Covenant' or 'action as the result of a decision taken by the Assembly or Council of the League of Nations'. It also provided for peaceful means of settling disputes, closing the 'loophole' by which the Covenant permitted war. The Union considered its draft treaty in terms of its possible acceptability to American opinion.[30]

Secretary of State Kellogg's proposal to enlarge a treaty renouncing war to include all the principal states in the world made the task of reconciling outlawry with the Covenant more urgent by the end of 1927. In the context of the LNU disarmament campaign and its attacks on Chamberlain's foreign policy, the

Kellogg proposals were important in another way. After the collapse of the Geneva Naval Conference it was important to improve Anglo-American relations. The Foreign Office did not seem to be active in doing this, so LNU leaders tried to drum up support for the Kellogg proposals to show Whitehall the way. It promoted the project of a joint all-party letter in support of the Kellogg proposals; Murray cajoled Lloyd George into going along, but he failed with MacDonald so no letter materialized.[31]

The Union was cautious in its advocacy, because it feared that Washington might back out if Britain pushed too hard. When the LNU circulated its own draft treaty, it made it clear that it did not expect it to provide a model for something Britain should submit to the United States. Given the realities of American politics, the Senate could hardly accept a British proposal without changing it. Hence the Union only wanted to provide some helpful guidelines for the Foreign Secretary in his negotiations with the Secretary of State.[32]

As Kellogg moved his proposal along, the LNU kept up a stream of enthusiastic statements. At the same time it kept reminding people that the renunciation of war was no substitute for the League. Grosvenor Crescent encouraged branches to work for the acceptance of the Kellogg proposals while addressing themselves to the 'misunderstandings' which had developed about them: that the proposals would interfere with the right of self-defence or prevent the implementation of sanctions under the League or the Locarno Treaty.[33] Cecil wrote an article for *The Spectator* explaining why the outlawry proposals would not threaten the Covenant. Coercive action under the Covenant was *international*; had the Americans wished to forbid such action they would not have limited their proposal to the limitation of war as an 'instrument of *national* policy'.[34] Cecil and the Union did not encourage over-close scrutiny of the proposals or hair-splitting discussions about their practical effect. They scorned Chamberlain's efforts to pin reservations to them and to ascertain what their impact would be on the Monroe Doctrine. This was no ordinary episode in diplomacy to the LNU. 'Now and then in the affairs of nations what is termed "a venture of faith" is called for and justified. All the omens point to the conclusion that this is in fact one of those rare occasions.'[35]

The reasons for this almost excessive show of enthusiasm for the emerging Pact of Paris are not hard to find. It represented progress, badly-needed motion of a sort which Cecil's resignation had not generated. Cecil revealed this direction in his thinking when he said that the Union's aim was not just to induce acceptance of outlawry, but 'to make its acceptance a fresh starting point for the movement towards arbitration and disarmament'.[36] The pact was to serve as a springboard, and *Headway* admitted that if it did not lead to disarmament then 'all the hopes the Pact has inspired to-day will be largely illusion'.[37] Extravagant praise for the pact and hopeful talk about the fundamental change in the climate of world affairs it had ushered in were all a preface to the Union's real demands: signature of the Optimal Clause and an all-inclusive arbitration treaty, international disarmament, the withdrawal of foreign troops from Germany, and other measures.[38]

The logic of this argument, that the Pact of Paris was a marvellous source of inspiration which should help the LNU achieve its other objectives, led down a blind alley. It encouraged efforts to bring the Covenant into harmony with the pact. Philip Kerr, using his authority as a specialist on American affairs, pressed for such an effort even before the pact was ratified at the end of 1928. Kerr joined the Executive Committee and laboured on a report suggesting amendments needed in the Covenant to bring it into line with the pact. His report suggested eliminating mention of war as an instrument of national policy in Articles 12 and 15. More important, he suggested a new interpretation of the all-important Article 16. Because it was 'almost impossible in a crisis' to determine who had broken the Covenant, Article 16 should not require members to apply sanctions against an aggressor. Instead, they should combine to prevent a resort to hostilities. The Pact of Paris had, after all, outlawed resort to violence as a way of settling disputes.[39]

These changes were more than Cecil and most other LNU leaders could support. They doubted Kerr's assertion that this sort of thing would impress the Americans. The Union's Revision of the Covenant Committee rejected the idea that the Covenant should be harmonized with the pact, citing practical problems. The LNU preferred to view obligations under the pact and the Covenant as concurrent, and leave it at that.[40] Kerr protested against the Committee's lawyers, who said the pact had such slight legal weight that it could be dismissed as a mere 'international kiss'.[41] But his effort had failed.

Union leaders saw the effort to modify the Covenant as potentially dangerous, something which might split their organization and egg pacifists on against Article 16 and collective security.

Within the LNU, as in the Labour Party, the allegiance to the League's sanctions machinery remained more formal than real. An effort to bring the Covenant into line with the pact could start many members questioning first principles, and that was risky. But the issue would not go away. The British Government proposed to the 1929 Assembly that the Covenant be amended in order to pledge members to renounce war except in self-defence. In 1930 Cecil was on a Government committee studying how the Covenant might be altered to do this. By then he was very wary of the proposal and spoke out against watering down the Covenant. Though it might please the Americans it would alienate the French.[42]

The LNU did not oppose the Government's proposals directly, but many members of the Executive were unhappy with them and the Union was very restrained on the subject.[43] Moreover, the Executive insisted that it would support changes in the Covenant only after a new disarmament treaty took effect and after the Assembly passed a resolution which made it clear that the Council must not recommend measures involving acts of war, except against a party which had itself resorted of war.[44] The revision issue divided Union opinion, so when the attempt to bring the Covenant into line with the pact failed in 1931, there were no tears shed at Grosvenor Crescent.

Whitehall did pursue naval agreement with France in the summer of 1928, but this was not the kind of initiative in disarmament which the LNU wanted to flow from the Pact of Paris. The Union disarmament campaign revived and began to have some effect on the public by the end of 1928. Conservative Party leaders were now worried about the electoral impact of the League issue. Sir John Power, a Conservative who tried to serve as a bridge between the party central office and the Executive Committee, suggested that if Cecil were invited back to the Foreign Office he would be worth a million votes.[45] However Baldwin attempted to neutralize League opinion by making an overture to Grey instead. In January 1929 he asked him if he would be willing to serve as Foreign Secretary in a new Conservative Government.[46] When this got no response, Baldwin went into the May elections unmoved on disarmament and security questions and pledged to keep Chamberlain at the Foreign Office.

By the time of the elections Labour had warmed up to the League considerably, chiefly because of Henderson's patient work within the party leadership. The 1928 party programme, *Labour and the Nation*, had a section on international affairs which omitted the old demands for revision of the Versailles Treaty. Henderson's emphasis on collective security through the League still faced opposition from pacifists and leftists. But the prospect of Labour victory now was a very different matter for LNU leaders from what it had been in 1924. The Union could not take direct electoral action, but Cecil issued a well-publicized letter urging voters to support only those candidates who could be trusted to back a 'vigorous and progressive peace policy'. Cecil issued the letter as an individual and not as President of the LNU, but the distinction was not one the average Leaguer was likely to make. Cecil *was* the LNU to most people, and in the context of his resignation it was clear enough which way voters were being asked to turn.[47]

When Baldwin was ousted and a new Labour Government took office, a hopeful era began in League policy. The LNU moved back into its usual posture as a sympathetic supporter of the Government. Henderson became Foreign Secretary and brought Cecil into the Foreign Office as Chairman of a Committee on League Affairs. Cecil, still a nominal Conservative, finally got the desk in the Foreign Office which he had coveted for so long. Noel-Baker became Henderson's PPS while his friend Hugh Dalton became Under-Secretary. Cecil's relations with Prime Minister MacDonald remained cool, and Philip Snowden was very hostile to him. Snowden tried to keep this 'Tory Jesuit' out of the Government because of his leadership of the LNU, 'a most harmful organization'.[48] However, Henderson supported Cecil and they worked well together until the Government broke up in 1931.

Some questions remained about Henderson's ability to implement his plans, given MacDonald's record and the divisions in the Cabinet. Then there was the question of whether Foreign Office officials would let their new chiefs have their way. When Will Arnold Foster was brought in as Cecil's Secretary, Dalton noted 'We are rapidly building up a superiority of gunfire over the officials.'[49] Noel-Baker speculated on the need to launch a movement against the influence of the bureaucrats; Cecil was less worried about the Foreign Office than about Hankey's continuing influence on the Prime Minister.[50] These suspicions of Hankey were well founded. The Secretary of the Cabinet later admitted that his hostility to the League and collective security had been consistent since 1916.[51] Cecil talked about pushing Hankey out of office, but Hankey kept MacDonald's confidence and was never really threatened.[52]

Foreign policy was not the exclusive concern of the Foreign Office. The Services, the Treasury or the Board of Trade had decisive influence on some decisions in the inter-war period. There, especially in the service departments, the LNU had few friends. The hostility of officials to the League was rarely overt. It was easier to ignore the new institution at Geneva than to attack it. But resentment was there, beneath the surface: at Cecil, with his frequent attacks on bureaucrats, at the high salary scale of League officials, at amateurs intruding into the foreign policy domain of professionals.

Most officials accepted the need for the League, just as most politicians did. By the late 1920s they did not advocate a return to the old diplomacy. Most were willing to listen to new approaches. Appeasement did represent a new approach to foreign policy, after all. Yet Grosvenor Crescent and Whitehall remained far apart on the substance of League and armaments policy, and generally on the issue of where the emphasis should be in foreign policy. Nevertheless the context of the LNU's relationship with the Government at mid-point between the wars was quite different from what it had been in 1919. The League had become established. Robert Vansittart, who became Permanent Head of the Foreign Office in 1930 seemed almost sympathetic compared with Crowe, who held that position before 1925. Vansittart had been touted as a traditionalist within the Foreign Office, but he could write privately in 1931 that the League was the keystone of British foreign policy and that there was 'much thinking and struggling ahead of us if the old pernicious doctrines of the balance of power [were] not to creep back'.[53] Vansittart impressed LNU leaders favourably at first; after meeting him in 1933, Murray still found him 'very sensible and strongly pro-League'.[54]

With Labour in office, League supporters moved to realize their long-deferred dreams. Within the LNU, advocates of a pooled League force dressed up their proposals and started anew under Davies's leadership. The development of air power—talked about as the ultimate weapon in the 1920s—gave them fresh ammunition. A book by William McDougall attracted wide support in 1927 for the case of establishing a League air force with a monopoly of high-speed planes, while relegating only slower craft for commerical purposes.[55]

The Union was divided on the international force idea, with Conservatives and pacifists generally hostile. At the General

Council in June 1929, advocates were able to push through a resolution asking the Government to 'seriously consider, with a view to arresting competition in air armaments, whether it would not be possible to internationalize the whole or a proportion of national air forces as an instrument for the defence of the international order'.[56] Davies and his supporters on the Executive (Major Buxton and Lady Layton) made other attempts to advance the international force idea, but they did not get much further until hope for disarmament faded.

Disarmament was still the chief objective of the General Council in 1929. It urged the new Government to press for naval agreement with the United States so as to achieve a drastic reduction in all classes of warships.[57] During MacDonald's American visit, *Headway* spoke in glowing terms about the progress that was being made on reaching understanding with Washington.[58] When Anglo-American discussions broadened into the Five Power London Naval Conference in January 1930, Union leaders were hopeful. They said that Britain should be ready to disarm so long as she kept equal to any other naval power.

The London Conference led to a treaty which extended some of the Washington agreements of 1922, and brought some progress in other areas such as the construction and use of submarines. But in many ways the conference proved unsettling to Grosvenor Crescent. It was not just that France and Italy kept their old naval rivalry alive and eventually failed to sign the main London treaty. Nor was the problem simply that Britain and France failed to resolve their differences. The main difficulty the LNU had with the proceedings in London was that they still seemed to be based on the old assumptions about the probability of war and 'of each State having to provide unaided for its security by means of its own armaments'. The Union had hoped for the abolition of submarines, the scrapping of many existing capital ships and a ban on the construction of new ships of over 10,000 tons.[59] Instead it got only some limited regulation, far less impressive than the treaty reached in Washington in 1922. In the past the LNU had explained away failure at the disarmament conference table as the result of lack of commitment by Whitehall. Now Whitehall was committed, so its failure was not so easy to dismiss.

The London Conference experience prompted a measure of reappraisal in the Union. People asked again if sanctions belonged in the Covenant. The LNU's June 1930 statement on international policy said that the conference had shown the difficulty of reconciling American isolationism with European insistence on maintaining 'prearranged mutual assistance between nations for the defence of international order'.[60] A more fundamentally pessimistic critique began to find expression in Union meetings and the pages of *Headway*. In his article, 'The Danger of War: Are we Taking it too Lightly?' in the August 1930 *Headway*, C. Delisle Burns berated those advocates of League methods who 'are so certain of their own virtue that they do not notice the smokers in the chemical works, or, if they notice, they only ask them to join the Union'.[61]

If there was anything to be optimistic about after the London Conference, it was that Henderson had clearly not given up on disarmament. At the 1930 Assembly Henderson spelled out his demand for further progress in disarmament, and underlined it by linking British agreement to the General Act and Treaty of Financial Assistance to the completion of a Disarmament Convention. LNU leaders backed this move, for they knew that Henderson, unlike some other Labourites, was a strong supporter of international sanctions and was not trying to use the League's failures with disarmament to dilute British security commitments.

The old uneasiness between LNU leaders and the Prime Minister persisted. MacDonald rebuffed Cecil's many attempts to meet him, and in his correspondence with Cecil on disarmament he revealed attitudes that were heretical at Grosvenor Crescent. For instance, MacDonald expressed concern about British weakness in world affairs and said that others might perceive British zeal for disarmament as a sign that Britain could not afford to arm anyway.[62] British world leadership was still an article of faith in the Union. Cecil had privately speculated about whether disarmament by the naval powers without corresponding reductions by the military powers might not undermine Britain's position, but he felt obligated to deny any sign of weakness now, lest he give ammunition to Hankey and other opponents of disarmament.[63] In any case, MacDonald kept his Government committed to disarmament despite mounting right-wing opposition.

Union leaders were divided on how deeply they should commit their organization to disarmament in the autumn of 1930. Murray was very doubtful whether, after years of campaigning on it, the Union could now rouse the nation to the cause. He wanted to turn to other issues, international co-operation on economic matters in particular.[64] Cecil and Noel-Baker fought hard to keep the priority on disarmament, and they had their way. In 1931, during the year's hiatus between the disappointing close of the preparatory commission and the opening of the World Disarmament Conference on 2 February, 1932, the LNU campaigned more vigorously than ever before for disarmament. Even this was not enough to satisfy Cecil, who complained to Murray that Union people were not throwing themselves into the campaign with enough zeal.[65]

The approach which the Union hoped to realize at the World Disarmament Conference was based on two main planks. One was to win recognition for Germany's right to equal status with other powers. The other was a 25 per cent reduction in armaments budgets world-wide, to be carried out within five years. The Peace Treaty's restrictions on German armaments provided the starting point for the effort to gain equality for Germany. The LNU called on other States to scale down their forces in line with the restrictions placed on Germany and, most significantly, to prohibit the production of the 'aggressive' weapons denied to Germany by the treaty (warships over 10,000 tons, tanks, submarines, heavy artillery, and military aircraft). The Union's approach thus combined qualitative and quantitative features. It was capped with a call for assurances that the strength of all would be used for collective defence.[66]

At the meeting of League societies held in Brussels in mid-February 1931, Cecil tried to win support for the LNU programme. Despite the opposition of the French delegate, who contested Cecil's view that the failure of the Disarmament Conference would mean disaster for the League, Cecil got the International Federation committed to abolishing certain classes of weapons. At home, the Union was pleased to be in step with Basil Liddell Hart, the influential military affairs expert. Liddell Hart's memorandum, 'The Problem of Land Disarmament: A Solution—Simple and Complete', also suggested abolishing heavy guns and heavy tanks.[67]

The LNU had more difficulty winning support from other sections of the British peace movement. To pacifists, the Union's programme, promising a mere 25 per cent reduction in armaments over five years, could hardly be called disarmament. Still the LNU did its best to overcome its own corporate jealousy of other peace groups in order to get peace movement support. In an uncharacteristic gesture, it urged members to co-operate with the Women's International League for Peace and Freedom in obtaining signatures for a 'Disarmament Declaration'.[68] It played down mention of sanctions in order to encourage pacifists to go along with its arms reduction programme. This aspect of the Union's campaign, and more broadly the idea of subordinating all other issues to disarmament, was to complicate things when events in Manchuria made the question of sanctions less academic.

The Union used every resource at its command to win public support for the Disarmament Conference. It published leaflets such as 'Arms and the People', bombarded the sympathetic sections of the press, such as the *Sunday Times* and *Weekend Review*, with press releases, and addressed countless trade union, Rotary Club, and Co-operative Movement meetings in support of its objectives.[69] It provided its branches with model resolutions for town meetings they were told to sponsor on the subject. Cecil and Murray tried (without success) to get funds from the Carnegie Endowment to publish an international bulletin on disarmament. They were able to get the endowment to help stimulate Armistice Day public meetings in the United States to arouse American opinion.[70] They also set to work on a great international congress in Paris, which launched the conference with an appropriate flourish of speeches by dignitaries (former Premier Herriot, M. Titulesco, and others) and demonstrations.

All of this activity helped trigger opposition from the right. The *Evening Standard*, the *Daily Mail*, and above all the *Daily Express*, became more vocal in their opposition to the Union and the League. *Headway* tried to be patronizing about their attacks, comparing them to the hecklers at Hyde Park Speaker's Corner who stimulated interest in a speaker's case without influencing any 'serious' person.[71] Other attacks could not be dismissed so lightly. The former Under-Secretary for India, Earl Winterton, spoke in Parliament about the need for force in keeping the Empire. Admirable speeches by Lord Cecil and Professor Murray, he said, would fail to convince rebellious tribesmen of their error.[72] The Union's critics often lumped all pacifist, uni-lateralist, and disarmament arguments together, so that *Headway* had to put a notice in bold print into its October 1931 issue that 'Disarmament, in any reference to the subject in *Headway*, must be understood to mean the reduction and limitation of national armaments by international agreement.'[73]

Some of the dissension spilled over into the Union. When Norman Angell prepared a pamphlet, *The Foreigners' Turn to Disarm*, he aroused stiff internal opposition. Military men who were co-operating with the LNU tried to refute some of his arguments and they forced Angell to make some changes. One of them, Admiral Herbert William Richmond, circulated his critique of Angell's case to the Executive Committee. Richmond stressed that Britain had sacrificed so much in naval strength already that it could not afford further reductions—even if other nations made proportionate sacrifices.[74] Another, Lieut.-Gen. Hugh Jeudwine, led a group of the Union's military members in publishing a paper which emphasized that the Union did not want one-sided disarmament by Britain or British disarmament 'by example'.[75]

Before the end of 1931 a number of events had altered the context of the campaign for disarmament. The fall of the Labour Government and the consequent loss of Henderson as Foreign Secretary, the Japanese action at Mukden, the formation of two National Governments and the deepening depression—all turned attention away from disarmament. Now there was no avoiding involvement in the world economic crisis. Murray had been pleading for the Union to do something in this area since 1930.

The LNU's only platform on economics in the late twenties had been support for the World Economic Conference of May 1927. This meant support for lower, stabler, and more uniform tariff barriers essentially. It was not free trade—a cause dear to the hearts of Cecil and other Union leaders—but it was for 'freer' trade. When the depression fuelled the drive for higher tariffs in Britain, Murray wrote to Baldwin restating the LNU's commitment to these policies, and hinting that in any controversy over the tariff question, the League movement would be 'thrown . . . almost entirely on the Free Trade side'.[76] Murray urged a regular system of international conferences as the alternative to tariff wars and wanted the LNU to campaign for international economic co-operation.[77] Cecil was worried that such a campaign might leave the Union open to the charge that it was blocking imperial preference. More importantly, it would detract from the disarmament campaign, still his chief concern.[78] He dissuaded Murray from pursuing his plans, at least for a while.

Events were on Murray's side, as Britain left the gold standard and the crisis deepened. The Executive was at last ready to propose to the League Assembly that it convene a World Conference of Prime Ministers and Finance Ministers 'for the purpose of considering (without limitation of any kind) the present grave and dangerous economic and financial situation, and of inducing or causing the nations to adopt whatever measures are essential to its adjustment'. The LNU did not propose any specific solution, beyond the need for the conference to 'discover and adopt the remedies, however fundamental'.[79] Murray was a bit more specific in October 1931, arguing that with an immediate armaments truce, the cancellation of war debts and a lowering of the barriers against trade 'the social order may yet be saved'.[80]

The economic crisis forced the LNU to divert its attention from disarmament. The internal problems of the Union organization which arose at the same time had much the same effect. The LNU appeared on the surface to be at the peak of its success in 1931. It had a total membership of 406,868 in some 2,982 branches throughout Britain. Union leaders talked about their success in getting British acceptance of the Optional Clause and General Act in 1930 and in other areas. Yet a sense of frustration and failure underlay the difficulties at Grosvenor Crescent.

Chapter V

The Manchurian Crisis

During the controversy about Germany's admission to the League in 1926, Winston Churchill had written to Austen Chamberlain berating 'certain supporters of the League who intended it to create a heaven upon earth, provided human beings and events would allow an interval of fifty years, say, to occur in which to build this wonderful edifice'.[1] The interval in fact lasted only a decade. The depression and a series of international crises changed the political climate in the 1930s. The LNU was slow to respond to this new situation with new policies. Instead it kept pleading for the adoption of its familar prescription, which policy-makers and the public did not want.

It is a commonplace that the same views can change meanings in different contexts. For instance, the liberalism which was a progressive force in the nineteenth century was left in a more conservative role in the twentieth. This was the fate of many LNU policies which lost their validity in the 1930s. Disarmament and the appeasement of Germany represented, arguably, a reasonable approach to the problems of the post-war decade. However, with the rise of Hitler they took on a new meaning. Union leaders cannot be faulted for failing to prepare their country to fight Hitler in the twenties, but they can be for their hesitancy about fascism in the early thirties. They did begin to make the necessary transition in 1935, during the Ethiopian crisis, but the debate on rearmament continued until 1938.

From the start, the Union had placed emphasis on the role of world opinion and on pacific means for settling disputes. It had had been loath to suggest to the British public that such tactics—a League-sponsored economic boycott, in particular—might fail or lead to war. Collective security was thus not understood to involve risks, or even to be the basis for the defence of Britain. It was talked about instead as an alternative to war, a policy which by mobilizing the strength of the law-abiding nations would elimi-nate the need for large national armies. This helps to explain why League supporters saw no contradiction between advocating it at the same time as they pressed for disarmament.

All of these tendencies were evident in the LNU's response to Japanese actions in Manchuria. The Manchurian crisis, which began in September 1931, is often seen in retrospect as the first decisive challenge to the international system established after World War One. For those who later criticized British foreign policy and urged that Britain take a firm stand against aggression, the temptation was very great to say that they saw it all coming and had urged that the stand be taken since 1931. When LNU staff members prepared a history of their organization in 1939, they described how 'the Union realized how much was at stake in this test case for the League. From the beginning it vigorously contested the widespread delusion that this was merely a local squabble which would soon settle itself without affecting the rest of the world. Failure to restrain Japan, the Union urged, would be a dangerous encouragement to aggression elsewhere.'[2] One could argue that Manchuria started a reassessment of old policies within the LNU, but it is not possible to accept Grosvenor Crescent's version of events. Historians surveying the Union's response to the crisis in East Asia have told a very different story.[3]

If 1931 has rightly been called 'the decisive turning point in the history of post-war Europe',[4] then it was, for the Union, a turning point which failed to turn. Far from seeing the Japanese action in Machuria as a clear case of aggression from the start, the Union was uncertain about what was going on there. It did eventually advocate resistance to Japan, but only by breaking diplomatic relations and boycotting Japanese goods.

The LNU had paid little attention to Asia in the years before the crisis. In the spate of surveys and long-range predictions which *Headway* published in 1930 the analyses of the situation in East Asia were fairly reassuring. One article, 'Where Awakening Asia is Going', asked whether Japan was a force for peace or war, and concluded 'distinctly, at the present moment for peace. The country sets a high value on the position it has secured and can be counted on to do nothing that would lower its reputation in the eyes of the world. Its loyalty to the League of Nations is unfailing. . .'[5] Another piece, 'The League in 1940', said that the League should do more to bind Asia to it in the future through its financial, health and social work.[6] Murray talked about the international situation in February 1931 and concluded that 'no war at present is in the faintest degree probable'. However, he warned, 'if it were once believed that an aggressor could calculate on the indifference of the League and the isolation of his victim' there might be danger.[7]

When the crisis began in September 1931, Cecil was at the League Council as Britain's substitute representative. In October he got the Foreign Secretary's permission to create an informal committee to see what could be done if Japan proved obdurate. This committee reported that sanctions might have to be invoked against her under Articles 15 and 16 of the Covenant. It also said that American co-operation was needed for a sanctions policy to work; hence Washington's attitude was critical.

This sort of recommendation for sanctions was not what the Foreign Secretary, Lord Reading, wanted to hear. He asked Cecil to drop this line of inquiry and Cecil complied.[8]

Because at a later stage in the crisis Cecil became openly critical of the Government, it is easy to imagine that he would have been a critic from the start were it not for the restraints of his office.[9] He was, indeed, ready to consider imposing economic sanctions while Whitehall was not, and he had not ruled out consideration of stronger measures under Article 16. But this was a very different thing from being willing to use force, which no one wanted, or to act without the co-operation of Washington, which was not ready to co-operate in imposing major sanctions.[10] Therefore it is very doubtful if Cecil was held back by external restraints; he was feeling his way towards an answer rather than holding one back.

What is more important about Cecil's presence in Geneva was that it helped determine the public response to the crisis. The National Government could point to Cecil when asked whether it was pursuing a proper League policy. When Angell asked in the Commons if the Government was doing everything possible to uphold the Covenant and secure its observance in Manchuria, Anthony Eden replied that *Cecil* had done everything possible.[11] The initial response of the LNU to the crisis was to support Cecil's work in the Council.[12]

The Union continued quiet and vague in its response to Manchuria in the autumn of 1931. It sent a telegram to the Chairman of the Japanee League of Nations Association asking it to use its influence with the government for peaceful settlement of the crisis. This was a gesture rather than a serious initiative, coming as it did after years in which no real foundation for co-operation had been built. The response came not from the Japanese society, but from the Foreign Minister, Baron Shidehara, who explained that the complex Manchurian situation prevented 'the facile application of normal standards'.[13]

Strangely, some LNU leaders continued to express regret that the Japanese League society was proving so partisan and nationalistic.[14]

On 15 October the Executive passed a resolution that 'the Manchurian dispute is a crucial issue for the whole future of the League and more especially for the success of the Disarmament Conference'. It praised the Chinese Government for placing itself 'unreservedly in the hands of the League', and the Americans for their co-operation with the League Council. Since the United States had not co-operated in setting up a League Commission of Inquiry this praise was more wishful thinking than anything else. The LNU ended with the by now ritual gesture of asking Britain to do all that was possible to uphold the League's authority.[15]

Union leaders continued to be extremely cautious. Murray wrote a letter to *The Times* of 14 October which described events in the Far East as a 'complicated tangle' requiring skilful handling. Cecil privately praised the new Foreign Secretary, John Simon, for his views on Manchuria, and stressed how dangerous 'any violent or too outspoken action on our part' might be.[16] At the end of November, Cecil even professed optimism as to the outcome of affairs. He thought that League machinery was adequate to resolve the crisis, despite the fact that the Chinese had invoked only Article 11 (which dealt with the prevention of hostilities) instead of Article 15. Cecil agreed with Simon (as did Grey) that Britain should not act unilaterally but through the League Council.[17] Cecil, to Murray's disappointment, did not even feel that a case should made against Japan for breaking the Covenant. While Murray would have liked a special meeting of the Assembly, Cecil wanted only an inquiry and quiet pressure for a cessation of hostilities.[18]

The Union's non-committal position drew some fire from the press. First the *News Chronicle* of 23 November belaboured it for failing to organize public opinion behind an effective League policy; it did not explain what that might be. Then the *Manchester Guardian* in early December criticized the LNU for its passivity.[19] The Executive still failed to be more specific about violations of Chinese territorial integrity or the sort of measures needed for a solution. In a resolution of 24 November the LNU did express a concern about the supply of weapons to Japan and China. This was to become an important aspect of the Union's approach as the conflict went on. Its main point though was to call for an independent League commission of inquiry to be sent to Manchuria to encourage negotiation or arbitration.[20]

This policy was in line with Cecil's advice and contained nothing to upset Whitehall. It was too innocuous to satisfy many Union members, however. Manchuria did not become a major focus of concern in these opening months, but dissidents in the LNU wanted a more forthright effort made to curb Japan. Noel-Baker was not a dissident, but he was the most outspoken member of the Union's front bench pressing for vigorous LNU action. He talked about Manchuria as a great opportunity for the League, especially because it might bring America into co-operation with it, and prodded Murray into writing letters and pressing for action in the International Federation to show public concern.[21] Alfred Zimmern of the Executive was even more direct in his criticism of LNU policy and the Cecil line. The nub of the difficulty, as he saw it, was that Cecil really believed that the Japanese would soon evacuate, so the Union could not yet act. Sooner or later, when these hopes proved false, it would have to take sides. Zimmern wrote to Gwilym Davies of the collective security-conscious LNU Welsh National Council to prepare for that moment.[22]

Murray tried to chart a course for the Union which would keep it clear of criticism of the Government and Cecil but which would satisfy the increasing demands for the LNU to speak out. The supply of arms to combatants was the right issue for this purpose, and Union leaders explored a campaign on this theme.[23] They made this part of a resolution presented to the December 1931 General Council meeting. However, tempers ran high at this meeting, the first held under the new rules for selecting Council representatives, and *Headway* had to admit that speeches by Grey and Cecil left many members with their doubts 'undispelled'.[24] After the Council, *Headway's* editor, H. Wilson Harris, tried to block publication of those speeches because of the divisive effect they might have. It was not Cecil, he said, but 'obviously Zimmern[who] voices the opinion of a very large section of League supporters throughout the country'.[25]

One interesting facet of the discussion at this phase of the crisis centred on the role of public opinion. There had been so little public interest in Manchuria that Union leaders were beginning to wonder about the efficacy of opinion now that it was being put to the test. Cecil blamed public apathy on the difficulty of finding out what was happening. He wrote to Drummond in mid-December complaining about the secrecy of League proceedings. The Secretary-General was anxious not to embarrass Japan and kept counselling discretion, however.[26] Murray wrote that the real moral of Manchuria was that public opinion had failed. The Japanese could read in the British or French press that the League did not matter, that Western sympathies were with them or that treaties were meant to be broken.[27]

These second thoughts about opinion seem odd in a way, when we consider the LNU's reluctance to give the crisis anything like the emphasis given to disarmament. Union leaders could not complain about the public failing to support the imposition of sanctions; they had not asked for them yet. Zimmern raised questions about guarantees to China and strict enforcement measures under the Covenant, but even he wanted only 'some signal demonstration of the Council's disapproval' of Japan such as a withdrawal of Ambassadors from Tokyo or a boycott.[28] That the failure of opinion could be talked about as the 'real failure' by Murray only points up his exaggerated notion of what it should have been doing.

Manchuria became a subject of intense public interest in Britain with the Japanese bombing of Chapei on 20 January 1932. The LNU now began to move into a more outspoken position. It announced that it would give prominence to the Far Eastern dispute along with disarmament so as to 'awaken public opinion to the crucial character of these issues for the future of the League'.[29] Its first move in this direction was to urge the Government to propose calling a special Assembly to deal with the crisis.[30] On 12 February it renewed this request and elaborated on a policy for settlement. This asked for Article 16 to be applied with 'whatever pressure of a diplomatic or economic character' was needed against whoever rejected settlement proposals. Such measures might include an embargo on the export of arms, a boycott of exports from the 'violator', the refusal of financial facilities and the withdrawal of diplomatic representation.[31]

The Executive made it clear that it wanted Britain to work in conjunction with the United States—the proposal for a 'special' Assembly implied that the United States would be invited. However, it did not criticize Whitehall for failing to respond to American initiatives in January. In a covering letter to the press the LNU did not say that American co-operation was needed for an embargo or other steps to work. It merely stated that: 'the present instance is particularly favourable for American co-operation, a rare opportunity unlikely to recur if we have trouble in Europe'.[32]

The Union sent a deputation to the Foreign Secretary on 16

February to leave him with some suggestions on how to stop the 'humiliation' of Britain and the League. Murray advised Simon that Japan could not resist joint pressure from Britain, France, and the United States. In any case, Britain must emphasize that she would not recognize illegal Japanese gains.[33] Cecil soon gave the same advice, arguing that Japan would be stopped by action short of war *if* there were American co-operation. If Washington would not co-operate, then Cecil saw no other option than to turn away from the whole business.[34] Simon left the deputation unhappily convinced that even if the Americans were co-operative, the Cabinet did not intend to apply pressure on Japan under Article 16 and restrain her from further aggression.[35] The word 'aggression' was now being applied at Grosvenor Crescent to Japan's action; Cecil told a meeting on 27 February that since 3 February Japan was the aggressor.

The LNU still did not give public opinion any clear lead. *Headway* described the 'wide publicity' given the Executive's 11 February resolution, but in fact it had little impact.[36] Of the papers which did mention it, the *News Chronicle* and the *Manchester Guardian* found it a bit late or a mild gesture of atonement for past inaction.[37] Union leaders were increasingly critical of the Government, but uncertain about what would work. Cecil disliked the idea of boycotting Japanese goods which Murray favoured, chiefly because he feared that lack of public sympathy ('the richer class is very unsound') would lead it to fail.[38] Noel-Baker was especially critical of Drummond and encouraged Cecil to write to him urging condemnation of Japan.[39]

The Union tried to hammer out a policy members could agree on at a special General Council at the end of February. Members had been voicing doubts about the LNU recommendation to embargo arms shipments to both China and Japan, because they feared this would work to Japan's advantage.[40] Cecil met the anti-Japanese sentiments of the Council half-way, presenting the case for a moderate sanctions policy. The League, acting with the United States, should insist on an armistice and create a neutral zone—policed by neutral troops—between the combatants. If Japan did not agree, then diplomatic and economic pressure should gradually build up against her to force a settlement. None of this, Cecil explained to a questioner, would necessarily lead to military action.[41]

In March the LNU tried to encourage support for this sort of approach. *Headway* responded to the familar comment that there was no British interest in Manchuria by arguing that in East Asia there was really a close connection between interest and duty. Imperial interests were involved in India and in Japanese pressure to send colonists to Australia.[42] On 7 March Cecil and Grey addressed a big meeting on Manchuria in London. Cecil felt that preparations for the meeting had been inadequate and he had misgivings about holding it at all.[43] The meeting was indeed of doubtful value, but it was revealing for what it showed of Grey's view of the League. In this last year of his life, Grey remained committed to the League's paramount importance, but sceptical about the possibility of doing anything about the Far Eastern Crisis. After all, nothing could be done without American co-operation and this was not forthcoming. Cecil, probably trying to counter the impression Grey created that little could be done, played down the importance of the United States. 'It was', he said, "ridiculous to say that the Assembly, representing some fifty nations, was not perfectly able to insist on the cessation of hostilities if it chose to do so.'[44]

LNU leaders were optimistic about the prospects for settlement once the League Assembly adopted a resolution on 11 March to bring about a solution under Article 15. With the worst of the Shanghai fighting over and an armistice expected there soon, the crisis now appeared to be near an end. Murray wrote to Drummond that 'one breathes again after the resolution of the Assembly' and that a real League triumph was in sight. His faith in public opinion now restored, Murray concluded that boycotts and blockades 'will always be the mark of failure'.[45] These views were similar to those which John Simon and Samuel Hoare were expressing privately that week: that the Manchurian crisis had shown that sanctions could diminish the influence of the League (Simon) and that the League should be used more like the modern Papacy rather than like the armed papacy of the Middle Ages (Hoare).[46] Even the LNU activists, Noel-Baker and Zimmern, were now pleased. Noel-Baker talked about the unseen role Grosvenor Crescent had in the Assembly's triumph. Presumably this referred to LNU encouragement of the principle of non-recognition which Simon had advanced.[47] Zimmern found reason for hope in the thought that while the struggle was not over, time was on China's side.[48]

The commission which the League had dispatched to the Far East earlier in the year was at work, and the tendency in Geneva was to mark time until its report came in. Since the Chairman of the commission, Lord Lytton, was a member of the Union Executive Committee this tendency was even more marked in Grosvenor Crescent. Cecil now wanted to drop Manchuria and return to campaigning on disarmament exclusively. 'It is as much as you can do', he wrote to Noel-Baker, 'to get an ordinary branch secretary to understand one set of points. If you ask him to understand two, he will either muddle them both, or drop one of them.'[49] Some Union members were restive over this proposal, and several staff members took the unusual step of writing to Murray to urge the Executive to give a 'powerful lead' on Manchuria. Specifically they wanted to press Whitehall to suggest ways of applying international pressure on Japan to show Tokyo that the collective system was a reality.[50] The Executive instead held to its policy of supporting the League Assembly in its commitment not to recognize Japanese gains, and standing ready, if need be, to apply diplomatic and economic sanctions.

Murray was not about to launch any new campaign on Manchuria. He appeared to be in a mood of self-congratulation at the June 1932 General Council, contrasting the 'miserable' mood in the Union when the crisis unfolded, with the present when public opinion did 'take the right line'.[51] He seemed content to leave it at that, to let members assume that sound opinion would be transmitted into sound policy. The question of whether the LNU was having any impact on British policy on Manchuria was obviously more complex than that. The most recent historian of the crisis has concluded that in this first year 'domestic opinion was not taken consciously into account, either in the Foreign Office or Cabinet, when shaping British policy. . . .'.[52] No matter how outspoken League advocates might be (and most of them were not), Whitehall could always write them off as an unrepresentative minority. Vansittart noted that outside of LNU circles, civilized opinion was pro-Japanese.[53] In the same way, Simon agreed with Hoare that it was only a noisy minority, 'worked on by League of Nations Union progaganda', who favoured sanctions. However Simon showed that he did not intend to ignore that minority in September 1932, when he said 'that we must avoid getting into a position of antgonism and keep in the middle of the road'.[54]

By then the Lytton Comission report was completed, bringing to an end an awkward period of waiting for the Union. Anticipating the situation if the Japanese were hostile to the report, the Executive first said that: 'deplorable as the withdrawal of a State member from the League must always be, it is better that a State should withdraw if it is not prepared to carry out its obligations. . . .'[55]

When the report became public in October, the LNU led the chorus of approval. Lytton was now the man of the hour at Grosvenor Crescent and the inclination was to defer to his judgement on Manchuria. Since Lytton was as anxious to avoid provoking Japan as Murray and the majority of the Executive were, this did not mean a shift in policy. Lytton hoped that the Japanese effort could be undermined by a series of lesser measures such as passive non-recognition and an end to loans.[56]

By October, with a Japanese puppet state, Manchukuo, established in Manchuria, these minor steps were all that were being contemplated at Grosvenor Crescent. Not only was 'no one . . . seriously contemplating the use of force', *Headway* observed, but it even doubted that 'concerted economic pressures will be brought to bear'.[57] Lytton wanted to restrain the Union from action. When the International Law Committee reported that 'on the facts disclosed in the Lytton Report the Japanese Government is responsible for action inconsistent with Japan's obligations under Article 10 of the Covenant', he kept them from demanding a punishment to fit the crime. After all, Lytton said, his commission was not the final tribunal and its findings had not yet been accepted by the League.[58]

The LNU followed Lytton's course and avoided provocation. It was ready to ignore its own warning that Japan would have to leave the League. Lytton said that the critical need was 'to preserve unanimity in the League' and get American co-operation. 'To urge that China should not accept Japanese advisers in Manchuria, or that Japan should insist on the complete independence of those provinces, would be equally detrimental to the cause of peace . . .'[59] A *Headway* editorial picked up on cue and disparaged the 'many who talk of boycott or blockade'.[60] The LNU asked the Government to press the League to accept the Lytton Report and then call on both China and Japan to confer on the basis of the report's findings.[61]

Behind the scenes dissatisfaction increased in the Union over Japan's behaviour. Cecil now was unhappy with Simon; the Foreign Secretary's 6 December statement before the League Assembly seemed dangerously pro-Japanese to Cecil.[62] He was prompted to write a letter to *The Times*, warning against a policy of drift. On Manchuria as on disarmament, he said, Britain's atti-

tude was vital, for 'the world is still hoping for a clear and coura-
geous lead from us . . .'[63] It was obvious that he did not think that
Simon was providing it.

In this situation, Murray tried to find some way for Britain to
give moral leadership and support for the League.[64] He wrote to
Simon on 14 December to warn him that LNU opinion was
'worked up' over the crisis. 'They fear', Murray reported, 'that
you are going too far in the direction of conciliation . . . and that
any failure to stand firm for the Lytton Report . . . will result in a
betrayal of the League and the whole new order in international
politics.'[65] This warning was not exaggerated. Davies had mobi-
lized considerable support, especially in Wales, for the cause of
imposing sanctions against Japan. Simon responded by inviting
Murray for a private visit later in the month and assuring him that
the Government stood behind the Lytton Report. As subsequent
events made clear, Simon took Murray's letter seriously; it led him
into support of an arms embargo to the Far East.[66]

The arms embargo had been a key Union demand for a year,
although opinion at Grosvenor Crescent was divided about
whether it should apply to both countries or to Japan alone. By
early 1933 Union sentiment had turned towards punishment of
Japan, and Zimmern was gaining support for proposing strong
action against her under Article 16.[67] Murray brandished this
extremism at Simon when he met him at the Foreign Office on 31
January. Impatience was building up, as well as 'a great desire in
the Union that [Japan] should not be allowed "to get away with
it" '. In this discussion Simon was not yet ready to go along with
the idea of an embargo; he said it was useless for Britain to prohibit
the export of arms if they continued to pour in from elsewhere. At
its next meeting on 2 February, the Executive pressed its demand
for an embargo anyway.[68]

The embargo proposal, which would end the export of arms to
any countries breaking their Covenant and Kellogg Pact obligations (that is, to Japan), was a moderate gesture in the context of
discussions at Grosvenor Crescent. It helped prod the Government into a statement which was more moderate still on 27
February. This suspended the export of arms from Britain to both
China and Japan while international discussions on Manchuria
were in progress. LNU Conservatives, now led by Austen
Chamberlain, who had joined the Executive at his party's call in
February 1932, were pleased with this policy. On the other side,
Davies denounced it (and Simon's whole 'cowardly' policy) in a

letter to *The Times*, for putting Japan and China in the same category and thereby stultifying the Lytton Report and the Assembly's decisions. Cecil and Murray went along with the embargo, although Cecil had misgivings that China would be hurt by it more than Japan.[69]

The embargo proposal had been intended by Murray to serve an internal purpose, unifying the LNU behind a policy most could agree on. However, it proved no more effective with Union dissidents than with the Japanese. Murray and Cecil, with failure at the Disarmament Conference and in Manchuria now hanging over them, agonized over what to try next. Murray wrote to Cecil on 7 March that if Japanese advances continued then some 'emphatic protest' against the Government's 'vacillating and insincere policy' might be in order.[70] Cecil agreed that a strong stand might become essential and that 'the period of neutrality is rapidly coming to an end' for the LNU.[71] The Union's frustrated left now concerned Murray and Cecil less than its Conservative right, which might prevent the LNU from taking the sort of strong stand it needed.

Specifically, they wondered how much longer Lytton should have his way. In the weeks after the embargo was announced, Lytton had played down the possibilities for League action in a way that undermined LNU morale. He warned people not to expect the League to be able to interfere in a conflict or force armies to withdraw.[72] Lytton often talked about the League's value in bringing about a just solution in Manchuria. Even Murray began to ask if this 'just solution' was not a chimera, made unrealizable by Japanese conquests.[73]

Lytton still had the support of Union Conservatives, however. Chamberlain played down events outside of Europe and counselled extreme caution. He made a point of standing up to Cecil, who, he said, 'would drive so hard and so fast that he endangered and might easily wreck the machine'.[74] Cecil in turn tried to muster support against Chamberlain, citing the risk of 'finding ourselves completely immobilized. His power of doing nothing amounts to genius.'[75] Murray agreed with Cecil that Chamberlain should not be allowed to 'muzzle' the LNU and he worked on Hills and other Conservatives. He emphasized that as against the opposition ('Beaverbrook or Rothermere or the average member of the House of Commons') the Union's Executive was united on fundamentals and should stop wrangling over methods.[76]

Chamberlain grew upset with the LNU, which called for action all the more loudly now that the Manchurian situation was beyond repair. Japan had answered the League's condemnation with a notice, given on 27 March, that it was going to quit the world organization. In view of this, Chamberlain saw no point in pursuing further action which would only create Japanese resentment against Britain. Cecil, on the other hand, explored the idea of a general embargo on imports from Japan and wanted the Foreign Office to sound out Washington about it.[77] This seemed unrealistic to Chamberlain, who wanted to concentrate on Europe where something useful might be accomplished. Even the mild resolutions of the December 1933 General Council, which urged non-recognition of Manchukuo, a general embargo on arms shipments to Japan and acceptance of the League Assembly's settlement plan, went too far for Chamberlain. He called it a futile and dangerous gesture, which might thrust Britain 'into the forefront of a conflict on behalf of the League'.[78]

The Union seemed determined to show that it had learned something from the experience of 1931/2. Where it had been silent, it was now vocal in favour of diplomatic and economic sanctions. Union leaders did not contemplate war, only 'perfectly bloodless sanctions'.[79] However since the most effective of these, a boycott of Japanese goods, required international co-operation to be effective, little came of the LNU effort.

With no possibility open for effective action against Japan, the Union took refuge in symbolic gestures of disapproval. In 1935 the Executive pressed for China's admission to the League Council. When the Japanese launched full-scale war against China in 1937, the LNU encouraged an unofficial boycott of goods from Japan.[80] The December 1937 General Council also urged the Government to help China with financial assistance and supplies of food and medicine. When the boycott idea was badly received by businessmen, Union leaders played up the importance of direct aid.[81] Cecil doubted the value of a boycott so he wanted the League to aid China openly, with munitions as well as other supplies.[82] Only in July 1939 did the Executive finally recommend direct measures against Japan. The Japanese invasion had to be repelled in the interests of world order and lasting peace. The Government should 'take every possible step to secure this result, and in particular to follow the lead of the United States in giving notice for the abrogation of our commerical treaty with Japan'.[83]

Manchuria had shown that the recognition which the League had won from Whitehall was very limited. The crisis did not have

any immediate impact on British official thinking about th\
League, but it did gradually takes its toll. Those who had warned against the dangers of over-commitment felt that events in the Far East had confirmed the wisdom of their views. In any case, the net effect of the Manchurian crisis was to move Britain away from the League. This is not to say that the 'old diplomacy' had taken hold again in Whitehall. It is just that the League, especially after Germany and Japan had left it, was no longer seen as a very helpful forum for solving critical international problems.

The LNU's credibility as the voice of the British public in foreign affairs was badly weakened by the events of 1931 and 1932. Its cautious and uncertain response to the early stages of the crisis cancelled out the kind of 'League opinion' which might have prodded the Government towards a different course. When the Union did exercise its influence with Whitehall, it was unable to make its advocacy of an arms embargo effective in 1933. This episode was as instructive for what it showed about the limitations of the LNU's methods of wielding influence as for the deference the Foreign Secretary was willing to accord Grosvenor Crescent.[84]

There is no particular date which marks the end of the era of good feelings between Grosvenor Crescent and Whitehall. There were swings back and forth in the thirties. However, the context of the relationship had clearly altered in some significant ways during the Manchurian crisis. The Union, with its membership now falling, could not speak with the same authority it had once had. As new groups arose within the peace movement and as the issues of sanctions and rearmament drove members from the LNU, it became weaker still. In Union publications it is easy to detect signs of this new attitude towards the Government. The old tone of confidence based on the belief that the future was the League's and that official recalcitrance would be overcome ebbed away. Cecil's reaction to one Baldwin speech in 1934 was that the Government was now 'anti-League' and that 'mere Hankeyism at its worst had triumphed'.[85]

The Union was put on the defensive *vis-à-vis* the Government on a variety of issues. For instance, in the periodic debates on British contributions to the League, the LNU had to conduct a holding action. The amounts were usually minuscule. The British attack on excessive League expenditures in 1933 brought a net saving of £6,000, of which Britain's share was £600. That the League should be begrudged such a sum was hard for its supporters to accept. In vain they held up the modest amounts being spent on the League against the billions being spent on armaments.[86]

It seemed almost unfair to Union leaders that the position of influence which they had established with Whitehall should be undermined by the failures of the League. They sometimes tried to retrieve the situation by redoubling their emphasis on the independent importance of the LNU. *Headway* argued in 1934 that while

> people often talk as though the future of the League of Nations Union depends on the success of the League of Nations. It would be truer to say that the future of the League of Nations depends on the success of the Union . . . Even if the League were to go under, even if war were to break out in Europe, this movement must continue until international cooperation has become as natural to the nations of the world as already it is to the nations of the British Commonwealth.[87]

When critics attacked the Union, *Headway* reasoned that they were trying to destroy the League's main bulwark. 'First the Union, and then the League, was their calculation. If they could smash the one, they believed, they would be more than half-way to smashing the other. . . .'[88]

The Union's importance rested ultimately, according to this perspective, on Britain's importance. British Leaguers assumed that if their country stood by its obligations under the Covenant, then the League could keep the peace. Until the mid-thirties it was further assumed that peace could be kept without resort to force. The role of the LNU, building public opinion in Britain to keep the Government steadfast, was thus vital. With the Union strong, 'this country will be an immovable rock in whose shelter the League will find safe mooring in any weather, and where . . . Britain goes forward the nations of Europe will not hold back'.[89]

The Manchurian crisis did not shake this belief in Britain's central importance to the world. It should have, for it was a good demonstration of the limits of Britain's—and the League's—power to enforce a global peace. Instead, Britain was counted on more because the League had to be counted on less.

Chapter VI

The Early 1930s

If the Manchurian crisis did not change the perspective from Grosvenor Crescent fundamentally, then neither did other events in the early 1930s. The LNU continued to press for disarmament even after the withdrawal of Germany from the World Disarmament Conference. Its leaders gradually saw the need for British rearmament, but they were very cautious in their advocacy of it. They began to talk about 'collective security' in this period, but they did not link this concept to the use of force. They answered critics of the Covenant, who said it might lead Britain into war, by re-emphasizing the importance of pacific means of settling disputes.

Within the LNU, as within the peace movement as a whole, there was uncertainty about how the League should operate.[1] Pacifists divided on the question of whether they could continue to support the Union. *Headway*'s columns were alive with discussions of how Union membership was compatible with absolute pacifism. 'Surely', one exchange of letters in 1934 concluded, 'the difference of opinion is mainly one as to which article of the Covenant is most important. The Union obviously has a place for all who want peace'.[2] The LNU reassured potential defectors while encouraging a false sense of how the peace might be kept. It bought consensus for a while, but at a high price.

On the eve of the World Disarmament Conference, scheduled to begin in Geneva in February 1932, Union leaders were not sanguine. Before most earlier international conclaves they had usually managed to appear confident if not enthusiastic. Now, after years of campaigning, they knew that optimism would be misplaced. Their final efforts to drum up support for disarmament had not gone well. Cecil tried in vain to get financial support from the Carnegie Endowment in the United States to start a monthly international bulletin on disarmament.[3] He sponsored an international conference on armaments in Paris, which attracted 2,000 representatives from twenty-eight countries, only to see it broken up by right-wing counter-demonstrations. The turn-out had been impressive enough, in any case, to encourage further use of the same organizing technique in the future. Instead of working through the international League movement, Cecil had invited representatives from many voluntary societies through the good offices of the British Rotary Movement.[4]

The LNU tried to prepare for the conference in another way, by showing how its success could help solve the economic crisis. Late in 1931 the Union devoted many articles and meetings to the depression, usually emphasizing the ways in which it was linked to war debts, reparations and disarmament. In January 1932 it issued a new policy statement which put the need for financial and economic co-operation, along with arms reduction and defence of the international order, as its top priorities.

The Union tried hard to answer the charge that disarmament would throw some workers out of their jobs. It devoted its annual industrial conference in February 1932 to the subject of 'Disarmament and Unemployment'. John Bromley, President of the Trades Union Congress and Ramsey Muir, Chairman of the National Liberal Federation, spoke at the session on 'What might be done to settle the displaced worker?' Other topics included 'What is the armaments industry?' and 'International Aspects of Disarmament and Unemployment'.[5]

The preparations for the Disarmament Conference in White-hall made LNU leaders uneasy. They were unhappy with the report of the three-party committee set up early in 1931 by the Prime Minister. Cecil tried to get the Government to take a forthright position in favour of arms reduction by trading off his agreement to serve as a delegate to the conference.[6] However, the Prime Minister had been thinking about dumping Cecil already and was not willing to make concessions to win him over.[7] The Foreign Secretary had to leave for Geneva without Cecil, and without a clear idea of what Britain's disarmament policy should be.[8]

Cecil, now excluded from the conference which had been the main focus of his life for so long, showered Simon with suggestions on what to do. He got little encouragement in this, and became gloomy in his predictions. It might now be too late for disarmament and things could only get worse later.[9] Murray, no more hopeful about the prospects for over-all arms reduction, hoped the conference could at least prohibit air warfare and win arms equality for Germany (with other powers accepting the Versailles Treaty's restrictions).[10]

Even though LNU leaders privately admitted that a percentage reduction in armaments was not possible, the Union kept its demand for a 25 per cent reduction in arms budgets world-wide. Its January 1932 policy statement stressed other goals as well: the need for economic co-operation, for international security arrangements and for better ways to resolve disputes peacefully. Before setting off to discuss disarmament with the French it seemed only prudent to say something about security. But what? LNU leaders hesitated here, well aware that anything they might say about strengthening Article 16 would give isolationists ammunition against the League. Moreover, they did not want to bargain with existing security arrangements to get disarmament.[11]

In the opening phase of the conference, after the French presented their new plan for an international police force and security system, the LNU encouraged co-operation with the Quai d'Orsay. The dilemma for Whitehall was the familiar one of having to make commitments and pledge collective action through the League if it wanted the French to disarm. However, Britain now saw it as the foreigner's turn to bear sacrifices and the foreigner's turn to disarm. Despite the best efforts of the LNU, and Cecil's urging his staff on to 'harry' MPs and put as much pressure on the MacDonald Government as possible, Whitehall's fear of new foreign entanglement prevailed.[12]

The French plan did not win complete acceptance in the Union. It allowed nations to keep bombers, battleships, heavy artillery, and other 'offensive' weapons which the Union wanted to ban. The international force proposal pleased the Davies wing of the LNU but displeased the Conservatives and pacifists. Murray was upset by the way a 'coalition' of pacifists and Conservatives had formed in opposition to this proposal.[13] Nevertheless, he was convinced of the paramount need to reassure the French, so he backed the League force idea.

Although he was moderately optimistic about the conference's prospects by the spring of 1932, Cecil worried increasingly about the possibility that its military representatives might wrangle away any chance for agreement. Anxious to forestall the damage, Cecil emphasized in speeches that service experts should not be allowed to decide whether the abolition of some weapons system is desirable; they should simply implement policy and not try to make it.[14] Cecil remained unhappy about the excessive influence of technical advisers to the conference, and in 1933 accused British advisers of sabotaging the abolition of aircraft and of bombing.[15]

In the hope of a fresh start, the Union seized on the American proposals of 22 June, 1932, which called for the abolition of offensive weapons and the reduction of the remaining land forces by one-third. Bombing was to be forbidden and substantial reductions imposed in naval tonnage. The LNU urged Britain to accept President Hoover's proposals in broad outline, and 'thereafter to take the initiative in a further advance towards the establishment of the principle of "equality of status" regarding disarmament between the vanquished and victorious powers, as well as the principle of "collective security" '. Cecil hoped that the directness of the Hoover proposals might appeal to the public and that this might save the conference. The public, he told Simon, was more advanced than its respective governments on the question of disarmament.[16]

Simon did support the American initiative, although asking for some modifications of its naval tonnage proposals, but this was not enough. France still wanted some guarantees for her security, Japan remained intransigent, and the conference was quickly bogged down again. The Union's rank and file was frustrated at this new failure; the LNU *Newsheet* reported in July that members were 'tired of the maze of words and definitions leading nowhere'.[17] They had seen disarmament as a crusade imbued with high moral purpose, and they could not bear to see these ideals discarded.

The situation at Grosvenor Crescent grew tense, as leaders began to scrap unrealizable demands and followers began to object. Cecil, Murray, and other leaders had privately retreated from the LNU programme months before; it made sense to them to emphasize realistic goals so as to salvage something from the conference. However, when the Executive Committee passed a new disarmament resolution on 4 July which did not reiterate all the old demands, it provoked a sharp reaction in the Union. Branches talked about challenging the Executive's leadership. The London Regional Federation was typical in its call of protest at the country's 'entirely inadequate disarmament proposals'. Its leaders urged Murray to convene a special General Council meeting in September so that they could explain how the LNU disarmament campaign should be run.[18]

The Executive turned down the request for a special Council, but tried in other ways to reassure the membership. It issued a statement on the progress made at the conference in repudiating bombing, prohibiting chemical warfare, accepting the principle of budgetary limitation and of supervision by a permanent dis-armament commission.[19] The Executive was itself divided on how to proceed though. Lloyd George, an Honorary President of the Union, heated matters up by putting in a rare appearance at Grosvenor Crescent and proposing a sharp rebuke to the Govern-ment. This tactic seemed too provocative for most the Executive, which, after many discussions, prepared an ambiguous statement which pleased no one.[20]

Cecil concentrated on the cause of German equality and urged the Prime Minister to press for the abolition of all weapons denied to Germany. MacDonald had certainly been committed to this cause a decade earlier, but now he was unresponsive. Cecil grew more outspoken in his criticism of the Government for not giving a lead on offensive weapons. 'We have lost much of our faith in some of the delegations—notably, alas, in that of Britain.'[21] The Cabinet responded on 30 September; it agreed to a meeting to consider how to bring Germany back to the Disarmament Con-ference.[22]

The Union kept campaigning for disarmament in the autumn of 1932 in increasingly discouraging circumstances. Deputations to Parliament got a cool response. Even LNU questionnaires which were framed to get a positive response (Did they agree to the urgency of averting failure for the Disarmament Conference, to the recognition of moral obligations to Germany? . . . etc.) got fewer than one-third positive answers from MPs. Within the Union too, opinion divided more sharply on the wisdom of dis-armament. Branches complained to Grosvenor Crescent about the way the disarmament campaign cut into their normal work. Conservative-dominated units, such as the Hampshire Federa-tion, protested against the policy of sending out deputations to lobby for a particular disarmament proposal.[23] Union leaders now feared that the Union would break apart if the conference failed completely. Cecil feared that many disappointed members would turn towards extreme pacifism and the cause of unilateral renunciation of armaments.[24]

When in March 1933 Britain presented a new draft convention to the conference, LNU leaders seized on it eagerly, like drowning men seizing a life-preserver. Much of it was merely a summation of things already agreed to at the conference. It prohibited mobile land guns larger than those allowed Germany under the Versailles Treaty, limited tanks to sixteen tons and proposed an extension of the London Naval Agreements for three more years. More importantly from the LNU perspective, it put the prospect of German equality in sight at last, for at least on land after five years Germany was to be subject only to the same restrictions as everyone else. It even held out the promise of more security to the French, although Cecil doubted if this would be enough.[25]

Hitler's assumption of power in Germany at this juncture did not prompt any change in Union disarmament policy. Instead it was used to justify the rightness of the LNU policy of equality for Germany. There was something to this—if Germany had been treated better she might not have turned to the Nazis. But the new situation of 1933 required more than a recital of past inequities. The General Council which met in June 1933 continued the call for prohibition of all weapons forbidden Germany to 'deprive Germany of any excuse for re-arming'.[26] After Hitler pulled Germany out of the conference in the autumn the LNU called on the British Government 'to secure an immediate first measure of disarmament on the part of the Powers from whom it is due in fulfillment of the pledges made to Germany fourteen years ago'.[27]

Germany's departure from the conference and the League swept away the assumptions on which disarmament had been based. The Disarmament Conference kept on meeting sporadically and to little purpose until April 1937. The Union's continuing insistence on disarmament in the winter of 1933/4, its claim that progress was still somehow possible, made it seem out of touch with events. Where voices now called for British rearmament, the columns of *Headway* rang out in denunciation. Noel-Baker in December 1933, for instance, denounced the 'myth' that Britain was disarmed and weak. He surveyed the naval and military situation and concluded that Britain was relatively stronger than she had been in 1914.[28] Rearmament, by implication, was unnecessary.

The Union insisted more and more loudly on the need for collective security, but its opposition to rearmament weakened that demand. Collective security remained an abstract, poorly thought-out notion in the minds of most Leaguers at this stage. The LNU's support for slogans such as 'No rearmament for Germany' only confused things more. Some leaders of the League movement began to demand more rigorous thinking about where the old policies would lead in the new international climate. Lord Allen of Hurtwood criticized the LNU, as well as the Labour Party, for demanding disarmament, for wishful thinking about Germany, and for talking about economic sanctions without explaining the consequences if they failed.[29]

Instead of heeding this line of advice, the LNU searched for ways to arouse new enthusiasm for its cause. The public had lost interest in disarmament as such, although the traffic in armaments by the 'merchants of death' remained a popular target of the left. Murray suggested in October 1933 that if the LNU championed the case against private armaments manufacture it would have a popular appeal which disarmament lacked. Such an effort, which could take the form of a demand for ratification of the Arms Traffic Convention and the fulfilment of Article 8 of the Covenant, might have the added attraction of keeping restive left-wingers in the Union fold. 'They would rally again to an attack on the armaments firms.'[30]

The Union had paid little attention to the arms trade in earlier years. It had urged that the Arms Traffic Convention of 1925 be put into effect, and its leaders had occasionally fulminated against the influence of armaments firms in British politics.[31] When *Headway* had discussed Britain's role in the arms trade in 1930, when the sale of tanks to the Soviet Union was being debated in Parliament, it pointed out that the sale of munitions overseas was not illegal or even necessarily bad. It asked that export licences be issued only for sales to governments and not to those involved in armed insurrections.[32] One reason for caution on the issue was its political awkwardness; it had an anti-capitalist edge which left non-Labourites uncomfortable.

Nevertheless, the Union began to move from mere advocacy of control of the arms trade into a more advanced position, in order to revive the disarmament cause. In November 1933 the Executive passed a motion introduced by Cecil 'that it is contrary to the public interest that the manufacture and sale of armaments should be carried on for private profit'. A longer version of the resolution prepared for the General Council recommended vigorous international control along the lines of the Arms Traffic Convention of 1925 and of the French proposals of the previous May at the Disarmament Conference 'for the purpose of establishing supervised limitation of the manufacture and trade in war material'.[33] The LNU planned to launch a campaign against private manufacture at a big rally in London set for 6 February.

The Union issued a number of publications on the theme of private manufacture. One of these issued by the London Federation, George Innis's *Dealers in Destruction*, was particularly sweeping in its denunciations of 'private traffic in the implements of war' and the 'constant peril to peace' it posed. Simon complained to the Union about the one-sidedness of its attack,[34] and Conservatives in the Union mounted their opposition to the new policy. The appearance of a new Government memorandum on disarmament gave the Executive an excuse to beat a hasty retreat. On 1 February, it reversed its position and amended its motion against private manufacture. It decided to use the big meeting later in the week to call for collective security and all-round disarmament instead.[35] Private manufacture remained a lively subject of controversy within the Union. The Executive limited itself to very modest initiatives on the subject. In July it called on the Government to support the draft articles on the manufacture and trade in arms which had just been adopted by the Disarmament Conference.[36]

In the first months of 1934 the Union continued to respond to new initiatives at the Disarmament Conference as if they could make a difference and calling for controlled international disarmament as an alternative to rearmament. It was done in a subdued way though, as if without much hope of success. Tom Jones, the Deputy Secretary to the Cabinet, noted this mood after a luncheon he had with Cecil, the editor of *The Times*, and several others on 1 March. There was agreement, he recorded, that Whitehall felt that the Disarmament Conference had failed, that the League counted for nothing, and that Britain would soon rearm.[37] Nevertheless, Union publications kept up the call for controlled disarmament along with collective security. *Headway* proclaimed in July that the policy of isolation—and not that of disarmament or the League—was the victim of the Disarmament Conference.[38] Union leaders knew better. In answer to a report from Geneva that some agreement might still be reached, Cecil replied that 'as long as we have a British Government presided over by MacDonald, of which the Foreign Secretary is Simon, the chances of any real success either for Disarmament or for the League are very small . . .'[39]

Although the Union remained nominally committed to disarmament, it was obvious that the real issue had become rearmament. Within the LNU, just as in the Labour and Liberal Parties and many organizations of the left, the transition from supporting disarmament to something more than a grudging acceptance of rearmament was slow and difficult. The Union might of course simply avoid taking a position on the kind or amount of weapons needed for national defence. It was not, strictly speaking, a matter of League policy. However, the General Council had in 1934 enunciated a position that there should be no unilateral rearmament. The point of its resolution was to encourage a policy of collective action rather than to keep Britain at a low level of armaments. When the Government instead acted on its own in proposing increases in the RAF in July 1934, the LNU felt bound to oppose the move. The Executive lamely suggested that if the Disarmament Conference succeeded, it would 'render such increases unnecessary'.[40]

The alternative which many internationalists wanted the Government to adopt, especially as disarmament became less and less likely, was some kind of international police force. In 1932 Davies helped found an international organization, the New Commonwealth Society, to work for this idea and for an equity tribunal to supervise changes in the international situation.[41] Davies hoped it would attract a large world-wide membership, but it soon broke down into a federation of relatively small national societies, with the British the most important. Davies had a considerable following in the LNU, and the New Commonwealth soon began to function as a kind of pressure group at Grosvenor Crescent.

The formation of the New Commonwealth was given a mixed reception by the LNU. *Headway* welcomed the appearance of its magazine in November 1932, while raising doubts about whether an international League force would be much help in attaining security. However, it concluded that 'almost anything would be better than the spineless and dishonorable wobbling with which many Powers have been of late subordinating their treaty obligations to their private convenience . . .'[42] With G. N. Barnes as President of its International Section, Davies as Chairman of its Executive Committee, and the sympathy of many LNU leaders, the New Commonwealth was bound to have an impact on the Union. Its creation reflected dissatisfaction with the LNU. However, it was not precisely another League society; its lack of support for the existing Covenant became an important part of its appeal. It was still able to gain standing in the International Federation of Nations Societies and hence could be in contact with the League movement in other countries as well as in Britain.

The demand for an international police force centred on the demand for a League air force. While the Disarmament Conference held out the prospect that national military air forces might be abolished, the League air force proposal appeared to be a logical way to build collective security on the basis of disarmament, so to speak. It was a divisive issue for the Union, but too much in the minds of the Union's branches to be swept under the rug.[43] The June 1932 General Council passed a resolution recommending 'that the international organization of aviation under the auspices of the League of Nations and the creation of an international air force should be carefully considered'.[44]

The Executive responded slowly to the popular pressure for a League air force. It finally decided in April 1933 to follow the Council resolution and push for such a force. Chamberlain and the other Conservatives contested this decision even more bitterly than the one against the private manufacture of armaments.[45] Cecil tried to dismiss their objections, arguing that since it was not a question which was capable of compromise, Conservatives should simply agree to disagree with LNU policy.[46] Chamberlain reluctantly did just that.

In 1934 the battle lines on the issue remained in place. Cecil accepted Davies's invitation to become a Vice-President of the British section of the New Commonwealth Society.[47] He was not active in the organization and used his position to keep New Commonwealth in line with the LNU.[48] The New Commonwealth's 'special relationship' with the Union provoked controversy when Davies asked for permission to send his circular letters directly to Union branch secretaries. The Executive granted it to him, but only on conditions which he refused. The row over this produced recriminations all round.[49] With controversy on party lines growing agitated on a number of issues and the prospect of Conservative defections looming ahead, moderate leaders such as Murray and Courtney tried to defuse the League air force issue.[50]

The December 1934 General Council took this course. It considered a proposed section on 'Aerial Disarmament and a League Air Force' in the lengthy Executive policy statement, "Collective Defence Against Aggression'. After very sharp debate, with Allen and Adams leading the supporters of the force and Chamberlain and Hills opposing, the issue was shelved for consideration at the next Council. In the meantime the Union was to hold a conference on air disarmament, with representatives from the Royal Aeronautical Society, the National Peace Council and other groups invited. This was to study the international air force question, as well as the subsidiary questions of how to prevent the misuse of civil aircraft for military purposes. The conference was held in early April in London and the proceedings summarized in a booklet, *The Problem of the Air*.

The delay before this meeting helped Union leaders iron out their differences on an international force. Everyone then agreed that air disarmament, the internationalization of civil aviation and a League force were all feasible, if the political will to achieve them existed.[51] More to the point, events in the spring of 1935 made Conservatives more amenable to an arranged solution. The triumphant conclusion of the LNU's Peace Ballot and the publication of the White Paper on defence in March both pushed the Baldwin Government and its Union backers into a more obliging position. If LNU support for rearmament might be conditional on a show of good faith in disarmament and collective security, then Conservatives were ready to provide appropriate professions of good faith. Accordingly, at the July 1935 General Council, Chamberlain seconded a resolution proposed by Allen which had the unanimous support of the Executive. This asked the Government to press for the abolition of national air forces, to publish its own proposals for the international control or internationalization of civil aviation and to examine the desirability or organizing an international air force to guard against the use of civil aircraft for military purposes. A deputation presented this resolution to the Foreign Secretary and got a sympthetic hearing but no commitments.[52] The Ethiopian crisis then imminent made the whole thing academic from Whitehall's perspective.

The Union's failure to adjust adequately to the new situation of the 1930s was evident on other issues besides rearmament. It remained very hesitant about economics, rarely venturing beyond modest suggestions for improvements in working conditions or the expansion of the League's social work. The free trade sympathies at Grosvenor Crescent crept into LNU statements on tariffs and other 'hindrances to international concourse', but never in specific calls for abolition. Instead, the Union said tariffs should be set by international agreement in line with World Economic Conference recommendations.

The LNU as an organization did not go much further than this in the critical years of the depression. It pointed to the League as offering the machinery for international co-operation which could provide the way out. It tried to demonstrate its concern for workers by sending deputations to the Ministry of Labour to lobby for adoption of the Washington Hours Convention and the Coal Mines Convention. It also pressed for ministerial level representation to ILO conferences, in order to emphasize the importance of the League's efforts in this field.[53] But it did not try to develop a new conception of what the League could do in economic and social development or international planning. As individuals, many LNU leaders were part of the movement of 'middle opinion' which emerged, chiefly from the peace movement, in the early thirties to encourage co-operation across party lines and planning for economic progress.[54] The Union itself stayed away from this effort.

The ineffectuality of the League in the world economic crisis was apparent, and when Clement Attlee lectured in Geneva in 1934 on 'The Socialist View of Peace' it was this that he stressed. He said the old socialist criticism of the League had grown in the previous three years. There was hostility to the League because it 'was built on the assumptions that economic questions would continue to be primarily a matter of private concern' and that the existing social order would prevail.[55]

Many fervent internationalists wanted to update the Covenant so that a strengthened League could lead the world out of economic and political chaos. There had always been some who felt that the League, with its reliance on sovereign states, had not gone far enough and was bound to fail. The case they put forward was not new; suggestions to limit national sovereignty or pledge individuals to the support of some central authority were common currency in the peace movement. In the LNU there had been a bid to institute a pledge in 1920 which raised this question. Members were to vow that in any international dispute they would not support any country—their own included—which refused to submit its case to arbitration,[56] The resolution, and others like it, were defeated as the leadership steered the Union on a conservative path.

When things had been going well, Grosvenor Crescent could afford to ignore this current of opinion. The Covenant did allow for peaceful change, after all, even though the political realities at Geneva militated against it. The proposal for an Austro-German Customs Union in 1931 posed in sharp relief the question of whether the League system was in fact hampering peaceful change. The news of the project, which would have contravened the provisions of the peace treaties designed to prevent *Anschluss*, was handled clumsily by the Germans. As a result, the LNU followed most of British opinion in criticizing the way the project emerged. Yet the proposal itself seemed reasonable, and the

Union soon supported it. When the international court ruled out the project later in the year, the LNU response was almost one of surprise 'that political considerations had played a large part in arriving at the decision . . .' The LNU *Newsheet* noted that 'the verdict came as rather a shock to League opinion in this country in general'.[57]

The response to this episode, and to the series of shocks which followed it, was to increase the pressure for changes in the League. Some zealous internationalists began to argue that a deep and abiding personal commitment to the League might restore the situation. When Beverley Nichols's popular book *Cry Havoc!* raised the question 'My country or my world, which should come first?' in 1933, some Union members were prompted to think about ways to reaffirm their loyalty to Geneva. Union leaders tried to side-step the matter when it was raised at General Council meetings. Cecil said he could not envisage any case in which Britain would engage in a war contrary to the Covenant, so a choice would never have to be made! *Headway* admitted that 'the Union does appear to be dodging this issue'. It tried to set things right by stating that many members 'would put loyalty to God before loyalty to King and Country. Between loyalty to God and loyalty to Country many would put loyalty to man, and interpret this as meaning loyalty to the League of Nations as the entity most nearly representative of all mankind.'[58]

The question of how the Covenant should be revised to allow for peaceful change had to be faced sooner or later. After the withdrawal of Germany and Japan from the League it became a major concern at Grosvenor Crescent. *Headway* ran many articles on the subject in 1934. However, the Union could not decide which way to move, as contradictory advice came in from all sides.

Philip Kerr (Lord Lothian after 1930) had been one of the most prominent advocates of Covenant revision for years. Unlike Davies, or those who wanted to tighten up League enforcement procedures, Lothian had advocated keeping the League flexible enough to invite American co-operation. Although he held only minor office in the National Government in the early 1930s, he had the ear of Lloyd George and could not be ignored by LNU leaders. In the House of Lords and in correspondence with Union leaders, Lothian kept pressing for revision as one 'in favour of the League . . . but opposed to the Covenant.'[59]

One Union response to demands for revision was to try to detach the League from the peace settlement in people's minds. In

1935 *Headway* countered the allegation 'that the League is responsible for the terms dictated at Versailles'. If the Covenant was written into the peace treaties, it was only for 'tactical reasons' which had 'ceased to be important'. The league was not committed to defend the treaties any more than any public law. It wanted change, but peaceful change.[60]

In 1935 the LNU launched an intensive study in order to satisfy critics, especially in the key area of how the peaceful change of outdated treaty arrangements could be brought about. The 'Report on Reform of the League of Nations' it produced called for a number of minor steps to tighten League procedure, but no major overhaul. In cases where a Member State asked the League to reconsider a treaty because it had become inapplicable or a threat to peace, the report said that the Assembly could appoint a commission of inquiry to recommend action. The Assembly would then offer its advice to the League Members party to the treaty. If they did not act within a reasonable time then the Council would consider the matter under Article 11.[61]

Lothian and others who wanted special concessions to the United States got no encouragement from the report. It did say that a 'system of collaboration' was developing between the USA and the League, because an American observer was on the League Council when it dealt with Manchuria in 1931. However, it said that this co-operation should develop naturally and not be embodied in some written document.[62] Despite the extreme caution of these recommendations, they managed to upset Union Conservatives. Yet they were too cautious to arouse enthusiasm among those who wanted change. The Executive eventually decided to drop the issue, instructing its delegation to the June congress of the International Federation of League of Nations Societies to avoid discussing reform of the League and to persuade others to do the same.[63]

By now revisionism had become so entangled with other divisive issues that Union leaders were more wary of it than ever. Many of these leaders were ready to support British rearmament and they did not want to encourage the notion that there was a cheap and easy alternative to collective security. They knew it was chimerical to hope, as so many in the peace movement did hope, that Hitler could be sated by some new economic realignment. Despite their arguments, sympathy for revisionism, for peaceful changes of boundaries, and even the transfer of colonies, remained strong in the Union's rank and file.

The dialogue on revisionism within the League movement led to an interesting change in the Union's perspective on the empire. For years, leftist members had railed against the LNU's imperialist stance and pointed to the way the empire had blocked progress. As one member put it in 1934, 'Is it possible to be a loyal supporter of the League of Nations Union and remain a staunch imperialist?'[64]

When talk about grievances and 'have nots' began to dominate discussions of empire, Union leaders opened *Headway* and their platforms to new arguments on the subject. They astutely ran articles which took a progressive line on colonies, in that way bolstering their own case against trying to buy off Hitler. One of these on 'The Demand for Colonies' set forward the case that the possession of colonies had no necessary connection to poverty or wealth. Hence Hitler's claim that the Germans deserved more territory was pointless.[65] Another article suggested that the problem was how to abandon the whole theory and practice of imperialism by international agreement. 'Opinion within the peace movement', the author said, 'has already reached a point at which it discerns that the colonial problem is much more than what Hitler calls the equality of colonial rights. If we are to speak of have-nots . . . they are the indigenous inhabitants of colonies.'[66] This line of argument, which insisted that subject peoples should be consulted about their fate, was a convenient response to Hitler. However, even those like Allen, who wanted to respond sympathetically to German grievances in 1935, were affected by it.

The widespread demands to make the League more responsive to international economic needs did evoke a reaction in the British peace movement. The National Peace Council began in 1935 to develop new ideas on how the League could become a major organ of reconstruction and transform the mandate system so that it could provide equal access to raw materials and markets and reduce economic competition. The LNU sponsored discussions on these subjects and issued pamphlets such as C. A. Macartney's 'Social and Economic Planning' in 1935. It set 'World Planning' as the topic of its annual industrial conference in February 1936. However, the Union was a late comer to these issues, and it remained cautious in adopting new proposals.

Chapter VII

Educating for Peace: LNU Propaganda Methods

In the early 1930s, as the League cause grew more controversial and the Union came under fire, the mood at Grosvenor Crescent became increasingly introspective. Membership, which had grown continuously in the 1920s, started to decline in 1932. The circulation of *Headway* was about 100,000 in 1930, but then fell off sharply to 60,000 in 1932. LNU leaders began to wonder if their programmes and publicity efforts were adequate. They sponsored discussions and invited the opinions of 'experts' as to why the League cause did not have wider appeal.

The verdicts were unsettling. The publicist Sir Charles Higham was one of many who said that the Union had not been 'boosting peace' correctly. He suggested lively advertisements in the press, cinema, and radio.[1] Others suggested making *Headway* more appealing. Some talked about dull formal LNU meetings at which workers would only feel bored, self-conscious, or patronized. One 'asked some young workers in a Westminster garage if they attended LNU meetings. No, they did not like meetings . . . If I had the choice between seeing Eddie Cantor or going to a dance or listen to someone droning about peace, what would I do?' The problem was different in the countryside where there were few rival attractions to meetings, but hesitation about mixing with the 'upper crust'. Farm-workers did not want to spend their spare time with the people who typically ran things in their village, with the clergymen, teachers, businessmen, and retired army officers who were probably in charge of the local LNU chapter.[2]

With their public falling away, Union leaders wondered if they had worked to realize their goals in the right way. They remained convinced that their message was vital. As Lord Queensborough, long-time LNU Treasurer, put it they were 'trustees of a gospel . . . the world must learn or perish. But how can it learn if there is no one to teach?'[3]

The gospel had been carried to the public through a vast range of activities. From summer schools to films, books, and children's camps the Union tried almost everything to bring its message to the people. It had been most interested in reaching the nation's leaders, and few politicians could have escaped contact with its literature and meetings. At times about half the members of Parliament were members, yet it would be misleading to make too much of the LNU's success in attracting politicians. The gesture of belonging to this non-party organization was so easy, with no commitment as to how one would vote implied, that it had little value in assessing influence. The most one can say is that members did receive Union literature, so they probably knew what Grosvenor Crescent policy was, even if they did not agree with it.

The fact that so many politicians were insiders may have been a disadvantage. Large membership rolls were meant to impress them, but they soon realized that if Union members were numerous they were also divided or apathetic. They might attend LNU meetings and emerge with heightened doubts about the organization.[4] In the same way, LNU deputations to Whitehall could not argue that Union opinion was squarely behind them. Everyone knew that on the issues that counted, party affiliation and not membership in the LNU was decisive.

A more sophisticated way to use League opinion to influence the Government was to emphasize the very splits in the Union which were known about in any case. LNU leaders might warn that extremists in the branches were about to pass an embarrassing resolution if the Government did not bend a bit in their direction. Murray often used this tactic, and it was not simply a ploy for him. He was genuinely concerned about keeping the Union on an even keel and preventing it from splintering.[5] However, as Murray's experience with Simon during the Manchurian crisis showed, this sort of appeal could be turned round easily. The LNU needed the Government at least as much as the Government needed it. Unlike a stop-the-war movement, or a pressure group based on one issue, it was not trying to force one specific change, one policy for which it was willing to threaten and sacrifice support. Its leaders were reluctant to say anything which might wear out the welcome mat for the next deputation.

Deputations were also used a great deal on a local level. Circulars to branch secretaries provided model questions for MPs ('He might be asked whether he is in favour of using all the powers of the Covenant to prevent war between Italy and Abyssinia') and laid down the ground rules for Union deputations.[6] Branches were advised to form their deputation from the same party as the MP, to keep their discussions away from party politics and to make sure that each candidate or MP was lobbied only by his own constituents. The LNU polled candidates at election-time and published the results, but without comment. There was no LNU coupon or seal of approval for candidates. The closest equivalent to that was a letter of commendation from Cecil, which some actively sought. Harold Nicolson was refused one in 1935, ostensibly because he was not on the Executive Committee.

The Union started using election questionnaries in the 1918 General Election and got such an encouraging response to its questions about the desirability of establishing a League, abolishing conscription, disarmament and other measures that it kept using the technique. It drew up lists of questions for candidates so that no by-election would find the Union unprepared. The questions ranged from the very general to the specific, as these questions distributed to branch secretaries in 1921 show:

1. (a) What are your views on the League of Nations?
   (b) If elected, will you use your influence in Parliament to support and strengthen the League of Nations?
2. What is your attitude with regard to the admission of the remaining ex-enemy states into the League of Nations?. . .
5. Are you in favour of the principle that the territories of Asia, Africa and the Pacific Islands which were taken from Turkey and Germany should be entrusted to mandatories . . .?[7]

In the 1922 General Election the Union prepared for a major polling effort. Branches could adapt the questions sent out from headquarters and add questions developed locally. They could also choose the means of confronting the candidates, either in joint meetings, with deputations, or by writing. The only requirement Grosvenor Crescent imposed was that if a local election meeting were held it should be attended by all the candidates or none.[8] Since all the parties included a statement of support for the League, it was easy for candidates to oblige with positive comments. The results of the tally of 1,386 candidates were almost unanimous, with only three declared opponents of the League registering their opinion.[9]

Politicians did not have to be deceitful to give positive replies to the LNU. The questionnaires were drafted to make it difficult for them not to be positive; moreover, most accepted the League as a 'good thing'. Since the League issue remained somewhat peripheral it is not surprising that in the 1920s the Union could report triumph after triumph. Still it was not possible for most LNU members to sustain much enthusiasm for this 'political' work, since everyone supported the League.

In another sense, victory was always out of reach because nothing stood behind the questionnaires. When *Headway* polled its readers in 1930, asking 'Does the attitude of a Parliamentary candidate gain or lose him votes on any substantial scale?' a clear majority said that the League was not an electoral issue. No matter what a candidate said about the League, there was no guarantee that he would stand up for it, especially if it meant opposing his party.[10] The most one can claim for LNU questionnaires is that they made it difficult for politicians to ignore the League. By helping establish the League as an issue and encouraging statements of support for it, they made it possible when crisis came, as in 1935 over Ethiopia, for the Government to support sanctions.

The Union's political work was based on grass roots support. Large and active branches were the key to the whole effort, and for most members their branch *was* the LNU. It was quite possibly the only organization in town concerned with foreign policy, peace, and war. The branch was the logical place to work for one's views on world affairs. The political disposition of branches varied. Some were inert or determined only to block any resolution against the Government. Others, like the Montague Burton industrial branch at Leeds, one of several organized in factories, took a radical stand on most issues.

Branches did not always rubber stamp policy recommendations from Grosvenor Crescent or wait for their monthly letter from headquarters before deciding on a course of action. Some branches with many pacifist members co-operated with local Peace Councils and other activities of the National Peace Congress, even though this was discouraged by headquarters. The Executive Committee wanted support from the branches and not political guidance. Hence, while an independent-minded branch might go its own way in its own locality, it could not make its mark on the Union as a whole.

Moreover, independence was the exception not the rule. Only rarely, and then only late in the LNU's history, were there significant shows of dissidence, with some Scottish non-co-operation in the Peace Ballot and Youth Group activity discussed below. Branches displeased with some LNU policy usually did not challenge it directly; they were far more likely to complain instead about the way the Union was organized. The 'Gordonite Revolt' of 1931 was typical of this.

The structured and hierarchical organization of the LNU

inhibited dissent. If some secular pacifist groups, the No More War Movement for instance, emphasized the independence of the individual unit or even the social development of the branch, Union branches did not. The rules governing branches were routine enough for a voluntary organization. However, it is easy to see where some of Grosvenor Crescent's suggestions about how to start out might lead, especially its support for municipal auspices and honorary officerships clearly intended for local dignitaries. Branches launched in town halls, with the Mayor in the chair, supported by local MPs and clergymen, were thought of as safe and quasi-official.[11] Such a branch would probably not become a centre of controversy or the nucleus of a movement to upset the Union leadership.

Since many branches were wholly financed by headquarters their dependence on it was increased. Larger branches were organized as 'Central Branches' and could raise their own funds, pay for their own propaganda work and turn in to headquarters whatever was left over. The subject of capitation grants—branch payments to headquarters—was a delicate one, with branches often resentful at the way most of what they collected went to Grosvenor Crescent. The difficulties over resources reflected the broader running dispute over whether the Union was too centralized.

The structure of the LNU explains something about its internal dynamics, but the people who ran it explain even more. The stability of the Union's leadership and Cecil's domination of it were both remarkable. The continuity of Cecil's leadership had never been based on the absence of opposition to his views. However, those who disagreed with him strongly found it easier to quit than to fight. Cecil's national reputation made it difficult for others to challenge him successfully on the Executive Committee, the centre of power in the Union. Chamberlain was a notable exception from 1932 to 1936; he was as adept at threatening resignation as Cecil himself, and represented Conservative interests at Grosvenor Crescent unflinchingly. Cecil was no longer a major political figure by the 1930s, but his leadership of the International Federation of League of Nations Societies and the International Peace Campaign, his Nobel Peace Prize in 1937 and probably his age too made him a grand public figure, harder than ever to challenege.

Those who worked well with Cecil enjoyed careers in the LNU which were happy—and long. Murray continued as Chairman until 1938 and thereafter became Co-President with Cecil until 1945. Lytton succeeded him as Chairman and also stayed until the end. Lord Queensborough remained as Treasurer from 1922 until 1936. Others on the Executive Committee, such as Noel-Baker and Kathleen Courtney, worked tirelessly on LNU affairs for most of its twenty-seven-year history. Dr C. W. Kimmins, London County Council Chief Inspector of Schools, presided at the LNU Education Committee's first meeting in 1919 and was still in the chair twenty years later. The staff of over 100 at Grosvenor Crescent was also noteworthy for the long years of service its members gave. J. C. Maxwell Garnett was a vigorous and imposing chief of staff as Secretary from 1920 to 1938.

Garnett left his post as part of the Union's only major shake-up in personnel, just when Lytton was taking over as Chairman from Murray. Garnett had been an Examiner for the Board of Education and then Principal of the Manchester College of Technology before becoming Secretary. He threw himself into his work with a sense of mission which reflected, as did his books *World Loyalty: A Study of the Spiritual Pilgrimage Towards World Order* (1928) and *A Lasting Peace* (1940), his deep religious commitment. As Secretary, Garnett's first impulse was to run everything himself. Murray, putting it as tactfully as he could, warned him against overworking and suggested that if he delegated more to his staff they might 'work with more heart and pleasure'.[12]

A man of strong personality who did not take criticism lightly, Garnett was master of a tightly run ship at headquarters. He was at his best in educational work and sometimes showed resentment when this was subordinated to the Union's political activities. Over the years he attracted a chorus of critics on the Executive Committee, but there were also many, especially educators, who defended his administration. Cecil was critical at times, but he knew he would have trouble finding an adequate replacement.

The LNU's recruitment policy secured the control of Grosvenor Crescent over the membership. By constantly adding more and more names to the rolls, it in effect guaranteed that it would attract the apathetic and inattentive.[13] Membership turned over rapidly. Even in the 1920s, when membership increased by between 74,000 and 100,000 a year, the number of old members who stopped paying their dues was very high. Membership totals were still large in the 1930s, but once they were in decline they were no longer a source of pride or a sign of growing strength. The obsession with growth, always doubtful, backfired. By 1938 membership had fallen to 264,180 from the 1931 peak of 406,868.

It had always been hard for the public to follow LNU announcements about membership because of the odd form of double book-keeping which Grosvenor Crescent used. The figure publicized was the total of all members who had ever belonged and not known to have died or resigned, rather than the more usual figure of current dues-payers. When in March 1933 the Union celebrated topping 1,000,000 in total membership, its total of subscribers was under 400,000 and in decline. In defence of this procedure, the Union pointed to the inadequacy of its collection procedures, and then after the depression it pointed to the difficulty people had in parting with their dues. The good will of the public was perhaps still there, even if the subscriptions were not.

There was a more plausible reason to argue that subscription figures did not give an adequate idea of the Union's popular support. Apart from individual subscribers, the Union also had corporate members, groups affiliated with it in one way or another. Church congregations, professional and community service groups, trades unions and co-operative societies brought hundreds of thousands of their members into the fold, or at least within reach of LNU literature. There were 575 corporate members by 1923 and 3,058 by 1930 when membership was at a peak. Corporate membership declined along with individual membership in the 1930s, and the total dropped to 1,936 by 1938. Nevertheless, many organizations that were not corporate members of the Union still kept close contacts with it, sending delegates to LNU conferences on industrial, educational, or religious topics and disseminating LNU literature to their members.

Membership figures do not, then, tell the whole story of the LNU's work or influence. What they do indicate is that a great effort was made in the 1920s to build a mass membership. As some feared at the time, a high price was paid for this. *Headway* instructed branches in 1922 that 'the primary object of our meetings is to get new paying members'.[14] Inevitably, this emphasis discouraged those who wanted to tackle controversial issues or explore the implications of League membership with thoroughness. Some LNU leaders worried about these recruitment tactics. Violet Bonham Carter complained in 1923 that people joined and then took no further action.[15] Norman Angell argued in 1926 that popularity could be dangerous for the Union, because so many members had not really considered what the League involved.

These 'Leaguers' might prove fickle in the future.[16]

Within a few years it became apparent that Angell's diagnosis was correct. However, the routine of activity in the branches stayed about the same, despite bouts of soul-searching in head-quarters about the way things were run. Typically, this routine included Study Circles, groups of six to twelve meeting regularly to discuss a selected subject with the aid of leader and textbook, inter-branch debates, essay contests, and numerous activities for children.[17]

Above all, the Union depended on public meetings, giving as much emphasis to the number of meetings it held as to member-ship.[18] It has a staff of speakers, as well as long lists of volunteers ready to address local meetings. Frederick Whelen, The LNU's chief speaker, had by 1929 addressed more than 3,000 meetings during a decade of service. Some of the speakers were pegged to address only certain audiences: the list of volunteers to speak to Labour meetings had more than one hundred names.[19] They could draw on *Speaker's Notes*, a series of pamphlets the Union constantly updated for their benefit. In 1931 the selection of these included: 'The Manchurian Crisis', 'The U.S. and the League', 'The Armaments Truce', or 'ILO Notes'. When the meeting ended, the Union carefully tabulated attendance figures and brief descriptions of the event ('A good meeting. The chapel was crowded with enthusiastic people. Chorus gave musical items . . .').[20]

At Grosvenor Crescent, there was constant introspection about how the meetings were conducted. Were too many branches trying for 'Fame', a few big-name speakers, instead of balanced programmes? How could partisan, inexperienced, or poorly informed volunteer speakers be weeded out? Was the LNU preaching only to the converted at most meetings? Should it run meetings at all or try to place speakers in the meetings of outside groups? Would it help to run debates, with different viewpoints defended instead of talks?[21] Veteran speakers, including that stal-wart who had the Hyde Park Corner stand for the Union, contri-buted their expertise: 'the speaker must watch for the slightest tendency of the members of the audience to shuffle away, and on seeing such signs should at once invite questions as though his address were at an end . . . Interrupters, properly handled, are his best friends in spite of themselves. Even on a cold evening the audience will remain to listen if there seems any likelihood of "fun".'[22]

The endemic weakness of meetings—dullness—was hard to overcome, however. 'Why', asked one LNU staffer, 'should we have to suffer so much to support a good cause?'[23] The Union tried to combat dullness by urging branches not to hold too many meetings, for if it is 'to dispose the public or the Press . . . and influence the Member of Parliament, it is essential that it should be a local event of some importance'.[24] Nevertheless, by the late thirties, even when Churchill and Eden had joined Cecil, Angell, and the others in the front ranks of Union speakers, audiences often complained of boredom after hearing the same lines being delivered by an all-too-familiar cast of players.[25]

An LNU campaign on a special topic, disarmament or whatever, was orchestrated so that meetings were backed by a mix of pamphlets, press releases, and topical books.[26] The Union produced over 400 pamphlets, most of them timely, concise discussions of a current issue. These were cheap, many for one penny like the 'Penny Pocket Books' distributed in the early thirties, and popular in level. There were not free, however, for the Executive judged that people would be more likely to read and respect something they had paid for than something given them.[27]

The problem with these publicity campaigns was that the press usually did not co-operate, so there was never enough League coverage to satisfy Grosvenor Crescent. In the early 1920s particularly, events in Geneva were not—from an editor's viewpoint—good copy. The Union made some clumsy efforts to convince them that there was an audience eager to read more about the League, in one case in 1922 asking members to write to editors about it directly. Thousands of letters duly poured in to newspaper offices and irate editors complained about being the victims of an inspired campaign.[28] The LNU did not have much better luck with developing a world-wide 'League of Editors' to encourage better attitudes in the press.[29] The situation did improve in the mid-twenties, as the League prospered and more correspondents were assigned to Geneva.

Overt hostility to the Union was not the problem in the 1920s. The *Morning Post* aside, most newspapers, even the *Daily Express*, were very restrained in their criticism of the League in its heyday. *The Times* was not at all hostile until the 1930s, but its editor, Geoffrey Dawson, was not anxious to co-operate with the LNU. Murray was rebuffed in his efforts to get the paper to establish a 'League News' section to parallel its 'Home News' and 'Foreign and Imperial News' sections.[30] *The Times* was especially reluctant to print letters to its editor which were duplicates of letters sent to other papers, yet its letters columns were still indispensable. Hence Union leaders had to chose between writing instead to the sympathetic *Manchester Guardian* or *Yorkshire Post* which the right people might not read, or risking rejection by *The Times*. The *Daily Telegraph* was a good compromise choice in the thirties.[31]

The Press Section at Grosvenor Crescent was too small to help much with the major daily papers. Its three or four staff members could not issue current news releases, so instead they prepared short feature articles on League or LNU affairs, or general articles on health or labour topics which weaved in mention of Geneva. From 1922 until 1938 the LNU issued a weekly news bulletin of international affairs. It also prepared 'specials', syndicated articles exclusive to one paper in a circulation area, which had a reasonable acceptance rate.[32] The provincial weeklies were the best customers for LNU material.

When the Union started, the idea of setting up a League news-paper had been mooted, and in 1921 Cecil suggested that a weekly publication might be possible. Even this was beyond the LNU's means, however.[33] The Union's first house journal was a monthly, the *League of Nations Journal*, which was sent free to members who had subscribed at least 5s. a year. A more ambitious venture appeared in October 1919. It was the *Covenant*, a highbrow quarterly with over one hundred pages of articles on world affairs, selling for 3s. 6d. an issue. Designed as the chief organ of the LNU, it faded within a year.[34]

The Union's main emphasis after that was on a shorter monthly magazine aimed at a less select audience. This started as *The League*, changed names in 1920 because of the confusion it caused football fans, to become first *Today and Tomorrow* and then *Headway*. Grosvenor Crescent also turned out a number of more specialized periodicals. *Church and Home* (later *Church and World*) was issued half-yearly as an inset to church and parish magazines. *League News* was aimed at teachers and older primary schoolchildren. It came out three times yearly and had a circulation of 20,000. At various times it launched other publications, chiefly to meet the needs of members who had not subscribed enough to get *Headway*. Apart from the news-letters of the various LNU branches and regional organizations, the major Union publications had a peak annual circulation of over 2,000,000 in the 1930s.

Headway's circulation fell from 100,000 in 1930 to level off at about 60,000 for most of the following decade. Its actual readership was well below that, for the perpetual complaints about it from members established that many did not read it. *Headway* could never quite carry out its multiple functions as the channel between headquarters and members, as a serious journal of world affairs, as a 'parish journal' of LNU activities and as bait for attracting members, while remaining readable. Members complained that it was the stiffest reading that entered their homes but Grosvenor Crescent gave them little satisfaction. Its editor insisted that 'support of the League qualified by the condition that everything dull or abstruse about it must be avoided like poison is a singularly half-hearted affair'.[35]

The editor from 1923 to 1932 was H. Wilson Harris, a journalist who tried to keep *Headway*'s 'house journal' functions minimal. His efforts to encourage a lively diversity of opinion in the signed articles were restricted by the touchiness of the Executive Committee's members. In 1927, for instance, he caused a row when he playfully printed a declaration of faith in the League by the king alongside some sceptical comments by Viscount Lascelles (the king's son-in-law) under the heading 'Family Jars'.[36] Even the advertisements were scrutinized minutely by the Executive. They rejected advertisements for the Rationalist Press in 1923 and a Royal Military Tattoo in 1925 so that no one would be offended. A more tricky issue arose in 1926 when Arthur Ponsonby ran a series of advertisements for his peace letter campaign. *Headway* readers pointed out that the letter campaign was not consistent with the Covenant and Ponsonby was turned away. Thereafter the Executive elaborated a policy of excluding all advertisements from political, religious, or social organizations.[37] Within weeks the committee found that it still had not eliminated the possibility of controversy; it felt obliged to reject an advertisement for a book on birth control.[38]

Headway took more than its share of blame for the failures of League propaganda in the early thirties. Murray's son Basil drew up a critical 'Report on Publicity' in 1932 which helped ease Harris out of the editorship. Sir Norman Angell was offered the job but turned it down.[39] As a member of the Executive Committee and Chairman of the Publicity Committee, Angell remained at the centre of the Union's effort to revamp its propaganda. His views on *Headway* were in fact quite similar to Harris's: vital and interesting reading matter could never placate all critics. Anything that aroused eager approval was bound to arouse equally emphatic disapproval. Angell called for a more precise targeting of the Union's propaganda. Mere advocacy of the League or 'peace' were no longer good enough; one had to show why the League was indispensable.[40]

Angell worked to strengthen several facets of the LNU's publicity effort. He tried to attract first-rate editors and publicists to his Publicity Committee, only to find that most of them did not like the idea of playing second fiddle to the Executive Committee. Nor did he manage to overcome the Union's problems with the press. He tried the personal approach with dinners for newsmen, and he launched a new series of 'Disarmament Notes' for fourteen local London papers. Angell also tried to get more LNU releases into print by angling them for the women's pages or such gossip columns as 'Londoner's Diary' in the *Evening Standard*.[41] He made more progress in improving posters, especially for the disarmament campaign. These posters effectively developed themes which Angell had discussed in his books. They dealt directly with the fears and anxieties which people had about disarmament in order to convince them they could be safe in a disarmed world.[42]

Headway remained an uncertain weapon in the Union's propaganda arsenal, never able to meet the conflicting demands placed upon it. If it improved the quality of its paper and put on a heavy cover, printed more cartoons and photographs and did the other things to make it attractive for news-stand sales, then it would be too expensive to produce and mail to Union members who subscribed only 3s. 6d. yearly. So dissatisfaction with it persisted for one reason or another.

That *Headway* and the Union's other vehicles for disseminating information should be under constant scrutiny is not surprising. By the standards the Union had set for itself it was failing, and in the 1930s failing badly. Its expenditures, which averaged about £40,000 a year in the inter-war period, may have looked substantial by the standards of the peace movement but were hardly up to the LNU's ambitions.[43] Garnett lamented that he was supposed to educate the whole British people on a budget smaller than that of many schools and colleges.[44] If the message was not getting across it was easier to blame propaganda methods than anything else.

There were only two areas in which the LNU felt it was doing really well: in the churches and the schools. The churches provided the Union with its most sympathetic audiences. From the start, LNU literature had encouraged the notion that the League was 'the one piece of practical Christianity which the war has left us'.[45] Its first mass mailings were sent in 1919 to clergymen throughout England and Wales. The Archbishop of Canterbury was so helpful that Bryce could comment in 1919 on the support the League was getting from leading bishops, now 'more liberal than their clergy'.[46] The Lambeth Conference of 1920 called on clergy to act so that 'the whole Church of Christ might be enabled with one voice to urge the principles of the League of Nations upon the peoples of the world'. The LNU presented the practical way to fulfil this resolution:

Every church can best assist the cause of the League of Nations by joining the League of Nations Union as a corporate member. The next step would be to appoint a special officer to look after the League of Nations work of the Church . . . This League of Nations Registrar . . . would see to it that every member of the Church or congregation was asked to join the League of Nations Union, and was given good reasons why he or she should do so.[47]

The Union's Christian Organizations Committee, which included representatives from all leading denominations, issued a wide range of materials for use in churches. Litany, prayer, and hymn sheets were provided for selected dates such as Armistice Sunday, the birthday of the League and the Sunday nearest the anniversay of the signing of the Peace Treaty. It also sent out Sunday School lessons which stressed that interest in the League was 'the natural outcome of the application of the teaching of Jesus to wider human relationships'.[48] The LNU succeeded so well with this sort of appeal that by 1929 it pressed ahead to enforce a resolution 'to the authorities of all places of worship in Great Britain that prayer for the League of Nations should form a regular part in their worship'.[49]

The Lambeth Conference of 1930 then adopted resolutions on the duties of Christians to support the League. Religious leaders were reminded that war was incompatible with Christ's teachings and urged to 'promote those ideals of peace, brotherhood and justice for which the League of Nations stands'. More specifically, they were also told 'to help actively by prayer and effort, agencies (such as the League of Nations Union) which are working to promote goodwill among the nations'.[50]

The LNU's success was even more obvious in the chapel than in the church. The nonconformist minister was generally the first person a Union organizer would call on in a new town, and chapels—especially in Wales—were a hub of League activities.[51] The Free Church Council in 1921 expressed 'its conviction that in the League of Nations lies the only hope for world peace . . .' In

1922 the National Council of Evangelical Free Churches launched its own campaign to boost support for the League and the Union.[52] The LNU statistics on corporate church membership show that nonconformist support was consistently high. In 1934, when a record high of 2,656 congregations were enrolled, the totals were:[53]

Methodists	805
Congregational	529
Anglican	511
Baptist	238
Presbyterian	213
Unitarian	26
Independent Methodist	19
Society of Friends	19
Roman Catholics	14
Other denominations	30
Free Church Council	23
Sunday Schools	11
Church Brotherhoods	113
Unclassified	105

These totals make it clear that the Catholic Church represented something of a problem for the LNU. Cardinal Bourne, like the Archbishop of Canterbury and the Chief Rabbi, accepted a designation as the Union's Vice-President. But the coolness of the papacy to the League in the early 1920s hampered the LNU's work with Catholics. Even after the Pope indicated his willingness to co-operate with the League, many problems persisted in this area. One reader criticized *Headway* in 1923 for its 'half veiled contempt for Catholics' and the LNU for its 'distinctly Protestant tinge'.[54] The Union made progress with the Catholic hierarchy in the early 1930s, but this was soon undone.

Minor problems with other religious groups were more easily overcome. The pacifist tradition of the Society of Friends gave some of its members some hesitations about the League. But Quaker League supporters founded a Friends' League of Nations Society to win over their co-religionists at the end of the war. It disssolved with its mission successfully completed after three years.[55] Jewish League supporters sometimes objected to the emphasis on the Christian-ness of the League.[56] But if there was little Jewish congregational affiliation with the LNU, a number of

Jewish organizations, such as the Bayswater Jewish Literary and Social Group, formed Union branches.

The one big problem arising from the LNU's work in the churches was an offshoot of success. Here, as in the schools, the Union was typing itself as part of a moralistic crusade, high-minded and uncontroversial. It promoted the tendency to talk about the League as an abstract 'good thing', hardly linked to practical matters of foreign policy and defence budgets. It promoted the tendency at Grosvenor Crescent to remain above the fray and accept the easy platitudes of politicians about the League and peace. The Union's effort to 'educate for peace' had much the same impact, steering people away from the hard questions about what League membership might entail.

The history classroom was the focal point of the LNU's educational effort. If schoolchildren were taught only 'drum and trumpet' history, a narrow, nationalistic account of England's past, they would never be good citizens of the world. The old textbooks, with their emphasis on battles and kings, would have to be scrapped. History curriculum would have to be revised at all levels so that a new generation would grow up ready to support enlightened foreign policies and the work of the League. Moreover, history was to provide the ultimate justification for the League's existence. As one teacher put it, 'If history does not show that the League of Nations is a natural growth with its roots in the past, if we believe the League is an artificial structure, then it is a dangerous delusion and efforts to support it are a waste of time.'[57]

The LNU encouraged the study of international relations and of social history in order to show students the interdependence of nations. Because the British school system was very decentralized, the Board of Education could not do much to effect the changes needed. Especially in elementary schools, where there are no prescribed examinations, individual instructors had great freedom. The problem became one of reaching the teachers themselves, and of convincing them and local education authorities to reform. Summer schools and conferences for teachers, pamplets, visiting lecturers, films, a lending library, junior branches of the Union, and other devices were used in this effort.

Although Grosvenor Crescent was reluctant to revise textbooks itself, it did co-operate with the Historical Association in issuing a list of 'approved' books for teachers to consult. It also worked with publishers, advising them at conferences or exhibits when their books needed to be brought up to date: an 'up-to-date' text would include a chapter on the League. Just as importantly, it should not be narrow or biased in its coverage. Accounts of the war which blamed the 'evil genius' of Germany for starting it all were suspect.

With films as with books, the LNU tried to encourage what was good and discourage what was not. It produced documentary films in co-operation with the Historical Association which were seen by more than 1,000,000 schoolchildren. The Union also launched surveys on the influence of commerical motion pictures. One such inquiry, conducted in Bradford in 1928, analysed children's responses to 'What Price Glory?' and 'The Big Parade'. After studying the replies of some 4,000 children to such questions as 'What did the films make you think of war?' and 'What did you think of our side?', the pollsters concluded that the films did not have harmful effects.[58]

In the 1920s the Union's work in the schools went splendidly. The Education Committe was able to attract scholars of the calibre of Graham Wallas, Israel Gollancz, and Harold Temperley. It obtained generous co-operation from the local authorities. The London County Council arranged for mass meetings of teachers to hear talks by Cecil, and for lecture courses for teachers on the League at Evening Institutes. At Yeovil, education authorities specified that one afternoon each month be devoted to instruction on the League, and at Bolton the authorities established an essay contest on the League to stimulate student interest. In 1927 some 600 representatives of local education authorities met at a national conference and considered how to further instruction on the League in the schools.

Moreover, the teachers were responding with enthusiasm. Board of Education inspectors found that many, particularly history and geography teachers, were not only LNU members but branch officials as well. It was usually the history teacher who organized the school's junior branch of the Union, and such voluntary work was bound to influence his teaching. The changes in curriculum had been so well institutionalized that 'even the apathetic teacher who follows textbooks automatically will find himself encouraged to give League instruction, whether he mentions the fact in his syllabus or not'.[59]

The changes were not confined to the classroom either. From the mid-1920s on, the range of activities designed to introduce children to the League increased rapidly. Educators often argued that the extra-curricular approach—the League of Nations shelf in the library, the pageants, plays, and other activities—were more useful than the history lessons. Junior branches of the LNU, supplied by headquarters with copies of *League News* and a variety of pamphlets and other materials, were the best device for reaching students after school hours. They conducted contests, study circles, model Assemblies, League birthday parties, and other activities. Grosvenor Crescent circulated lists of plays suitable for performance by school groups. These included *Banish the Bogie*, 'an unusually quaint exposition of the way in which armaments manufacturers play one nation off against the others, so as to get orders . . .', *How the Cake was Shared*, 'an amusing analysis of the League of Nations' budget, symbolised by a cake', and a variety of tableaux on opium traffic, slavery, and other topics which showed the League in action.

The LNU also co-operated with the Boy Scouts, Girl Guides, Boys' Life Brigade, and other youth groups, supplying them with literature and lecturers. In 1933 it even launched its own scouting-type movement, the Nansen Pioneer Camps. Named after the Norwegian explorer and League official, Fridtjof Nansen, these camps were first designed as an alternative to the junior summer schools held in Geneva for children from 13 to 16 years of age. Pioneers spent two-week sessions camping out in the care of a staff 'selected for its ability to explain foreign affairs and the part played therein by the League . . .'. Camp life was supposed to demonstrate to the youngsters 'that the well-being of a community depends on the responsibility and good behaviour of its members, and this in ever wider groupings'. The camps were touted by *Headway* as 'a definite attempt to train for future leadership in our movement, and to create supporters for the League of Nations'.[60]

In 1927 the LNU established a Youth Section to provide activities for those too old for the junior branches but not yet ready for regular membership. It was suggested for sixteen- to twenty-five-years-old but included members in their late twenties. Youth Sections arranged debates on foreign affairs and a wide range of social activities. Comparable groups, branches of the British Universities' League of Nations Society, were set up in every university and most training colleges. Total university membership rose to over 7,000 in the early 1930s, with the Cambridge Society's 1,000 members and Oxford's 600 making them the largest clubs at each institution.

In the 1930s, as the Union became a more controversial body, its role as an educational organization was increasingly called into question. The men who had directed the LNU's school programmes saw their achievements threatened as the balance between political and educational work was upset. Educators complained about the Union being diverted from its main task. The Headmaster of Rugby was one of those who warned in 1938 that the Headmasters' Conference would break its ties with the LNU and that junior branches everywhere would soon fail if this did not stop.[61] Murray could only lament that the unrest of the world had even reached the teachers and the junior branches.[62]

Towards the end of 1938 agreement emerged on how to solve at least some of these problems. The Education Committee of the Union was to be made independent, in order to remove it from the taint of being a propaganda organization in the narrow political sense. In June 1939, the committee was reborn as the 'Council for Education in World Citzenship', a self-governing body, although still ultimately responsible to the LNU Executive. It was to publish *League News* and direct the junior branches, summer schools, camps, and conferences for teachers and students.[63] This arrangement proved workable, and the new Council continued to function during the war years.

Nevertheless, the basic difficulty with the LNU's educational programme could not be remedied by any organizational change. That programme had been designed to support the League of Nations, and by the late 1930s the League had collapsed. No matter how enlightened and internationally minded British schoolchildren might be, the fact remained that the world was on the verge of war.

Chapter VIII

The Peace Ballot

The LNU *Year Book* for 1934 said that 'there has probably never been a time since the foundation of the League of Nations when the whole collective system for the preservation of world order and peace were so gravely threatened as they are today'.[1] The failure of the League to meet the Japanese challenge in Manchuria, the collapse of the Disarmament Conference and the abrupt departure of Germany from Geneva had created a new situation. The Union was unhappy with the British Government's response to these events, but unable to offer credible alternatives. It had lost standing within the peace movement, for many pacifists were wary of the kind of coercive measures which the Union wanted to apply to Japan. More than that, it seemed increasingly out of touch with reality as it tried to combine disarmament and collective security—a version of collective security which was supposedly without risks.

The one strength LNU leaders thought they still had was the faith of the British public in the League. If they could call on this in some way and demonstrate to the Government that Englishmen stood squarely behind the League, then they might be able to retrieve the situation. The device they hit upon to do this was the Peace Ballot, properly called the 'National Declaration on the League of Nations and Armaments', which was launched in 1934 but not completed until the summer of 1935. Before it was over a new crisis erupted over the Italian venture in Ethiopa which put the League and its supporters to their greatest test.

In numerous historical studies and in the memoirs of Conservative statesmen, the Peace Ballot is mentioned as evidence of popular pacifism. Along with the East Fulham by-election of 1933 and that year's Oxford Union resolution not to fight 'for King and Country', the Peace Ballot was blamed for the failure to confront the dictators. Violet Bonham Carter said in 1941 that a member of the Government told her that Britain's unpreparedness for war and unwillingness to face it 'were entirely due to the peace propaganda and activities of the LNU, and in particular to the Peace Ballot'.[2] Here, as in Baldwin's comment that he owed his personal misfortunes to the Union, the tendency to exaggerate the LNU's influence is apparent. This is linked, as are the loose generalizations about East Fulham and the Oxford resolution, to one of the great myths which developed about British history in the thirties: that public opinion was pacifist and that this in turn prevented the adoption of a vigorous foreign policy.[3]

The idea of polling the public on some issue of international policy was a familiar one in inter-war Britain. The Union had co-operated with the Women's International League in 1932 on the 'Disarmament by Agreement' petition which got 2,150,000 signatures. the National Peace Council organized major petitions on the Washington Conference in 1922 and on arbitration in 1925.[4] It was obvious that the chief purpose of these efforts was to lobby and gain publicity for a cause, rather than to gauge opinion.

Several minor polling efforts were under way in early 1934. Vernon Bartlett of the League staff asked listeners to his radio talks to mail in answers to his question: 'Do you support a policy of international cooperation?' If there was anything surprising about the 21,000 replies it is that 10 per cent were against co-operation.[5] A number of provincial newspapers in the Rothermere group asked readers to vote on five questions about international relations, including 'Should Britain remain in the League of Nations?' Even though in this case the sponsor was anti-League, and used slogans in the poll such as 'Britain must be ready to defend herself' and 'Armaments mean peace', the results were overwhelmingly pro-League. The LNU capitalized on this: Angell wrote an 'analysis' of one such questionnaire for *Time and Tide* which ripped into the Rothermere press.[6]

The polling effort which most impressed Cecil was run by the Ilford *Recorder*, an independent local paper, in January 1934. The *Recorder*'s editor, C. J. A. Boorman, was a leader in his Union branch, and he discussed the idea of conducting a a ballot with Leslie Aldous, a staff member at Grosvenor Crescent.[7] The 'Peace-or-War Ballot', as Boorman called it, included the questions:

1. Should Britain remain in the League of Nations?
2. Should the Disarmament Conference continue?
3. Do you agree with that part of the Locarno Treaty which binds Great Britain to go to the help of France or Germany if the one is attacked by the other?
4. Should the manufacture of armaments by private enterprise be prohibited?

The results were overwhelmingly (5 to 1) in favour of League membership, and almost as strong in favour of the Disarmament

Conference continuing and the private manufacture of arms stopping. More surprising, certainly to Cecil who was still pro-Locarno, was the strong (3 to 1) negative response to the third question. This reflected the feeling that special arrangements to meet particular problems were wrong and did not benefit Britain.[8] What was most impressive about the results, which Cecil announced at Ilford Town Hall on 8 February was that some 26,000 responded—more than had voted in the last elections. Boorman also found that the ballot gave young people a chance to show their enthusiasm for the League.[9]

Cecil proposed an LNU referendum to the Executive Committee on 1 March suggesting that it could be combined with the continuing process of canvassing from door to door for new members. This raised objections because it would probably lead to so unrepresentative a sampling of opinion as to make the effort worthless. Then on 8 March Cecil tried with another proposal, this time to co-operate with other societies in polling the public on League membership so as to counter the Rothermere press efforts around the country. It was agreed that Union canvassing would not be involved and that the details of the effort would be worked out with the other organizations involved.[10]

On 27 March a conference of interested groups met at Grosvenor Crescent to discuss plans for a national referendum. A National Declaration Committee was established by the thirty-eight participating societies, not all of them 'peace groups', with Cecil as Chairman and Dame Adelaide Livingstone of the LNU as Secretary. The committee met on 11 April to begin planning the referendum. At this stage planners aimed for a vote of 4,000,000 or 5,000,000 and still weighed restricting the balloting to those regions here a large-scale result could be obtained.[11] Meanwhile Cecil worked to insure the LNU's full co-operation. He told the Executive that the cost of the operation to the Union, including Dame Adelaide's salary and that for her secretary, might run to about £4,000 but that outside funds would help pay this.[12] Some Executive Committee members still opposed the venture, arguing that it would fail because in areas without local LNU organizations it would be impossible to conduct.[13]

The ballot questions were ready by the time the General Council met in June, and raised objections of a different sort. The questions were:

1. Should Great Britain remain a member of the League of Nations?

2. Are you in favour of the all-round reduction of armaments by international agreement?
3. Are you in favour of the all-round abolition of national military and naval aircraft by international agreement?
4. Should the manufacture and sale of armaments for private profit be prohibited by international agreement?
5. Do you consider that, if a nation insists on attacking another, the other nations should compel it to stop by
   (a) economic and non-military measures?
   (b) if necessary, military measures?

The Conservative Party gave notice that it did not intend to co-operate in the balloting because these questions, 'except for one or two the reply to which is self-evident, are not such as anyone even with full knowledge of the difficulties of the problems with which they deal could feel justified in answering just "yes" or "no"'. Colonel George Herbert of the Conservative Central Office cited some more specific objections to the questionnaire. In the third question, for instance, that no mention was made of civil aviation. And in the fifth there was no indication of the way 'a' runs into 'b'—that is, that economic and non-military measures might involve a nation in military measures. The party allowed its local branches to decide whether or not to participate, but this decision was bound nevertheless to give the exercise a partisan cast.

Question four, on the private manufacture of armaments, was especially objectionable to Conservatives. Lord Cranborne, a leading Union Conservative and Cecil's nephew, had raised this matter with Murray in May, hinting that Union Conservatives and Baldwin were likely to be embarrassed by it. Murray replied that while the LNU could not drop the issue, 'he would ensure that attacks were not made on the Government in this connection'.[14] When in July Cecil conferred with Anthony Eden, Lord Privy Seal, who had supplied the Conservative Party's arguments against the ballot, Eden singled out the fourth question for criticism.[15]

Eden complained not only about the questions themselves, but also about the attached 'commentary' which was to be distributed with the ballots. This commentary soon became the cause of a major row in the Executive Committee which spilled over into the press. It restated the LNU's positions in a leaflet which was frankly designed to lead people into 'yes' answers. Conservatives objected to this tactic, and in the Executive on 19 July they asked that the commentary be replaced with a new and more balanced leaflet. Cecil argued that it was too late to replace the commentary, but that the Conservatives could draw up another leaflet of their own which would be circulated too. This compromise left several Union leaders worried, lest the Conservatives use their leaflet to attack the ballot itself.[16]

Austen Chamberlain was still upset over the way LNU branches could 'rig . . . the market' with biased instructions[17] and Murray's attempts to mollify him did not work. Cranborne was worried about the political threat to Conservatives posed by the ballot and unhappy that he had not been alert to the danger earlier; he advised Chamberlain that he was ready to quit the LNU and that others should take a strong stand on the issue too.[18] Agreement on a second leaflet (on blue paper) to accompany the original (on green paper) brought a temporary lull to this 'rainbow controversy', but only after news of the affair had generated public interest in the ballot.[19]

While this controversy raged, plans to organize the ballot took shape. In each locality the Union branch was to hold a conference for the representatives of organizations willing to co-operate. This conference was to appoint a committee, which ideally should include political leaders, churchmen, and other community leaders. Parliamentary constituencies, for which the LNU already had canvassing machinery, were to be the polling units with several grouped together under one committee in larger towns or cities. Volunteer pollsters were appointed by each committee and assigned to visit every household in their area twice: first to deliver the questionnaire and voting papers and then to collect them. These volunteers, some 500,000 of them in all, were periodically guided by speakers who advised then of objections which might be raised and suitable replies.[20]

Each committee was allowed to determine the best time to conduct its ballot, with an Easter 1935 target date suggested. While the first results came in on 22 November 1934, from Scaldwell in Northamptonshire (with huge affirmative majorities for every question), the big drive did not start in most places until after Christmas, when 1,000 local committees were at work, and the results were still dribbling in during the following summer. By the end of November, 60,000 ballots had been tabulated and by January the 1,000,000 mark was reached. Results from the big industrial cities pushed the totals up to 5,000,000 by the beginning of April. It was by then clear that the declaration was getting a far bigger response than expected, and the National Committee announced that a big turn-out would mean even more than a high percentage of affirmative answers. This was a moot point since the tendency of the hostile was not to take part. The final total reached by the summer of 1935 exceeded 11,000,000.[21]

The poll did not manage to get a truly nation-wide response, for LNU organizations in a few areas never co-operated fully. The response in any given area depended chiefly on the number of volunteers available to distribute the forms. Low percentages usually came from the areas where the Union and the co-operating societies were weak.[22] Early in the voting period, Wales and the north of England began turning in the highest and most positive results, and in the final tally the best eight constituencies were all Welsh while Lancashire and Yorkshire topped the English list.[23] Scotland posed the greatest problems, mainly because the Glasgow and Dundee branches were unwilling to co-operate. LNU headquarters tried to co-ordinate the effort in Scotland, but the results suffered. After the poll ended, Murray tried to force out the West of Scotland LNU Secretary and have the branch dissolved because of this experience.[24]

With the balloting under way, Union Conservatives began to feel more and more put upon. *Headway* appeared to taunt them in reporting that while 'the game of fault finding goes on, [people were] taking no notice of fanciful difficulties'.[25] The Conservative-dominated Finance Committee failed in its indirect attack on the ballot through complaints about excessive spending and loss of Union revenues.[26] It was indeed the case that subscriptions lagged with all energies devoted to the ballot. Conservatives on the Executive complained about the National Declaration Committee getting out of the Union's control, something which even Murray agreed was a problem.[27] Here, as in the roughly comparable dispute over the International Peace Campaign that this fore-shadowed, Cecil insisted that it was all worth while, and that Conservatives had been catered to enough; Livingstone and her second-in-command, Major Gordon Dickson, were Conservatives after all.[28]

Conservatives did not see it this way. The 'rainbow controversy' flared up again in the autumn, after it appeared that the agreement reached during the summer was not being followed. A third informative leaflet, this time in yellow, was issued by the Declaration Committee without being cleared by Chamberlain and other Union Conservatives. Chamberlain wrote a letter to *The Times* on 12 November complaining about the affair. Cecil insisted that he had cleared the new leaflet with Cranborne and that Chamberlain might do well to resign from the LNU if he really thought its leaders were 'all dishonest liars'.[29] The furore was over in a few days with Cranborne shouldering the blame for a misunderstanding.[30] Chamberlain was not ready to resign—yet. But his opinion of the LNU did not improve: 'I find all that body of public opinion with which I am associated more and more estranged from the Union', he said, even though 'the majority of the Executive do try to harmonize their views with mine'.[31]

The Conservative Party went on the attack, with its central office complaining about the way LNU fund-raisers used old letters of commendation from Baldwin.[32] The Prime Minister, in a speech on 23 November, criticized the Peace Ballot and warned that 'nothing could be more harmful to the League of Nations or to the League of Nations Union than that there should be a suspicion of their being drawn into the vortex of party politics. The Union was founded strictly on non-political lines. If it deserted those lines its influence for good in the country as a whole would be at an end.' More than that, he addressed the broader question posed in the ballot head on, and declared a collective peace system 'perfectly impracticable'.[33]

Cecil wrote to him remonstrating about his remarks on the LNU. Baldwin then backtracked a little, saying that the originators of the ballot might not have had party motives. The ballot could, however, be used for political purposes.[34]

These private reassurances did not lessen the impact of Baldwin's speech, which tended to make the ballot more of a referendum on the Government than it had been. Baldwin had linked support for collective security to the Labour Party. MacDonald too attacked the ballot as giving 'opportunities . . . to unscrupulous propagandists . . . for party politics of the lowest kind'.[35] Simon attacked the LNU as prejudiced and partisan in the Commons on 8 November winning loud cheers from the Government side.[36] Murray was concerned about these attacks and tried to reassure Conservatives that he was keeping over-zealous Labourite volunteers in bounds.[37] The Peace Ballot was designedly partial, so Murray's efforts to defuse it as a partisan issue could not achieve much.

The fact that by early 1935 the ballot was turning into a massive crusade, the biggest enterprise the Union had ever launched, made it a logical vehicle for the left to use against the Government. The *Daily Herald* touted it as a 'vote for peace' and in by-elections

Labour candidates could use the questions as a club against their opponents.[38] Even extreme leftist groups were included in the broad spectrum of over sixty undergraduate organizations supporting the declaration at Cambridge. They were not necessarily committed to securing affirmative answers to all the questions. Communists shared the objections of devout pacifists to the fifth question, although for different reasons. An alternative answer to questions five, a and b: 'I accept the Christian Pacifist attitude', was provided after the declaration got under way, but this did not meet the needs of extreme socialists. For instance, the Chairman of the Cambridge University Socialist Society could insist that:

Even such limited action as supporting the Ballot is in some degree an act of opposition to the war policy of the Government, and the C.U.S.S. calls on every undergraduate to register an emphatic 'yes' to the first four questions. The fifth question is on another footing. Wars between Imperialist Capitalist Powers are not caused by unprovoked attacks on one nation or another, but are the outcome of economic struggle for markets and raw materials which are inherent in capitalism, and every Power is an 'aggressor'.[39]

The ballot rolled to a triumphant conclusion in the summer of 1935, aided by heavy press coverage, with the *News Chronicle*, the *Daily Herald*, and the *Manchester Guardian* paying it almost constant attention. Even hostile comments from the right on the 'ballot of blood' drummed up interest in the effort. In the final weeks, the *News Chronicle* and the *Star*, as well as numerous provincial journals, printed their own adaptations of the questionnaire as a service to readers who wanted to vote but had not been able to.[40] The National Declaration Committee held a June meeting in London to announce the totals, which it then published in a sixty-four page 'official history' of the ballot. In a conclusion written for this, Cecil said the result 'exceeded our most sanguine expectations. . .'. Already he perceived 'a great change [coming] over the tone of public statements about the League. Up to a year ago official references to the League were rare and, when they did occur, they were politely sceptical . . . Now that tone has almost vanished. . . .' Nor was the change confined to speeches. 'The intervention in the Saar, the action on the Serbo-Hungarian dispute over the responsibility for the assassination of King Alexander, the insistence on a peaceful settlement of the Abyssinian difficulty are all welcome instances of a vigorous use of League machinery to solve international problems.' Cecil urged his followers to see their MPs and 'bring home to influential quarters full knowledge of what has actually been achieved. . .'.[41]

The decision to strike quickly and capitalize on the results of the ballot while it still enjoyed great publicity but before the votes were tabulated was in keeping with the conduct of what was, if anyone needed reminding, a propaganda campaign and not an opinion survey. The results in June, with over 11,000,000 replies in, were in line with the final results announced later in 1935 when all 11,640,066 ballots were in.

The first question, on whether Britain should stay in the League, drew the strongest positive response (Yes: 11,166,818; No: 357,930; Doubtful: 10,528; and No Answer: 104,790). The response to the second question showed that disarmament remained in favour (Yes: 10,542,738; No: 868,431; Doubtful: 12,138; and No Answer: 216,759). The third question, asking people whether they supported the abolition of national military and naval aircraft, got a somewhat weaker response (Yes: 9,600,274; No: 1,699,989; Doubtful: 17,063; and No Answer: 322,740). The fourth, on whether the manufacture and sale of armaments for private profit should be prohibited by international agreement, got a strong 'yes' vote. (Yes: 10,489,145; No: 780,350; Doubtful: 15,157; and No Answer: 355,414). The key fifth question yielded mixed results. It was in two parts, 'Do you consider that, if a nation insists on attacking another, the other nations should compel it to stop by (a) economic and non-military measures?' (Yes: 10,096,626; No: 639,195; Doubtful: 27,369; No Answer: 862,707; and Christian Pacifist: 14,169), and (b) if necessary, military measures? (Yes: 6,833,803; No: 2,366,184; Doubtful: 41,058; No answer: 2,381,485; and Christian Pacifist: 17,536).

The results were supposed to encourage resistance to aggression through collective sanctions. The wording of the questions, which asked about 'all-round reduction of armaments by international agreement' and 'all-round' abolition of aircraft 'by international agreement' showed that unilateral disarmament was not intended, and the separate category provided for Christian Pacifists further emphasized the distinction between the internationalist and pure pacifist positions. None of this stopped the ballot's critics from saying later—as Hoare, for instance, said—that it spread 'the impression . . . abroad that England was for peace at any price'.[42]

Certainly this was not the impression Eden tried to convey when he discussed the Ethiopian situation with the German Ambassador on 2 July. Hoesch recorded that Eden told him that

'British public opinion, [as] in the so-called "Peace Ballot", . . . would plainly not tolerate it if the British Government were just tacitly to accept a breach of the League of Nations Covenant by Italy or were to take part in an attempt at sophistically glossing it over'. Lack of support from the other powers might leave Britain isolated 'in the role of champion of an abstract League morality', Eden added, weakening the impact of his statement.[43] The following October, Hoare was even more specific than Eden had been in telling Hoesch that British public opinion had ranged itself behind the idea of collective security and that the 'Government were carrying out the policy of the people's will'.[44]

When a deputation from the National Declaration Committee headed by Cecil called at the Prime Minister's office on 23 July, Baldwin gave them the answers they wanted to hear. He slid past his old objections and said that he was 'glad to know that . . . the object of the Ballot was by no means to criticize the Government, even though some may have endeavoured to use the movement for this purpose, but rather to show the Government that we had a large volume of public opinion behind us'. He then assured the deputation 'that the League of Nations remains, as I said in a speech in Yorkshire recently, "the sheet anchor of British policy"'.[45]

The principal objection to the ballot was not that it fostered pacifism which in turn led to appeasement out of weakness. It was rather that it promoted an unrealistic view of collective security as a kind of abstract principle. Eden's original objection, repeated in his *Facing the Dictators*, was that the separation of economic and military sanctions in question five implied that economic sanctions could be applied against an aggressor without the risk of war. He doubted whether the people calling for sanctions against Mussolini were really aware that the brunt of applying sanctions would fall on Britain.[46] The vote for collective security had been impressive, but did the voters have a clear idea of what they meant by sanctions? Or did the ballot leave the British public with the impression that collective security was a high-minded but rather abstract goal in foreign affairs which involved no great risk or expense for Britain?

These questions troubled even the most steadfast supporters of the League. Harold Nicolson, for instance, told a story which cast doubt on the willingness of the British public to risk war in defence of the Covenant. During the 1935 General Elections he received a letter from a constituent asking for an assurance that Nicolson stood for the League and collective security and that he would 'oppose any entanglements in Europe'. Nicolson described how he read the letter aloud at various meetings and then observed the response. 'Only in rare and isolated cases', he recounted, 'did my audience at once see that the above formula was self-contradictory nonsense.' Nicolson and others found it revealing that the declaration was popularly known as the Peace Ballot, a title which only confirmed the impression of many ignorant voters that they were being asked to choose between peace and war.[47] The public's concept of collective security did not remain abstract because a potential target for joint action was lacking during the balloting. It was there, in Italy, but even the 7,000,000 people who voted 'yes' to question five (b) and supposedly wanted military sanctions applied against an aggressor may not have connected their votes to the situation brewing in Ethiopa.

The ballot had only confirmed the popular impression that collective security represented an alternative to war, a policy which by mobilizing the overwhelming strength of the law-abiding nations would eliminate the need for large national armies. Only if we recall this meaning of the term before the crucible of events helped give it a new significance, can we understand why it could still be linked to disarmament. This link was still there in 1935, and while the LNU was not flatly opposed to all rearmament, it qualified its support—making it dependent on the adoption of a collective security policy and an international disarmament agreement—in such a way as to make it meaningless. The White Paper on rearmament published in March 1935 clearly did not meet these tests.

Here, on the rearmament issue, was the most telling criticism of the ballot. Nevile Butler emphasized this when he briefed the Prime Minister before the 23 July meeting with the deputation from the National Declaration Committee. Many ballot supporters had 'condemned the Government for expanding the Air Force and for spending more money on the country's defence'. Since Hitler had reintroduced conscription and was building up his air force,

any British Government prepared to take a part in collective security was bound (1) to build up the Air Force, and (2) to take certain defensive measures against attack. Neither of these steps were likely to be popular, but they are essential not only to our own defense, but to our loyal and effective membership of the League . . . The Government therefore naturally asked itself to what extent the League of

Nations Union and other League supporting societies could be relied on to explain to people these disagreeable necessities.[48]

Rearmament in itself did not constitute an adequate foreign policy, but if Britain was to be able to implement a vigorous collective security policy with confidence, she needed rearmament. There is truth in Hoare's comment that the 'real question that should have been asked [in the ballot was] "Do you support British rearmament in the interests of peace?"'[49]

In terms of the Union organization there were other reasons to criticize the Peace Ballot. It cost the LNU some £12,000, and perhaps more important, interrupted canvassing for new members. Later Murray would lament that 'we plunged into a bold policy at the time of the Peace Ballot, and thought we should recover our expenditure through increased enthusiasm and membership. For various reasons the result has been the other way—a considerable drop among our rich subscribers, and since the Abyssinian debacle some loss of confidence in the League. If the League had succeeded we should probably be well in funds.'[50]

Despite all this, the Union judged the Peace Ballot to be its greatest success. After all of the doubts and reversals of the previous years, *Headway* described the General Council assembling 'in a mood of brave, if critical confidence' at the end of 1935. 'The immense popular success of the Ballot, the eager professions of all political parties at the General Election of their whole-hearted League loyalty, gave many thousands of Union members a new vision of the part the Union is called on to play in shaping the future of Britain and the world.'[51]

Others in the peace movement tried to copy the ballot's example. The Women's International League for Peace and Freedom initiated the 'People's Mandate' in April 1935, calling on governments to take common action in fulfilment of their Covenant and Kellogg Pact pledges. This was conducted in twenty-five countries and eventually received 10,000,000 declarations, with 1,250,000 in Britain alone.[52] In 1936 Bertrand Russell called on fellow pacifists to start a great effort to prove 'as the Peace Ballot proved, the overwhelming strength of public opinion against war, but not liable . . . to the kind of betrayal that befell [ballot supporters]'.[53]

Within the League movement too there were efforts to recapture the success of the ballot. The indefatigable Konni Zilliacus promoted 'a Peace Ballot for all who are of military age (18–35)' in

1935.[54] Noel-Baker suggested that the LNU launch another ballot in 1938, and he drew up questions which centred on the practical application of the principles presented in the first ballot to the Sino-Japanese War. In defending his proposal, Noel-Baker said that the Peace Ballot was worth repeating because it provided the only occasion when the Union had succeeded in getting a Conservative Government to change its policy on anything of importance.[55] Neither Cecil nor Murray liked the idea, however, Cecil fearing that its failure would destroy the LNU.[56]

Noel-Baker's comment about the policy change brought about by the ballot was of course a reference to the sanctions policy against Italy. This episode emerged as the biggest test of the Union. An accident of timing brought the ballot to a conclusion just as the Ethiopian crisis erupted. This conjunction of events gave particular significance to the LNU's polling effort, as did the presence in 10 Downing Street of a leader looking forward to a General Election.

The Peace Ballot had put the Union into a position unique in its history. It was more in the limelight than it had ever been and in the November 1935 elections it tried to capitalize on this. When Baldwin's commitment to the League appeared to fail in one speech at Wolverhampton, the Executive Committee was quick to protest.[57] The Prime Minister swallowed his doubts about collective security and continued to refer to the League as the keystone of his foreign policy.

This left voters with little to choose between the parties on League policy. All spoke freely in favour of the Peace Ballot's 'all sanctions short of war' formula but were vague on how this might be implemented. By pushing the Government into supporting sanctions, the ballot perhaps influenced the election in one way. Baldwin may have called it early because he realized that the Ethiopian War could only work against him in the long run. However, during the election, a confused affair fought chiefly over domestic issues, the LNU's impact was slight. The Peace Ballot shaped the rhetoric but not the reality of British policy.[58]

Chapter IX

The Ethiopian Crisis

League supporters had been equivocal in their response to the Far Eastern crisis. They did not intend to repeat their error in 1935. Fortified by the results of the Peace Ballot, the LNU adopted a vigorous policy of collective security. The Union's critics could now begin to call it 'the new war party'.[1]

The LNU was a 'war party' with a suspiciously ambivalent attitude towards armaments, however. In the Manchurian crisis, the Union—whether or not its prescription of applying diplomatic and economic pressure against Japan might have worked—was at least reasonably consistent. When in 1935 it advocated using 'the whole force of the League' to curb Italy while retaining its qualms about rearmament, its inconsistency became manifest. The League powers could no longer hope to cow opponents with a show of strength, and needed to be strengthened to meet the challenge of Fascism.

The point is not that Italy was so powerful an adversary that sanctions could not have been enforced against her if necessary. Later events confirm the view that Britain was strong enough to have pursued a sanctions policy with confidence, that Mussolini's bark was worse than his bite. The point is that collective security made sense as a policy only if it could apply to Germany as well as Italy. International law had to be enforceable for the strong as well as the weak.

F. S. Northedge, in his *The Troubled Giant*, found it 'a matter of some difficulty to explain why British opinion in 1935 was so firm in its demand for the enforcement of sanctions against Italy while Germany's far more dangerous breaches of treaties tended to be condoned'. He saw part of the explanation in the feelings of guilt which had developed in relation to the Versailles Treaty and part in fear of war[2]. So far as the LNU is concerned, the willingness to contend with Italy but not Germany was indicative of the prevailing attitude to collective security. The Covenant remained for most members 'an instrument for the prevention of war and the organization of peace', as it was often described, and not an instrument for coercion. It was painless for them to support sanctions against Italy, for Italy did not pose a direct threat to British security. Germany was another story, and the Union's response to the remilitarization of the Rhineland in 1936 was feeble by comparison.

For the British and French foreign offices collective security was being presented in its most unpalatable form in the Ethiopian crisis: they were being called on to direct sanctions against an ally labelled as an aggressor. The Four Power Pact of 1933, which the LNU had railed against when it was signed, provided a specific link with Italy.[3] More basically, with rising German power to contend with, diplomatic 'realists' wanted Rome's friendship. The Peace Ballot helped force Whitehall into action against its better judgement and it reacted by dragging its feet, never going the whole course into the kind of sanctions policy which might have curbed Italy.

In the British Cabinet there was almost unanimous reluctance to act against Italy.[4] Baldwin felt he had to respond to domestic opinion and brought the Government into line, but he remained fearful about British military weakness, not just because of the dangers posed by a revived Germany but also of Italy itself. Throughout the crisis the Prime Minister worried about the possibility of a 'mad dog' attack by the Italians on the British fleet. Drummond, now Ambassador in Rome, warned the Foreign Secretary of the danger of such an attack and counselled against a sanctions policy.[5] Churchill too was concerned about British weakness in the Mediterranean and while he did not oppose a League sanctions policy directly, he insisted that it should only be pursued if it had French support—an important qualification.[6] Eden, Minister for League Affairs during the crisis, had been critical of the LNU, but he was to emerge as the League's champion in the Government.

The response of the League Secretariat to the Ethiopian crisis complicated the LNU's position, Joseph Avenol, the Secretary-General, tried to keep the League from getting involved in the early stages. He acted partly out of the kind of pro-Italian 'realism' typical of French diplomats and also out of a desire to avoid taking action which might drive Italy out or prevent Germany from coming back into the League. When Avenol did become involved in settlement efforts, it was—from the LNU perspective—in the wrong way.[7] Union leaders could feel that a sanctions policy was more their own than the League's.

The LNU's perspective on Italy before the crisis had not been at all harsh. Individuals in the Union may have been critical of Fascism, but Grosvenor Crescent was not about to stir up trouble on account of it. *Headway* had for years bent over backwards to be fair to Mussolini. In the aftermath of the Corfu Incident of 1923, it assured readers that the League had nothing to fear from Fascism, which will either 'disappear, or, . . . more probably, will rapidly transform itself, dropping its affectation of savagery and becoming more and more reasonable, conciliatory, and sensitive to the good opinion of the world at large.[8] Pro-Italian articles appeared in *Headway* in the early 1930s. One in 1933 claimed that 'the days of a personal dictatorship are at an end' and saw Anglo-Italian friendship as a 'bulwark for peace'.[9] Even when the first reports of fighting in Ethiopia came in, *Headway* still cautioned readers against jumping to the conclusion that Italy was at fault. In June 1935, after the fighting stopped and the dispute was submitted to League arbitration, *Headway* praised Italy's 'loyal League service' and minimized the importance of the whole episode.[10]

At this stage, LNU leaders were trying to sound conciliatory to Whitehall as well as Rome. Baldwin had been playing up to them and they were ready to respond in kind.[11] Accordingly, the Executive Committee emphasized on 20 June that while it 'regard[ed] the prevention of Italian aggression upon Abysinnia as absolutely vital to the future of the League, is very anxious not to do anything which would hamper H.M. Government's action'. Union members were instructed on the importance of 'saying nothing which would add to the difficulties of the situation', and the Foreign Secretary was asked what kind of resolution from the Union he would like.[12] The Executive then picked up Haile Selassie's request that the League send observers to Ethiopia, or, that failing, that arrangements be made so that if it did decide to dispatch observers it could be done quickly.[13]

Cecil conferred with the Foreign Secretary on 26 June and told him that Mussolini would not dare face 'a collective threat from the League or a breach of British friendship'. He wanted to make sure that Rome was denied financial backing from British (and if possible American) sources and that League observers were sent to the disputed areas.[14] In the following weeks the Executive kept a low profile, while waiting for a Government lead. On 12 July it could not resist adding that while it 'realizes that the moment for action must be left to H.M. Government', Britain should say openly to the Council 'that we are prepared to fulfil our obligations under the Covenant and call upon all other Members of the

League to support us'.[15]

The question of what others, especially the French, would do was now critical. Cabinet members wanted to keep in step with their French counterparts. Neville Chamberlain, for instance, noted in his diary for 5 July that while the worst had to be assumed about Mussolini, 'if the French would not play, we have no individual (as opposed to collective) obligations, and we should not attempt to take on our shoulders the whole burden of keeping the peace'.[16] Murray went to France to sound out Bonnet and others. He reported to Cecil on 9 July that while French opinion could not be changed in time to help resolve the crisis, 'if England simply put forward faithful League policy at the Council the rest would inevitably agree and France be unable to oppose'.[17] Cecil was encouraged by this, but concerned about getting 'the British or any other Government to shew anything which distantly resembles courage and backbone'.[18] A Union deputation placed these concerns before Eden later in July and suggested a ban on the export of arms to the combatants.[19]

The Executive appeared to be clearing the decks for action in August. It sent Garnett and Noel-Baker to Geneva and urged the Government to tell the Council 'that the British nation will be ready to bear its part in any action, however drastic, that may be necessary for the purpose'.[20] Frank Walters of the League Secretariat wrote to Cecil when he read this resolution, expressing his doubts about it. It seemed to him to put what had been fairly certain in the light of statements by Hoare and Eden once again into doubt. Cecil's reply was revealing: the resolution was aimed at domestic opinion, which was not at all sure that the Cabinet would act. If the branches put pressure on in their constituencies, it would strengthen Eden's hand. It was, after all, an election year.[21]

The Foreign Secretary did not accept the LNU's advice to give notice at Geneva that Britain was ready to carry out its Covenant obligations. Hoare explained that he wanted to co-ordinate his policy with the French, and such a unilateral declaration might embarrass them.[22] Hoare needed no reminders that opinion in Britain was behind the League; he was ready to mention reports from his own press department to confirm this. Even the *Morning Post*, he noted, was growing restive at Italian arrogance.[23]

Cecil checked with Eden to see if there was anything he wanted the Union to do. There was not.[24] He again pressed Hoare to make a statement of intentions at Geneva.[25] While Rome continued to make threatening statements, the Union prepared for the storm ahead. Murray asked to see Hoare to get the arms embargo against Ethiopia raised. The Executive Committee launched an intensive study of sanctions, aided by Arthur Salter, who had won a high reputation as a top League official. Salter impressed the Executive on 29 August with an analysis stressing that mild sanctions could be as risky as tougher and more effective ones (such as blocking the Suez Canal). More importantly, diplomatic and economic sanctions alone would not be effective unless the aggressor believed that a collective determination existed to do more, if need be.[26] This perspective influenced LNU policy in the coming weeks; a policy paper prepared for the Executive by Angell, for instance, emphasized that economic sanctions should be tried 'with the realisation that naval force may, in the last resort, have to be employed'.[27]

In September the Union encouraged public discussion of the specific series of counter measures which would be taken if Italy carried out her threats. The Executive suggested that Britain should propose action to the Council under Article 16, beginning with the withdrawal of heads of diplomatic missions and a general boycott of Italian exports. Then, if this did not suffice, Italy should be denied use of the Suez Canal.[28] *Headway* compared Britain's situation now with that in 1914 when she 'went to war in defence of the international system'. It concluded that 'to-day, but much more flagrantly, there is threatened a refusal to fulfill treaties . . .'[29]

The Government finally provided the kind of clear sign that it would stand by the League which the LNU had been waiting for. On 11 September Hoare announced to an excited Assembly that Britain stood 'for the collective maintenance of the Covenant in its entirety, and particularly for steady and collective resistance to all acts of unprovoked aggression'. After this, the Executive was more anxious than ever to be helpful to Whitehall. Hoare was invited to address an LNU meeting on 24 September but when he said that he would prefer that no mass meetings be held, the Union obligingly cancelled it.[30]

Hoare's speech was read at Grosvenor Crescent as a triumphant postscript to the Peace Ballot. Union members were now assured that when the test came Britain would pass it: 'Loyal League members will first break off diplomatic relations with the aggressor. Next, they will apply economic pressure. Later they may find themselves obliged to repel force with force . . . (Britain) has set her hand to the Covenant; and she means to honor her obligations in full. She has adopted the League ideal.'[31]

Cecil was confident once Britain had taken her stand that other League members would fall into line. 'There will be', he predicted on 20 September, 'no difficulty in using whatever sanctions may be necessary unless the States go back from their present opinion . . .'[32] The Union's plans for collective security could at last be implemented.

When Italy rebuffed attempts at conciliation and invaded Ethiopia in October 1935, the LNU's time arrived. Cecil immediately counselled Cranborne, now Eden's Under-Secretary, to block the Suez Canal and cut off Italy's lines of communication.[33] On 3 October Cecil reported to the Executive that the Foreign Office had asked for the LNU's views on economic pressure under Article 16, encouraging the belief that Britain would implement sanctions.[34] By 10 October the League Council had declared that Italy had disregarded the Covenant in going to war. The Executive now predicted confidently that 'the great mass of the people of this country would support full use of the collective authority of the League to cut all communication between Italy and the African colonies'.[35] To prove that this support existed, the Union held a mass meeting at the Albert Hall in London on 31 October addressed by a three-party line-up of Austen Chamberlain, Violet Bonham Carter, and Herbert Morrison.

The LNU questionnaire for the General Election led with the question 'Will you support the use of the whole collective force of the League to put an end to the Italian aggression in Abyssinia?' To the dismay of some members, it went on to ask a lot of other questions, including one which asked if, when the war ended, the candidate agreed on the need for international disarmament.[36] This downgraded the crisis at hand, but then it fairly reflected the attitude that a challenge by Italy was not a matter of life and death. If Britain showed enough determination, it would all be easy.

The question soon became one of whether the Government would show that determination. Cecil wrote again to Cranborne, who was at the League, restating his plan for blocking the canal and warning against the use of minor sanctions, which might cause irritation but fail to stop the Italians.[37] A speech by Baldwin on 28 October and comments by Hoare and Eden in the Commons raised doubts at Grosvenor Crescent. The LNU warned the Government not to 'countenance any proposals more favourable to Italy than were obtainable by peaceful negotiation before the invasion of Abyssinia'.[38] The League response to Italy, embargoing the shipment of arms to her, urging a financial boycott, the withholding of some exports and the refusal of imports, was disappointing too. *Headway* complained that 'contrasted with the ideal League policy, the course actually adopted appears pitiably undecided'. Union confidence was weakening, as *Headway* pleaded that 'Italy must not be bought off at the expense of her victim. Her aggression must fail . . .'[39]

The war in Ethiopia raged on, as some fifty League members started to implement economic sanctions. LNU leaders grew more uneasy in November. The National Government won a large majority in the General Elections with pledges to support the Covenant, but it showed no interest in LNU proposals to block the canal and make those pledges count. The Executive tried to come up with some other way to stop Italy, and it settled on a ban on petroleum shipments to her. League countries sold Italy 90 per cent of her oil, and a League Sanctions Committee was to meet at the end of the month to decide what additional materials should be denied her. Concerned with the possibility that the United States might not co-operate in a League oil ban, Murray conferred with James T. Shotwell, a leading American internationalist. Washington announced on 18 November that it would keep its oil and other raw materials exports at normal levels in the spirit of the Neutrality Act. Hence—if American oil companies could be controlled by their government (which was questionable)—American supplies would not upset League sanctions.[40]

On 14 November the Executive urged Cecil to press the matter of an oil prohibition with Eden.[41] It followed this with a resolution 'that the supply of petroleum and its derivatives from sources under British control to Italy should be stopped immediately irrespective of the action taken by other countries'.[42] The need for a ban on the shipment of oil to Italy soon dominated Union thinking about Ethiopia. That Britain and other League powers should come so far and invoked Article 16, but still be reluctant to halt the supply of this one item and really stop Italy was infuriating. Cecil and Lytton discussed the matter with Hoare and Eden on 25 November but made no progress. Austen Chamberlain was won over to the idea of an oil embargo, although he did not think that Britain should have to get League permission to impose a ban.[43] The December *Headway* saw economic sanctions taking effect in Italy, but regretted the failure to add oil to the list.

'Why, then, is so right and decisive a step not taken?' The answer is simple. The plan to bribe Signor Mussolini to permit the world to live at peace, though repeatedly proved futile, has not yet been abandoned everywhere.'[44] This barb was aimed more at the Quai d'Orsay than Whitehall, for LNU leaders worried about the wrong kind of French influence. A British lead in imposing an oil sanction might have the added attraction of forcing France into openly taking her stand for the League or for Italy.[45]

News leaked out in early December that France *and* Britain had made their choice, in effect, for Italy. The Hoare–Laval plan to end the war by endorsing the transfer to Italy of the fertile Ethiopian plains won the approval of the British Cabinet. Then, with *The Times* leading the way, British opinion reacted sharply to this betrayal of the League. The LNU joined in, dispatching a deputation to 10 Downing Street, and calling on branches to do the same to every MP, rushing out press releases and setting a mass meeting in protest.[46] The public outcry—which has been likened to the campaign against the 'Bulgarian horrors' in 1876—was enormous.[47] Cecil later said that it was all 'remarkably spontaneous', and that the Union did little more than follow where the public led.[48] In a specific sense he was right, although the Peace Ballot and years of campaigning had no doubt prepared the way for it.

Baldwin was conciliatory with the Union deputation of Cecil, Murray, Chamberlain, Noel-Baker, and Lytton (who had just become LNU Vice-Chairman) on 13 December. He tried to justify his course by referring to the dangers of an attack by Mussolini and of a break with France, and got some support for his case from Chamberlain. However, on the main point, the Prime Minister insisted that League policy was still his policy. He not only agreed that sanctions would continue, but also would study the possible effectiveness of adding oil to the list.[49] With this, Cecil was ready to write off the whole Hoare–Laval episode as ' almost solely the work of Vanssitart'. Murray had his doubts. 'Are our present Ministers much better than our last, after all?', he wondered.[50]

The withdrawal of the Hoare–Laval plan and the replacement of Hoare by Eden as Foreign Secretary seemed to Union leaders a good chance to try again for a clear-cut collective security policy. Murray wrote to *The Times* urging a fresh start 'not from the proposals, but from the fact that the proposals have been so emphatically condemned by public opinion in this country and in Geneva'.[51] *Headway* said that the episode had given Leaguers new

confidence, and even dictators now knew that 'although governments go, the nations remain'.[52] Public support for the League
had been demonstrated, and at least in some quarters this was
perceived as important. Churchill drew the appropriate conclusion and explored the possibility of using the League against
Hitler.[53]

Whether Whitehall had learned anything was doubtful. A
public-relations gaffe had been committed. As Halifax put it,
while the French proposals were reasonable, they 'were too much
like the off-the-stage arrangements of 19th century diplomacy
. . .'[54] It had happened after and not before the election, so
Baldwin could weather the storm easily. Far from turning the
Prime Minister more towards the League, the incident only confirmed his view that Britain should be 'much more self contained',
and that sanctions led to dangers he was not ready to face. He was
frankly puzzled by the strong anti-Italian talk of Cecil and the
LNU.[55]

As the public pressure on him faded early in 1936, Baldwin felt
under no compulsion to strengthen his sanctions policy. Eden's
appointment and a string of promising statements about the progress being made in Geneva satisfied most League supporters.
Word reached Grosvenor Crescent that the Foreign Office now
felt that public interest in oil sanctions had abated, but Union
leaders remained hopeful that a ban might be imposed anyway.[56]
The LNU did not back the petition which Davies circulated,
which urged intensification of sanctions against Italy unless she
accepted arbitration (with the Lytton Commission recommendations on Manchuria cited as the precedent). This gathered
4,000 signatures by the first week of February.[57]

On 2 March Eden finally announced support for an oil embargo, which Britain would support if other League members
would do the same. This statement encouraged the LNU and
other critics at home, which is probably all it was meant to do.
That it was little more than a gesture was shown by the way
Britain then acquiesced to an indefinite delay in further meetings
of the sanctionist states in deference to French wishes. Paris was
fast losing whatever willingness it once had to go along with a
sanctions policy. The LNU called for an end to the 'dilatory
diplomatic manoeuvres' preventing the application of oil sanctions, but to no avail.

The Executive also advanced an elaborate set of principles for a
peace settlement. This stressed the preservation of an independent

Ethiopia, but allowed for the exchange of territory if she agreed. Ethiopia was encouraged to reform herself 'to prevent future annexation' and in return would be protected from foreign exploitation. The Executive divided on some features of the plan, specifically the provision for a League-controlled police force to implement the proposals, and for the economic development of Ethiopia.[58]

Hitler's denunciation of the Locarno Treaties and remilitarization of the Rhineland on 7 March changed the whole situation and rendered such plans academic, if they were not that already. It soon became apparent that with Germany on the march, Paris and London were not going to alienate Rome with more sanctions. For Grosvenor Crescent, the task began in earnest of giving collective security a new meaning and making it apply to Germany as well as to Italy. It would not be easy to convince the LNU membership of this, much less the nation at large. When the Executive discussed the Rhineland, Noel-Baker pointed out that the British people had such strong feelings about the right of Germans to equality that they might miss the point that international laws were being broken.[59]

At the same meeting Cecil mooted a resolution which established one kind of link between Ethiopia and the Rhineland. He proposed that the French should be asked to join Britain in stopping Italy in exchange for British co-operation in meeting any possible German aggression. This was dropped, but the Union continued to stress the similarities between the two cases. The special weekly, *Abyssinia—A Newspaper of the League in Action*, which the LNU had been distributing since mid-November, now became *The Crisis*, a supplement to *Headway*. It ran a piece on 'Two Aspects of one Challenge: Rhineland—Abyssinia'.[60] The Executive set a meeting in London for 8 May on the theme 'Stop the War in Abyssinia and Prevent War in Western Europe'. Grosvenor Crescent urged branch secretaries to alert their MPs to the danger that Mussolini might be allowed a free hand now that everyone was preoccupied with the Rhineland situation. 'Our people will regard it as an outrage if Italy's war is not promptly stopped on terms showing that aggression has not paid. When the League has stopped Italy's war, Germany will not challenge the League by aggression against the soil of France. . . .'[61]

The response to this was not very heartening, in the Union or out. Chamberlain, who had been chafing in his seat on the Executive since the election and complaining about the anti-

Conservative bias in the Union, sought to resign once and for all. He finally did on 5 May, announcing that he could no longer support sanctions because the danger in Europe was so great that a struggle inthe Mediterranean could not be risked.[62] At Murray's request Chamberlain held off resigning for a few more weeks, finally leaving in June when the General Council endorsed a policy of continued sanctions against Italy. The war in Ethiopia had at last ended, and Chamberlain said there was no point to sanctions, and no authority in the Covenant for maintaining sanctions as a punishment.[63]

There was now no hope for Ethiopia. Eden announced on 17 June that Britain would propose to the Assembly that sanctions against Italy should end. The LNU sought to get this decision reversed, and added a recommendation that Italy be expelled from the League. On 16 July the Executive sent the Government a series of resolutions on how to deal with the now victorious Italians: Britain should refuse to recognize Italian sovereignty over Ethiopia: it should give facilities to members of the defeated Government to return to their country and import supplies through British territory; it should lend no support to efforts to block the appointment of the Emperor's delegation to the League Assembly. Finally, repeating a call the Union had made months before when reports of the Italian use of poison gas were first seen, it should block the shipment of more gas to Ethiopia.[64]

In the aftermath of the war, the LNU conducted a rearguard action to get these recommendations fulfilled. It cited the precedent of Manchuria in support of non-recognition. The issue kept arising in 1937 and 1938, with Eden refusing to bind himself by any pledge not to recognize Italian sovereignty in Ethiopia. The Executive Committee made the rather unusual recommendation directly to the exiled emperor Haile Selassie, that he should refrain from sending a delegation to the Assembly in September 1937. If it was bad that Ethiopia should not be represented at the Assembly, it would be worse if she tried to claim her seat and was rejected.[65] When Italy announced that she was going to leave the League at the end of 1937, the LNU applauded the decision as leaving a more 'healthy' League.[66] While making these gestures, the Executive was wary of doing anything which might encourage the Ethiopians to resume the fighting. That could only lead to more useless slaughter.[67]

For months Union leaders had warned that Ethiopia would be a do-or-die test for the League. Now the test had been failed, but the question of what to do remained. One direction was indicated by Cecil's appeal in June 1936 that 'the Union may save the League'. That is, that if the LNU put enough pressure on the Government, Britain could still enforce sanctions, if not to save Ethiopia then at least to ensure that the League Council should approve of the peace terms there.[68] The Union, now racked by discontent and mass defections, was in poor shape to press such a policy and the Government knew it.

Another possibility was the one so often proposed by pacifists: to support a League without sanctions of any sort. The public was now more aware of the difficulties and dangers inherent in getting the Covenant system to work; it was now often said that the Covenant had been tried in the Ethiopian War but that it had failed. A speech by Neville Chamberlain, the Chancellor of the Exchequer, on 10 June said that the continuation of sanctions against Italy would be 'the very midsummer of madness', and encouraged this prospect of a more limited League. Many Union members, and not just pacifists or Conservatives, were attracted to it. LNU leaders, however, were staunchly opposed. Murray said in response to the Chamberlain speech that if sanctions were left out of the League it would finish the whole international system.[69] 'No sanctions', as *Headway* put it in July, 'means the rule of the gunmen.'[70]

The main hope of LNU leaders was that collective security could still be made to work in Europe. Sanctions had failed Ethiopia, they argued, because the big powers saw the war there as a peripheral issue which could escalate if it were linked to the powder-magazine of Europe. Some League supporters went a step further and hoped to make the coercive clauses of the Covenant a reality in Europe by repealing them elsewhere. They had little sympathy for the notion of transforming the League into a sanction-less agency for 'peaceful change'.[71]

These speculations on the Covenant were not academic, for the British Government was weighing the same issue. Whitehall was ready to change the League, but hardly to strengthen it. Instead, with the unhappy experience of sanctions against Italy fresh in mind, officials were trying to ensure that Britain was not dragged into another League venture. Sir Alexander Cadogan, who dealt with this problem at Whitehall, was particularly interested in seeing that nothing be done to make it harder for Germany to re-enter the League. He weighed the possibility of inviting Germany to send an observer to Geneva. Officials knew better

than to seek the Union's advice on this, and Cecil, althoug..
concerned about the situation, knew it would be useless to volunteer it.[72]

The June 1936 meeting of the General Council had to consider
Covenant reform in this new context. A sanctions policy had been
tried, but in a half-hearted way. Yet the failure of this inadequate
effort to stop Italy was now causing widespread disillusionment
with the League. 'Reform' was being proposed as the alternative
to collective security, as a way of destroying what little authority
the League had and buying off the dictators.

Chapter X

The International Peace Campaign and Rearmament

Union leaders reassessed their policies and moved in new directions after the Ethiopian crisis. They had relied on Whitehall and it had betrayed them. By mid-1936 they were becoming less deferential and more open in opposing a government which, as Cecil said, would not simply abandon the League, but would 'explain it away'.[1] They were ready to support a venture into popular front politics, the International Peace Campaign, which became more controversial than anything they had ever done. Their very closeness to the centre of power convinced them that they would have to use the weapon of the outsider, public opinion, in a more assertive way.

LNU leaders also had second thoughts about the way they had interpreted the League to their supporters. 'There is no doubt', Cecil wrote to Murray, 'that we are all a little to blame in not having made it plainer in the country that sanctions may lead to war.'[2] They began to tell their followers that the new international situation had made rearmament essential. To these leaders, it was obvious that a credible collective security policy now required armaments. However, the response to their proposal showed that many LNU members were not ready to make that connection. Despite all their tough talk about Italy in 1935, many League supporters had not really associated the crisis with their own country's defence. It was still a matter of Britain deigning to help others by sending the fleet. Now the League was presented to them in a new light, as a bulwark for British security, as something worth fighting for.

Grosvenor Crescent began to announce its support for rearmament gradually. *Headway* backed into the issue in March 1936 by declaring that British rearmament 'is necessary for the strengthening and efficient working of the collective system', but emphatically not 'if you are seeking individual rearmament outside the League'.[3] By August *Headway* gave clearer support to rearmament as the key to rebuilding the League after the most resounding failure in its history. 'In a period when the prospective aggressor is strong, those who are resolved to restrain aggression must be strong also . . .'[5] In October, the Executive prepared a resolution for the General Council to put the Union on record for rearmament: 'While admitting with deep regret that in the present circumstances an increase of national armaments has become necessary: Holds that no increase should be made except to enable us to discharge our duties under the Covenant; and urges H.M. Government to make it unmistakedly clear that their policy is one of collective security and international disarmament.'[6]

Even cautious wording and the invocation of disarmament did not make this resolution palatable to most Union members. In the rank and file of the LNU, as in the Labour Party, there was great suspicion of the Government's motives and a reluctance to back national rearmament unless it were somehow pledged to collective security. The emphasis, especially in the LNU Youth Groups, was less on the need for rearmament than on the shortcomings of the Government and the dangers of 'absolute rearmament'. *The Advocate*, a journal of one of these Youth Groups, was typical in its call for just enough arms for Britain to supply her quota of forces to the League to resist an aggressor. Anything more than this might lead to 'absolute rearmament', and a hopeless attempt to achieve isolation.[7]

When the Executive presented its rearmament motion to the General Council in December, it provoked angry attacks on the Government. The Council produced its own resolution which said that the Government 'will not have justified its demand for a large and indeterminate increase in armaments until it has made it clear that the purpose for which the Forces of the Crown are maintained is to fulfil our obligations under the Covenant of the League'. Until it had that assurance, the Council hesitated 'to commit the Union and thereby the Youth Groups, whose members would be chiefly affected, to approval of the rearmament and recruiting campaign'. The Council urged the Government to announce that its policy was one of collective security and disarmament, and that it would start consultations which could lead to an end of the arms race. It also asked the Executive Committee to prepare a recommendation for the next Council meeting that would substitute 'an international air police force for national air forces.[8]

To most members of the Executive, this resolution was evidence of a dangerous revolt within the organization. Cecil had no intention of reversing LNU support for rearmament, and he minimized the importance of the Council's action at first. 'Bodies like the Council continually pass foolish resolutions', he told Murray. 'What matters really is what the Executive Committee decides to do. . .'[9] When meetings of Union youth and university groups added other inflammatory resolutions opposing 'unilateral' rearmament the following month, the situation grew even more tense. A majority of the Executive wanted to overturn the Council resolution, but disagreed over the best way to do this. If they called a special Council meeting, it might attract extremists and exacerbate the difficulty.[10]

Conservatives were especially troubled by the way the Council resolution had revived the issue of an international force and used it as a way of blocking rearmament. Lytton, now the chief Conservative spokesman on the Executive, threatened resignation if the resolution were not overturned. It was all right for the LNU to try to keep pacifists happy, he argued, but if it came to a choice it was much more important to keep the support of Conservatives. Other Conservatives would follow his lead, Lytton predicted.[11] Murray, in his familiar role of mediator, seized on a statement by Eden and on Baldwin's New Year's message to the Primrose League as the very pledges to refrain from using force except in accordance with the Covenant which the Council had called for. This helped the Union reach a tenuous basis for agreement.[12]

First, a special committee was set up representing different factions in the LNU, including the Youth Groups. In effect, this body cancelled the impression left by the Council resolution by backing rearmament as a 'deplorable' necessity. It explained away the hostility which had greeted rearmament in the League movement as the result of 'suspicions based upon past disappointments'. It stated its belief that the Government 'could best restore the faith of others by showing that it has not lost its own. For this it must convince the public by its actions as well as speeches that British policy . . . is resolutely directed . . . towards the full development of the League system. . . .'[13] The way was cleared for the June 1937 Council to adopt a policy statement which backed rearmament, while insisting that general arms limitation was the condition of a lasting peace. Hostility to the Government and to the LNU leadership was not to be assuaged so easily, however. In 1938 the Union was still troubled by disputes between an Executive regretfully ready to rearm, while asking for appropriate vows of loyalty to the Covenant, and a branch (Manchester) which refused even to consider rearmament until the Government had given the pledge.[14]

The opposition to rearmament was not, as Lytton had portrayed it, pacifist in motivation. The very Youth Group leaders who were most vocal in attacking rearmament were also ready to champion the fight for the Spanish Republic. Many members were simply unwilling to trust a Government which had 'sabotaged' the sanctions policy against Italy by refusing to extend it to oil. They did not see the point in showing any kind of approval for the Government's defence programme, or in accepting yet another of its empty verbal concessions. Then too, members of a New Commonwealth persuasion were not happy with the way the January Council's declaration of support for an international air police force got swept out of sight in June. It had been shunted to a liaison committee established to co-ordinate the policy of the LNU and the New Commonwealth. They wanted rearmament— Churchill was now President of the British Section of the New Commonwealth—but they were losing patience with Grosvenor Crescent's efforts to reconcile diametrically opposed viewpoints on collective security.[15]

When LNU leaders moved cautiously towards rearmament, they found themselves working more and more closely with Churchill, their sometime adversary. Churchill had started to advocate an increased reliance on the League shortly after Hitler came to power. In one speech in November 1933, he urged a revival of 'the Concert of Europe through the League of Nations'.[16] However, at that time Churchill urged rearmament while the LNU emphasized disarmament; he was anti-German while Noel-Baker and other LNU leaders were working with the 'Anglo-German Group' which tried to secure German equality of rights.[17] Then Churchill had doubts about League sanctions against Italy. The League's failure in Manchuria and Ethiopia made it easier for Churchill to support the world organization, for by 1936 its theatre of action was Europe, which was what he wanted it to be. He judged that the British public would not back rearmament unless it was linked to a League policy, so he could now unhesitatingly champion such a policy side by side with the LNU.

The informal group, Focus, which began forming around Churchill in June 1935, attracted Cecil, Murray, and several other members of the Union Executive. Cecil had his doubts about Churchill's 'queer manoeuvres' early in 1936 and kept him at a distance.[18] Only later in the year, once the LNU had crossed the rearmament bridge, did Grosvenor Crescent court Churchill for the Executive Committee (unsuccessfully) and work closely with him to co-ordinate policy.[19] This co-operation laid the groundwork for the 'Arms and the Covenant' campaign.

A public meeting in London on 3 December 1936, launched this campaign. It was held under the auspices of the LNU which hoped to attract new members with it, although it was funded by the Defence of Freedom group which grew out of Focus meetings.[20] The meeting brought trade union leaders (Walter Citrine), Liberals (Violet Bonham Carter), Conservatives of an LNU stamp (Lytton), together with Churchill and his Conservative followers. Churchill declared emphatically that the League had never been so necessary and had never had so good a chance to win solid backing. He followed this with other meetings and then a speaking tour sponsored by the LNU in 1938. The hoped-for ground swell for 'Arms and the Covenant' did not develop, however, partly due to inadequate press coverage.[21]

There were problems with this alliance between Churchillians and the LNU on both sides. Many Union members of leftist sympathies remained suspicious of Churchill. Eleanor Rathbone of the Executive had to plead to others to overcome their prejudices against him: 'You may feel distrustful. So did I. I'm not certain yet. But I ask you to dispel prejudice and consider facts.'[22] When Churchill was meeting some LNU Youth Group members in 1938 one confessed that they still didn't trust him.[23] Other sorts of problems developed in the Union once *Headway* came under the direction of Focus in 1938. Teachers feared that this sort of involvement would undermine the Union's educational programme which required the appearance of non-partisanship.

Churchill was in turn wary about what too close an identification with the LNU might do to his standing as a Conservative. He shied away from signing one manifesto in December 1936 when he found that his co-signers would be 'nothing but the League of Nations Union notabilities'.[24] Although he finally agreed in 1938 to join the long list of Union Vice-Presidents, he did not join the Executive Committee. At Focus luncheons he reminded his LNU allies that he did not want to make party attacks or try to turn the Government out. He wanted to rouse and unite the country, not divide it.[25] The International Peace Campaign, which so preoccupied Cecil, Noel-Baker, and some other Union leaders from 1936 on, was making the League cause politically controversial. Churchill wanted to avoid association with this kind of 'popular front' movement, which might disturb his Conservative followers.[26]

The International Peace Campaign had developed out of talks Cecil had with Pierre Cot, Léon Jouhaux, and other French leaders in 1935. They discussed the possibility that the international peace movement might be revitalized with the help of existing voluntary societies which shared its objectives: trade unions, religious, educational, and youth groups principally. This tactic for building support for the League had been used to popularize the Covenant in France in 1920 and Cecil had used it in the disarmament campaign in 1931. At some meetings in his home in early 1936 Cecil gave the idea concrete shape as the IPC or 'Ralliement', as it became known in Europe. Eventually it spread to forty-three countries and brought together representatives of organizations which had some 400,000,000 members.[27]

To Cecil, Angell, Noel-Baker, and the other LNU stalwarts who became its British leaders, the IPC held an exciting prospect. Within Britain it could appeal to a broader spectrum of society than the staunchly middle-class LNU. More important still, it was to be a truly international movement which might succeed in mobilizing world opinion where the Federation of League of Nations Societies had failed. The Federation at its peak had a total of only about 1,500,000 members, while the campaign could claim to speak for hundreds of millions.

The LNU co-operated closely with the British National Committee of the IPC (which Cecil led). The LNU promised to support it financially, matching contributions to the campign from other organizations.[28] Delegates from many Union branches joined hundreds from other organizations at the first British Congress of the IPC in October 1937 in London. They set up a number of committees to direct peace work within their own vocational groups.

Co-ordination between the Union and this new campaign was not always easy, however, and many disputes raged at Grosvenor Crescent over the support being given the IPC. Although it described itself as 'non-political', the campaign was a popular front effort which included many Communists on the continent. Predictably, this became a political issue. From the first, the propaganda mills of Berlin and Rome attacked it as a Communist front, and Conservatives and the Catholic hierarchy regarded it with suspicion.

The Union inevitably caught much of the criticism aimed at the

IPC. The Prime Minister complained to Cecil about the leftist bias now apparent in the LNU, as evidenced especially by the 'Peace Weeks' and other activities of the campaign.[29] Cardinal Hinsley resigned as Vice-President of the Union over the IPC issue, and instructed Catholic representatives to withdraw from its Christian Organizations Committee.[30] Several Conservative members of the Union's Executive, including Cranborne, who rejoined after leaving the Government, were dismayed by the way the campaign seemed to splinter the already weakened LNU.

Despite these difficulties, Cecil and the campaign's other leaders felt it was too valuable to abandon. On the continent, it was proving to be, in their view, the most important effort for peace made since the war. If Communists were involved, they did not run things. Certainly Cecil did not think there was any justification for the attacks on the IPC or especially for the 'witch-hunter' mentality of British trade union leaders.[31] It provided the vigorous international backing which the League had always needed but never received.

Support for the IPC did not mean an end to LNU encouragement for the Federation of League of Nations Societies. Cecil donated part of his Nobel Peace Prize money to it in 1937 and continued to call for the strengthening of existing League societies. Garnett even pressed for a merger between the IPC and the Federation, although he did not get far.[32] A merger might have provided a way out of the danger which Garnett saw threatening the Union: that the IPC might establish local machinery throughout Britain and compete with the LNU for funds and support. If there was thus a certain logic to the proposal as seen from Grosvenor Crescent, it made no sense to the leaders of the campaign. They had nothing to gain by hitching themselves to the old League 'establishment'. The IPC had been established precisely because the Federation approach had been shown to be barren.

Whether or not the IPC could have had more impact if it had come earlier—a favourite topic for discussion at the time—it provided some grounds to hope that 'world public opinion', the League's lodestar, might be there after all. Its failure, and more broadly the failure of the LNU's newly aggressive policy, was not due simply to bad timing. The Union did not matter much politically by itself, so its success depended on its choice of allies and the way it co-ordinated its change in orientation with other opponents of the Government's foreign policy. The IPC was a liability in this respect.

The Union's choice of alliances proved especially unfortunate from the point of view of the Labour Party. Both Churchill, and his ill-fated 'Arms and the Covenant' campaign, and the IPC raised problems which kept the LNU separated from the Labour leaders who might have been its natural allies. Just at a time when Labourite proponents of rearmament were turning their efforts towards the conversion of their parliamentary party, they became very wary of co-operation with the LNU. Many years of patient work in cultivating Labour had put the Union into a position where the potential for such co-operation might have been great.

Although the Labour Party had championed internationalism and disarmament by treaty, many supporters of unilateral disarmament and other pure pacifists remained in Labour's ranks in the 1930s. One wing of the party, with George Lansbury as its leader, had no sympathy for a sanctionist League. Lansbury did not ignore the League; in 1935, on the eve of the Ethiopian War, he sponsored an attempt to have the League summon a world conference to discuss the reallocation of world resources.[33]

Another tendency within the Labour movement hostile to a League-based collective security policy was associated with Stafford Cripps and the Socialist League. The Socialist League, like the Independent Labour Party but unlike the Communist Party, had opposed the imposition of sanctions against Italy. Cripps reasoned that 'once the people are allowed to believe that a League of Nations and collective security can be operated to bring peace to an imperialist world, there is really no fundamental difference between Labour, Liberal and Conservative foreign policy'.[34] He resigned from Labour's National Executive to expound his own views and work through 'industrial action'.

At the party's 1935 Brighton Conference, often talked about later as the watershed marking the acceptance of a collective security line, these divisions within the party were left unresolved. Ernest Bevin dominated the proceedings, attacking Cripps for his resignation and Lansbury for his pacifism, but it was not yet clear that the party's course had been firmly set.[35] Only gradually was Bevin, working with his ally Hugh Dalton, the Chairman of the National Party Executive, able to swing Labour support to rearmament. Bevin tried to make this support broad-based by translating the problems of foreign policy into understandable terms. Just as a worker who enjoys the collective security of a trade union must be ready to take risks when a strike or lock-out looms, he said time and again, a movement which supported the League could not desert it in a crisis. With the Ethiopian sanctions fiasco, even faithful League supporters began to wonder whether Labour's foreign policy should be based on the League. Leonard Woolf urged a recognition of realities and an end to reliance on the League in his advice to the Labour Advisory Committee on International Questions in December 1936, prompting Noel-Baker's threat of resignation if the advice were followed.[36]

Bevin had to worry about the opposition of a 'United Front' which the Socialist League had forged with the Communists and the tiny Independent Labour Party. The IPC was thus coming at the worst possible moment to gain his support. The kind of popular front politics it represented was in itself an issue within the British Labour movement. Just as the Spanish Civil War issue had become a battlefield on which the left and right wings fought for control of the Labour Party, so the IPC was caught in this intra-mural struggle. The more conservative trade union and Labour Party leaders rejected association with Communists, and hence with the IPC. Communist leaders co-operated with the effort to keep the campaign 'non-political', and steered it away from such explosive subjects as the war in Spain. Kingsley Martin described how, at a 1937 IPC conference he attended, a spontaneous demonstration on behalf of Republican Spain was checked by the veteran Communist Marcel Cachin.[37] But Communist good behaviour did not overcome the suspicions of the Labour leaders (Bevin, Dalton, Citrine) who backed rearmament; at the same time the campaign's apolitical stance, avoidance of Spain and emphasis on the League made it seem irrelevant to their leftist opponents. Bevin made it clear that he would not help the LNU so long as it remained associated with the IPC.[38]

The Union's turn to a new conception of collective security and rearmament caused another great loss to the organization. It accelerated the tendency already evident after the Far Eastern crisis for pacifists to resign. When the IPC was launched it attracted the National Peace Council to its roster, but discouraged the participation of some secular pacifist organizations which had sent representatives to the IPC's charter meeting.[39] The National Peace Council, founded in 1905 but relatively inactive until 1933, tried to operate as an umbrella organization of the peace movement. But neither the LNU nor the Peace Pledge Union, the large secular pacifist group founded in 1935, joined it. Various attempts were made to cajole the LNU into participation with the Council nationally, and local Union branches did work with local peace councils. Garnett and Gerald Bailey, the National Peace Council's Secretary, were in contact and exchanged minutes of their Executive Committees. Relations were generally amiable between the societies, except in Scotland where the conservatively oriented Union organization refused to have anything to do with the Scottish Peace Council. However, from the time of the Ethiopian crisis, the two groups moved further apart. The NPC did not go along with rearmament, so Gerald Bailey did not get far with his pleas for renewed co-operation in 1937.[40]

The LNU, for its part, had shown great ambivalence about co-operation with pacifists. Pacifists in turn were confused and hesitant about the League of Nations.[41] During the Ethiopian War, many pacifists remained in the Union trying to keep their vision of the League alive. *Peace News*, a pacifist weekly started in 1936, supported this approach. While League policies 'based on armaments—on the war method—[were] discredited", the League still had a chance if it worked instead to remove the cause of war and all armament.[42]

The LNU's support for rearmament was for many pacifists the last straw. The Union could no longer convince them that it stood for peace. Union leaders made sporadic efforts to explain their policies in conciliatory terms. Murray described League sanctions against Mussolini as an act of pacifistic renunciation. To refuse Italy supplies was to refuse to participate in her acts of war; it should not be viewed as coercion, he argued.[43] Cecil explained that he did not want coercion, even of an aggressor. 'Only don't you think' he added, 'that, in dealing with the militarist mind, it would be a pity to say from the outset that come what may, we won't fight?'[44] Angell and Clifford Allen each pleaded for pacifist support for collective security. Angell warned pacifists that they were playing into the hands of right-wingers. Allen combined personal repudiation of war with similar views.

Most pacifists were no longer listening. Dynamic new groups such as the Peace Pledge Union got their attention. Meanwhile 'Non-Intervention' and 'No War' became slogans of the National Government. Some pacifists inevitably moved into sympathy with appeasement and launched attacks on the LNU and its conception of the League. For instance, Helen Swanwick argued in *Collective Insecurity* that a harsh attitude towards Germany and incessant talk about 'defending the Covenant' were only worsening the international situation and causing the arms race.[44] Aldous Huxley could explain the League's failure in his 1937 book *Ends and Means*, by saying that it was based on the wrong principles. 'Sanctions', he wrote, were objectionable 'for exactly the same reasons as war is objectionable. Military sanctions are war.'[45] Huxley did not like the Government's appeasement policies either, for to be both weak and rich is to invite attack. Hence he preached that Britain must give up her empire to find true security. Bertrand Russell, the pacifist hero to a generation of left-wing university students, also urged renunciation. He cited the case of 'defenceless yet safe' Denmark to show that unilateral disarmament was no visionary's dream but a practical policy. Could anyone seriously assert that Hitler would ever invade Denmark when it would gain him nothing and incur the world's wrath?[46]

The LNU was prompted by pacifist defections to reconsider its traditionally stand-pat position on Covenant revision. It issued two pamphlets on the subject in the summer of 1936, both suggesting that few changes were called for.[47] One of these picked up the notion then current in the peace movement of using the League to deal with international economic inequities. It suggested using Article 19 of the Covenant to establish Commissions of Inquiry which would examine grievances and then suggest appropriate revisions of treaties.

Rank-and-file Union members showed great sympathy for this sort of revisionism. They wanted some answer to the charge that they were warmongers who talked about resisting aggression without providing a way to alter the status quo peacefully. Many of them were attracted by the proposals Allen offered in late 1936. Before the General Council, in talks before Union audiences and in the December 1936 *Headway*, Allen tried to gain acceptance for a technique to deal with international grievances (dealing with boundaries, access to raw materials, colonies, and the like). This invitation to an across-the-board settlement was much more ambitious than the modest 'Commission' proposal under Article 19 which the LNU pamphlet suggested. It resembled the approach to Germany advocated by many in the National Peace Congress, but with a vital difference: Allen linked his appeal for considering grievances with a critique of those pacifists who attacked collective security.[48]

The Union leadership, under attack from members for being too cautious on Spain and too favourable to rearmament, gave way on this economic issue. Following the line of Allen's advice, it asked the Government in January 1937 to press for the creation of an International Fact-Finding Commission to look into the questions of access to raw materials and markets. This, however, did not close the issue for critics of the Union leadership who wanted the League to be part of a far-reaching programme of social and economic change.

In the Union's Youth Groups, which emerged during the Spanish Civil War as Grosvenor Crescent's most outspoken critics, there was increasing talk about the need for social justice as the foundation of peace. The Secretary of the Youth Committee wrote to *Headway* that 'when we talked about the ILO we have too often talked only about its international aspects, a subject apparently far removed from our daily interests or only about the evil conditions in other countries'. He described how the Youth Groups 'began faintly to understand our mistake at the World Youth Congress last year' and had joined in the international effort to investigate the social and economic conditions of youth in their own lands and prepare a National Charter of Rights.[49]

LNU leaders were not yet ready to move any further towards changing the Covenant. They stalled or offered elaborate answers to the charge that they had not been willing to respond to grievances. Cecil told the Council in December 1937 that he distinguished between the two types of grievances which had been generated by the Treaty of Versailles: the terms of the treaty itself, and whether they were carried out. So far as implementation went—extending disarmament from Germany to all the signatories, and living up to the commitments made on the Saar minorities and Silesia—the Union had fought to remedy injustice.[50] Noel-Baker, in a letter prepared for the press, argued that the League had encouraged peaceful change. which was now easier than in pre-League days. His major point was that 'revision' was not an alternative to collective security. No just revision could be carried into effect unless the means were there to enforce it.[51]

Their reluctance to support revisionism was grounded on the belief that Conservatives were ready to 'reform' the League out of an effective role in world affairs and should be fought. Since Conservatives now tended to disregard the League rather than worry about reshaping it, the LNU did not have to worry about them much. In any case, both pacifists and Conservatives were abandoning the Union in droves by 1937, so the internal pressure for a change in LNU policy eased.

Headway could describe the Union's opponents as a 'triple alliance' of isolationists, defeatists, and pacifists.[52] In the same vein Cecil referred to the ominous 'coalition between extreme pacifists, reactionaries and ex-diplomats' against the League. Outsiders saw humour in this shuffling of labels. Lord Castlerosse jibed that 'we are all pacifists now', yet while the heads of the army and navy were pacifist, he 'should not be at all surprised if Professor Gilbert Murray himself was not really at heart a pacifist'.[53] Murray lamented that the peace forces of Britain, after being defeated in foreign affairs, had turned to fighting among themselves.[54]

The Union tried to counter its growing host of critics with a campaign for signatures to the declaration 'Save the League: Save the Peace' and with locally organized 'Peace Weeks'. But by 1937, with the League itself near collapse, the LNU was losing members and could not reverse the trend. The 'Peace Weeks' prompted complaints from Conservatives, and eventually lost favour at Grosvenor Crescent because they were co-sponsored with other organizations and were difficult to control.[55] It was hard for LNU leaders to muster enthusiasm for new campaigns, as Angell's comments on alternatives to 'Peace Weeks' showed. 'We must provide rank and file of the movement some means of satisfying the itch to "do something about. . ."' he said. The Union's enthusiasts had to be 'kept busy on other forms of activity'.[56] Cecil, taking stock at the end of 1937, saw the Union's 'serious signs of loss of vitality'. 'Not only', he said, 'are our numbers and income going down, but the whole tone of the Council, the Executive and most of the meetings which I have attended is in a minor key.'[57]

Affairs at Grosvenor Crescent were increasingly troubled. Garnett and the Union staff were especially annoyed at the International Peace Campaign. They saw scarce Union funds going to support this popular front effort while their carefully nurtured education programme suffered. The Executive Committee too was divided over the wisdom of linking the Union too closely to the campaign. The tensions which had been simmering over these issues finally boiled over at the end of 1937. A satirical skit at the LNU office party turned out to be a bit too cutting, especially at Cecil's expense. John Eppstein, the staff member who put on the lampoon, caught the blame at first. Cecil demanded his dismissal.[58] Soon Garnett was under fire, because if the staff's morale was bad, then he was responsible.

Murray resisted dismissing Eppstein and told Cecil that staff tempers ran so high on the IPC issue that anything resembling an office purge would wreck the organization.[59] Cecil eventually accepted an apology from Eppstein, but remained determined to push ahead with a reorganization of the Union leadership. The LNU's loss of vitality was due to the bad morale at headquarters as much as to waning public confidence, he felt. His solution was to replace Garnett with a new Secretary and Murray with a new Chairman, preferably someone who could always be in London to supervise the office.[60]

Throughout January 1938, Grosvenor Crescent was in turmoil over these personnel questions. A sub-committee of the Executive studied the matter of staff loyalty, with particular attention to Eppstein and his skit. Staff members poured out their own resentments.[61] In between heated Executive Committee meetings letters flew back and forth on the merits and weaknesses of Garnett, Eppstein, and the IPC. Cecil had support from those (Noel-Baker, Livingstone, Arnold Foster) who were active on the IPC.[62] Murray at first hoped that the appointment of a Vice-Chairman who could supervise Garnett regularly would answer the demand for change, and then, characteristically, he came round to Cecil's way of seeing things. He agreed that Garnett should go, that Livingstone, the Organizing Secretary of the IPC and a focus of staff resentment, should leave the Executive and go on an extended fact-finding tour, and that he himself should become a co-President while Lytton became Chairman.[63]

It was typical of Murray to concede to Cecil, even when the issue was his own chairmanship. It was also to be expected that he would try to soften the impact of the changes, to try to make the LNU's only leadership crisis seem less like a crisis. Accordingly he suggested that Garnett be given six months' leave with pay and that the change of chairman should be delayed several months until the mext meeting of the General Council. Eppstein would stay, and Major J. G. Freshwater, who had been Deputy Secretary since 1920, could take over as Secretary of the Union.[64] This was the line of action taken; the staff remained uneasy about the IPC, but tempers were given time to cool. Murray stuck by his decision to leave the chairmanship, but he had second thoughts about easing Garnett out of office once the prolonged 'sick leave' ended. He talked about how much Garnett's 'intellectual drive' was missed in the office.[65]

In June Lytton became Chairman and Murray co-President as

planned. Then in July, Garnett returned, anxious to reclaim his position. The battle lines on the Executive formed again, with Garnett's supporters (Nowell Smith, Gwilym Davies, and others) generally viewing the issue as one of preventing undue political interference with the Union, or of preserving a balance between its educational and its political work.[66] They were upset when a majority of the Executive demanded Garnett's dismissal without giving him an opportunity to defend himself. There were recriminations all round when Garnett had to resign at last, and even Murray's best efforts at conciliation did not help.[67] Garnett felt he had been treated badly, indeed victimized, because he had blocked efforts to use the Union for agitation against the Government.[68] His departure seemed to mark the end of an era in the Union's history.

Chapter XI

A Spirited Foreign Policy: the Late 1930s

By the late 1930s the Union had adopted a policy of collective security and rearmament. It had lost enough Conservative and pacifist members so that a new unity of purpose seemed within its reach. However, new internal tensions arose as old ones faded and the LNU was not able to revamp itself successfully. It saw the defects in its old programme but was not able to agree on effective substitutes.

Over the years it had encouraged the British public to associate the Covenant and collective security with peace. Now that collective security was taking on another meaning, the Union had to clarify its position in the peace movement. Murray objected to 'Peace Weeks' partly because they were out of date. 'We are no longer', he said, 'a Peace Party opposing a Jingo Party. We are a "League of Collective Security" party opposing Pacifists, Isolationists, pro-Germans. We are actually for a "spirited foreign policy!" Hence a successful Peace Week with all the Peace forces well represented injures our cause, or at least muddles our supporters' minds.'[1]

Murray put forward ideas on the course the Union could follow at the end of 1937. Loss of membership was due to political causes which were beyond control, but some lost supporters might be regained. Conservatives could be won back by vigorous support for Anthony Eden; pacifists might appreciate a new emphasis on the conciliatory and humanitarian work of the League. The LNU's approach as summed up in the slogan 'Arbitration, Security and Disarmament' should be modified. Disarmament and the old campaign against the private manufacture of armaments would have to be shelved. Security was still a vital goal, but it was not realistic to talk about preventing wars around the world. Arbitration was still a goal, but it would be important to distinguish between willingness to settle differences and submission to aggression.[2] Most of Murray's suggestions reflected trends already under way in 1937.

The LNU committees addressing themselves to the membership problem agreed to a formula similar to Murray's. The Union should go to the country with a programme which urged that 'the members of the League, including Britain, must be as ready to use their strength in collective action . . . as in the defence of their own territories'. It should encourage the creation of machinery to revise unjust treaties and thereby allow for peaceful change. It should emphasize the advantages of fair terms of trade which League members enjoyed. Disarmament was not to be scrapped, but instead postponed until 'the regrowth of collective security permits international agreement to be reached on the subject'. Grosvenor Crescent wrestled with the problem of Peace Weeks, and considered renaming them 'International Defence Weeks', in keeping with these new guidelines.[3]

The need to appeal for Conservative support was pressing. Chamberlain's resignation in 1936 had not been a shock at the time, because Union leaders thought that Eustace Percy or some other Conservative of national standing could be brought in to replace him.[4] This had not worked out though, and other Conservatives including Lord Queensborough were leaving at the same time. This problem with Conservatives was on Cecil's mind during the leadership crisis at Grosvenor Crescent in early 1938. It helps explain the choice of Lytton as Chairman over Noel-Baker. While he was dynamic and respected, Noel-Baker was also a vigorous opponent to Eden in the Commons, and so rather controversial.[5]

Lytton was not active in Conservative Party affairs, however. Indeed, like Cecil, he had to explain why he had never become a Liberal.[6] Murray's suggestion to him that the best way for the LNU to influence Whitehall was through Lytton's personal conversations with Halifax was based on an optimistic estimate of Lytton's influence.[7] He failed to woo Conservatives back into the Union fold.

This failure might have opened up interesting possibilities for the LNU. That is, dissident members had been saying, almost from the time of the Union's creation, that the organization was held back by its Conservative and pacifist factions. Mosley in 1923, and others in his footsteps, had called for a more clear-cut policy which would carry League supporters into opposition to the government of the day when the situation demanded.[8] Eleanor Rathbone, the Independent MP, was the Executive Committee member who advocated this most forcefully in the late thirties. In books and speeches, she urged the LNU to discard its shop-worn disarmament slogans and put pressure on the Government for an effective collective security programme.[9] By 1938 Conservatives and pacifists were no longer the obstacle that they had been, and the Union was supposedly free to speak with one voice at last.

This did not happen, partly because the dissident factions kept some power, even *in absentia*. If the LNU wanted to win them back, it still had to consider their viewpoints. Then too, no matter how hostile Union leaders might have been to the National Government and how hopeful for a '1931 in reverse', a breakaway from the Conservatives to a new coalition of Labour, Liberal, and Tory dissidents, they could not do much with the LNU to further their goals.[10] It remained a chartered organization with limited aims and a tradition of political restraint. Moreover, its two sources of power, as the representative of a significant opinion bloc and as a focus for influential political leaders, were both badly eroded. Finally, the Union had not really won internal harmony once the Conservatives and pacifists left. Instead, the coalition of interests which comprised the LNU continued to unravel.

The Spanish Civil War provided the occasion for much of the controversy. Grosvenor Crescent seemed so hesitant about taking a position on Spain that it antagonized many rank-and-file members sympathetic to the republican cause. Noel-Baker was well ahead of the Labour Party leadership, outspoken from July 1936 in opposition to Franco and his British apologists.[11] Most Union leaders were very cautious though; Cecil's first reaction was that the League and Union should not get involved.[12]

The Executive Committee was forced to consider Spain in late August after weeks of hesitation. The Chairman of the LNU National Youth Committee, G. Raymond Gauntlett, had authorized Gabriel Carritt of the Union staff to attend the World Youth Congress in Paris. Carritt then joined the Congress's delegation to Spain on a fact-finding mission and appeared as a speaker on Spain on programmes which also featured Communists. Carritt had called for Union involvement on behalf of the Republicans, urging arms shipments to them and League action under Article 11.[13] The Executive censured Carritt, but backed away from the main question of League action.[14]

The Executive continued to avoid commitment in September, adopting only a resolution which said that a policy of non-intervention was 'necessitated' by the European situation. Britain should make it her business to keep that policy even-handed by inducing Portugal to co-operate.[15] This cautious statement kept the way clear for co-operation with Churchill, who was pushing the cause of strict neutrality through his friends on the Executive.[16] It was also designed to hold on to the allegiance of the minority in the LNU, chiefly Catholic, whose sympathies were nationalist. The first hesitant *Headway* editorials on the civil war had brought a letter of protest from twenty Catholic officials and members of the Union urging strict neutrality.[17]

The Executive was divided on non-intervention. Rathbone wanted to refer the question to Geneva and Noel-Baker to invoke Article 16 against the suppliers of weapons to Franco. They did not get far against Cecil and Lytton. The most the majority would agree to was a note to the Foreign Office on 6 October protesting alleged violations of the non-intervention agreement.[18] Murray assured Eden in November that the LNU supported Government policy in Spain, although he slipped in mention of Article 11, which might help in 'coping with these plots for stirring up civil war in foreign countries'.[19]

By 1937 it was clear that non-intervention was becoming a sham. The Executive took note of this in a resolution on 7 January and belatedly asked that the situation be referred to Geneva under Article 11. It also recommended that the League Council send a commission to Spain and added that British opinion would support League action to block the entry of arms and volunteers to Spain.[20] This cautious response did not soothe activist opinion in the Union. The National Youth Committee came out for the immediate withdrawal of all foreign troops in Spain, after first pushing a resolution calling for the ejection of 'all German and Italian troops supporting the rebel forces in Spain'.[21] Cecil now talked privately about the tenable case Spain could put before the League that the Italians had committed aggression against them. He asked Cranborne about the possibility of threatening a boycott of port wine so as to pressure Portugal into strict non-intervention.[22]

The situation within the LNU in 1937 was roughly comparable to that within the Labour Party. In both cases rank-and-file opinion was pro-Republican and impatient with a leadership which seemed to be as dilatory as the Government itself. The Labour Spain Committee, organized in March 1937, made as little progress in turning around the party's National Executive as did Rathbone, Noel-Baker, the Duchess of Atholl, and their supporters in the Union.[23] Even the terror bombing of Guernica did not stir the Executive. It suggested British aid to Spanish refugees but rebuffed Noel-Baker in his demands to fix responsibility for the bombardment and press for a report on violations of the non-intervention agreement.[24]

The Union's position remained essentially unchanged in 1937. At one June meeting Lytton scorned the failure of non-intervention, but the Executive suggested nothing beyond reference to the League Council and dispatch of a commission of investigation. When Rathbone in September urged the LNU to join with the National Peace Council, the Union of Democratic Control, the Women's Co-operative Guild, and other groups in a plea to both sides not to execute prisoners, the Executive turned her down, on the grounds that an appeal from societies of leftist political views would not achieve anything.[25] The Executive continued to back the Government's initiatives and was particularly supportive of the Nyon Conference.[26]

Dissatisfaction with the leadership grew more open in the LNU. The National Youth Committee, which co-ordinated the activities of the 281 Youth Groups, led the way in December. It said that the Union was so divided that it could not formulate a policy on Spain and that 'an attitude in accordance with the Covenant was not adopted until people had ceased to look to the Union'. It went on to issue a more general critique of the LNU as 'an organization of the middle-aged and middle-class'. The Union's biggest failing was its unwillingness to adopt any policy, 'even if a correct one, which would align [it] with Left organizations'. As a result, 'the working class and the young . . . feel there is no place for them'.[27]

Youth Group members had become exasperated at the kind of things the LNU was encouraging them to do: collect milk money for Spanish refugee children and the like. They had an almost unique position from which to oppose the Executive on a nation-wide basis, with their own quarterly journal, *Youth*, their own semi-annual conventions and their own leadership structure. When Raymond Gauntlett crossed swords with Cecil in June over some adverse comments Cecil had made to the press about the National Youth Committee, Gauntlett was in a strong position and could exact an apology.[28] Rank-and-file sympathies were with the Youth Groups. Many LNU branches co-operated with the IPC and were making increasingly open gestures of support for the Spanish Republic.

At the June 1938 General Council, hostility on the Spanish issue reached a peak. Cecil pleaded with the delegates that while his sympathies were with the Republicans, his only interest was in restoring peace to Spain. A victory for either side would settle nothing, he said, for it would only lead to renewed slaughter. This outraged many delegates, and one drew loud applause for her retort that peace must be founded on justice, that a halt in the fighting on terms favourable to Franco would not be peace. The Council settled on a compromise resolution calling for an armistice in Spain, the withdrawal of all foreign troops and technicians, and urging the immediate recognition of the right of the Spanish Government to import the arms needed for its defence.[29]

It was already too late to do much about Spain. By the summer of 1938 Cecil was preoccupied with central Europe and worried that Britain might play into Hitler's hands by getting concerned with Spain. He agreed with Churchill that Spain was a sideshow, a diversion to keep Britain and France turned away from German aggression. The Union Executive made a few gestures in the direction of its pro-Republican constituents, strengthening its questionnaires by asking if Britain should insist that Italy withdraw her troops as a condition for the confirmation of the Anglo-Italian agreement.[30] In January 1939 it asked the Government to withdraw the arms embargo in response to Noel–Baker's warning that the end was near for the Republic. It was too late to matter, either in Spain or in Grosvenor Crescent.

The Spanish Civil War fragmented the LNU in another less obvious way. It undid the bonds the Union had worked hard to tie with the Catholic Church, which in turn led to a loss of Catholic members. Eppstein of the staff had effectively cultivated the Catholic press and he tried to secure his gains during the war. He threatened resignation in October 1936 and sponsored the joint letter to *Headway* from LNU Catholics in an effort to keep the Union neutral.[31]

Cardinal Hinsley used his Vice-Presidency to keep the LNU from taking pro-Republican positions. He too threatened resignation and then dissociated himself from any political LNU resolutions.[32] However, by the end of 1938, with the IPC and the Union more clearly committed on the Spanish issue, Catholics felt they were swimming against the tide. Spain aggravated the problems which developed over the IPC and political involvement in general, and Hinsley went through with his resignation.

The Spanish Civil War was then too divisive an issue for the LNU to use in a campaign against the Government. Eden's resignation from the Foreign Secretaryship in February 1938 provided a much better opening for an attack. When Eden and

Cranborne left the Foreign Office, Union branches around the country held protest meetings. An emergency session of the Executive passed a resolution on 22 February regretting the way the resignations had created the impression that they 'were sacrificed to the hostility of certain foreign Governments, a hostility largely due to the support by these Ministers of the League of Nations and all it stands for'.[33]

The specific disagreement which triggered the resignations was over the timing of the Anglo-Italian conversations on the withdrawal of foreign volunteers from Spain. Behind this lay a series of differences on foreign policy between Prime Minister Chamberlain and Eden, with League policy as such not the main issue. But if the LNU leadership wished to use this occasion to challenge the policy of appeasement, this did not matter. Chamberlain had given the Union sufficient provocation; during the resignation crisis he said in the Commons that the League could not provide collective security, for instance.

It appeared for a while that the Union would enter the fray. *Headway* in March argued that a Government elected on Baldwin's collective security pledges could not in good faith carry out another policy. It added ominously that when the League was in danger, the Union must be free to oppose even the Prime Minister with all its resources.[34] For many frustrated Leaguers, this was the opportune moment to take political action. Speakers at Union meetings demanded Chamberlain's resignation. 'Let us not be Afraid of Becoming Political', an article by a branch secretary had urged in the December 1937 *Headway*.[35] Now the time had come.

Thirty local branch officials and members demanded Chamberlain's ousting from honorary leadership of the Union and put the case for political involvement in a petition to Cecil:

The practice of refraining from criticism of the government's policy, and the rule for keeping the Union out of party politics were formed in the days when British Governments honestly supported the League. This is no longer the case, and the Union's suggestions are patently ignored.

We, the undersigned, feel that there are worse fates for the Union than being involved in party politics . . .

We fear that, failing a clear and widely published statement, such members of the public who do not yet regard the Union, and far worse, the League, as totally negligible, may reasonably assume that the Union condones or even approves the government's foreign policies in Ethiopia, in Spain, in Europe and in the East . . .

We therefore protest as strongly as may be compatible with our respect . . . against the inaction which we consider the Union has been guilty for some time past . . .[36]

Murray was tempted by the idea of taking the Union into politics by running a non-party League-oriented candidate. Richard Acland, the Liberal MP, had encouraged this notion when he told Murray that if such a candidate did stand at Bridgwater both Liberal and Labour candidates would stand down and many Conservatives would vote for him.[37] Cecil doubted whether it would work, however.[38]

Many Union leaders had been involved in the various efforts so typical of thirties politics to cut across party lines and strike out in new directions. The Council of Action, which Lloyd George launched in 1935 and Harold Macmillan's Next Five Years Group had both endorsed a League-based foreign policy along with economic reconstruction. The LNU rejected a bid for co-operation from the Council of Action over the Eden resignation. The Council wanted LNU branches to co-operate in a postal ballot on the question 'Do you approve of Mr. Anthony Eden's stand for good faith in international affairs and will you support his demand for the re-establishment of peace and security through the League of Nations?'[39] It was natural for the opposition to think about using the LNU, the prototypical all-party group, as a vehicle against the Government. Even with its pared-down membership, it was still big.

A group of Focus supporters did win the Executive Committee's approval to use *Headway* in their campaign against Chamberlain's foreign policy. Angell was the chief intermediary in this friendly take-over bid to expand and improve *Headway* for news-stand sale and use it to campaign for collective security. Under the plan its editor, Geoffrey LePrevost, was to report not to the LNU but to a board consisting of Cecil, Angell, Wickham Steed, A. M. Wall, Violet Bonham Carter, and Sir Robert Waley Cohen. From October 1938 the new *Headway* was launched, with Churchill, Steed, Liddell Hart, Harold Nicolson, and others contributing. They did not attract the wider readership they hoped for; by March 1939 *Headway* had dropped to only 8,000 circulation and its Focus backers lost interest in it. The LNU resumed control and the experiment was declared a failure.

This was one of many instances which raised doubts as to whether the League had any potential as a political issue. It had once been possible to imagine a great political future for the League, the one great liberal idea to emerge from the wreckage of the war. In the immediate post-war era, when people could hardly remember the last 'normal' election, people thought it might overcome traditional party allegiances or at least reunite and strengthen the Liberals. Then the fall of Lloyd George's coalition had fostered a return to normal politics, and the League was effectively neutralized as a partisan issue. Subsequent events did not encourage the notion that the League was the right issue or the LNU the right organization with which to challenge the Government.

In any case, Eden and Cranborne did not want to see their resignations used that way. Some Union leaders tried unsuccessfully to get them to change their minds and give a series of speeches to rouse the country.[40] Murray agreed to respect Eden's wishes and keep LNU meetings from getting out of hand.[41] When he was pressed to convene a special Council meeting by members who wanted to oppose Chamberlain, Murray refused. The Government had not formally announced a change in policy, he said, so a censure move would be premature. Moreover, the proper business of the LNU was not to condemn governments, but to spell out League policy and then leave it to the voters to decide whether a government was satisfactory.[42] The LNU, after standing near the brink of electoral politics, had pulled back.

This was not meant to discourage 'League' candidacies in by-elections, and it probably made no practical difference. Although Vernon Bartlett, a Leaguer, was able to win at Bridgwater, the two other candidates most closely identified with the League cause were defeated in 1938. The Duchess of Atholl, after losing Conservative support in West Perthshire, ran on a collective security plank in Chiltern Hundreds so as to challenge Chamberlain's policies while keeping her seat. The efforts of Churchill, Cecil, Murray, Rathbone, and Bartlett were not enough to give her victory over a Chamberlain Conservative.[43] In a similar effort, A. D. Lindsay, the Master of Balliol, lost at Oxford. These experiences kept Union leaders shy of political involvement whenever the subject arose. In 1939 the Executive debated a proposal to blacklist MPs who had spoken or acted in opposition to the Covenant and to apply other electoral sanctions. Lytton objected on the practical grounds that 'it would be dangerous for a society which was not sufficiently strong to take sides in electoral contests without being able to influence the results'.[44]

The LNU leadership had overcome considerable rank-and-file opposition and determined what the organization would not do. In ruling against overt political activity, as on the Spanish Civil War issue, Union leaders kept to a safe course. Cecil berated the

Labour Party in 1938 for caring 'far more for the good of their organization than for the safety of the country or civilization itself'.[45] This sentiment was thrown back at the LNU by its frustrated members, and at many junctures in the past they would have been right. However, the Executive's caution was now founded on another calculation, that the Union should confine itself to the areas where it might have some impact. This meant concentrating on central Europe and the containment of Germany.

Some of the vagueness which had characterized the LNU's approach to collective security in earlier years was gone by 1938. In 1936 *Headway* insisted that 'the enemy is not Germany, nor Italy, nor Japan, nor Russia; it is the international anarchy . . .'[46] Now the Union was specific about who the aggressors were, so the lines could be sharply drawn between it and those who still wanted to satisfy Hitler's grievances. Allen parted company from Grosvenor Crescent and encouraged new negotiations with Berlin, to Cecil's dismay.[47] Lothian too announced that he was no longer sympathetic to an LNU which refused to meet Germany's legitimate grievances but talked about imposing League sanctions against her.[48] Lothian's criticism was a bit dated, for by 1938 no one thought that collective security could be based on the League alone. Murray indicated this in telling Lothian that while he thought there would soon be a war in support of the Covenant's principles, he had 'quite an open mind as to whether the fighting should be done under the Covenant or under some special regional pact . . .'[49]

LNU leaders talked increasingly in military terms. On Noel-Baker's suggestion, the Executive set up a committee (including Liddell Hart, and Generals Spears and Temperley) to study the relative strength of the League and non-League powers. This was supposd to combat the popular mood of defeatism which fostered appeasement, and to show that the advantage still lay with the League.[50] Cecil's riposte to those who talked about the difficulty of contending with German, Italian, *and* Japanese power was that Japan would not intervene in Europe if she could help it.[51] In the event of a military challenge in Europe, the situation was not hopeless, assuming proper co-ordination with the Soviet Union.

When Hitler began to move against Austria in February 1938, the Executive tried to encourage a stiff response. Austria had not asked Britain or France for assurances of military support, but the LNU issued a statement on the kinds of help which could be offered. 'If Herr Schuschnigg is still able to offer any effective resistance to further encroachments, diplomatic support from Britain and France might be very valuable; but not unless something more than remonstrance can be employed.' The statement described Hitler's 'New Technique of Aggression', by which he stirred up trouble as a pretext for intervention, and said that it could next be applied to Denmark, Holland, Belgium, and Poland. The Union also made it clear that the League could not help any more. Even though Germany's behaviour warranted calling her before the League Council, such a meeting 'might merely advertise the impotence of the League to protect Austria or to take any useful collective action at all'.[52]

Cecil tried to draw Halifax, the Foreign Secretary, into clarifying his policy on Austria.[53] The LNU stressed the need to assert Austria's right to independence; it praised Schuschnigg's courage in insisting on a plebiscite.[54] When the *Anschluss* which followed on 13 March failed to evoke a strong response from Whitehall, the Union reacted with predictable rage. Cecil angrily asked the Prime Minister if he now held 'that the use of material force is impracticable and that the League should cease to attempt "sanctions" and confine its efforts to moral force'.[55]

While nothing could be done about Austria, *Headway* responded to those who tried to minimize the importance of Hitler's action. It printed an article by an Austrian *émigré* which showed *Anschluss* to be something more than an alteration of the Versailles Treaty fulfilling the principle of nationality. Hitler had 'come with his troops like a conqueror of a hostile nation', the writer said, and now 'blood is flowing in Vienna, Austria is doomed'.[56]

There was time to look ahead to what might happen in Czechoslovakia and prepare for the next trial of collective security there. The previous November the Executive had called it a 'great danger spot' and set its Minorities Committee to work on the problem of the Sudeten Germans.[57] LNU leaders pressed after the *Anschluss* for a statement that Britain would place her forces at the disposal of the League to resist aggression. Especially if France intended to honour her treaty with Czechoslovakia, which seemed possible in March, then Britain had to commit herself or risk real isolation if France got into a losing war with Germany.[58] On the eve of the Czech crisis in August, Cecil again insisted that Britain should state that any German attack would not be tolerated. He prepared a proposal for the forthcoming meeting of the League Assembly to secure broad support for that policy.[59]

The Executive Committee spelled out this line of policy on 8 September. It urged Britain to 'do its utmost to resist any attempt by the German Government to settle the Sudeten question by intimidation or by military action', and to present the issue to the League Assembly. Lytton wrote to Halifax expressing consternation at the hints in *The Times* that Czechoslovakia might have to cede the Sudetenland to Germany. Britain should 'not [be] seeking peace by recommending surrender to German intimidation' or show 'nervousness in the face of threatened aggression'.[60]

When the Executive met again on 22 September the time for pleading had passed. A rush of events had revealed the nature of Chamberlain's appeasement policies unmistakably, and the only possible course for the Union was condemnation. In the harshest statement it had ever issued about a Government policy, the Executive repudiated 'seeking peace by surrender to force'. Not only was this policy 'disastrous to British interests and fatal to British honour', it would also 'in the end lead to war'. The German demands for the dismemberment of Czechoslovakia were 'part of a settled policy of domination in central Europe which will be carried out step by step unless the peace-loving nations resolve that it shall be stopped, and a return resolutely made to the maintenance of law and the resistance of force in the settlement of international disputes'. The words were strong, but the actions which accompanied them were weak. It was unlikely, Lytton admitted to the Executive, that the branches would be willing to organize protests with anything like the zeal of a few years before. The LNU set demonstrations for London and twelve other large cities but did not even call an emergency meeting of the General Council to launch a big protest campaign.[61]

On 26 September, as Hitler's threats made war seem inevitable, the Executive met again. It agreed to a resolution backing Churchill's suggestion that joint notes from Britain, France, and Russia should warn Germany that the invasion of Czechoslovakia was an act of war. Committee members divided over taking more far-reaching measures, such as calling for the formation of an all-party emergency Government which could command the country's support. This sort of thing seemed to be out of the LNU's province, in the view of many members.[62]

Cecil and Lytton were determined not to let this critical time slip away without a word of protest. If the Executive could not agree to this course of action, they decided to act without the Executive. They called a special meeting for 28 September to bring together LNU and Youth Movement leaders with a few opposition MPs and others in the peace movement. It began as a tumultuous gathering of about one hundred people in a Commons Committee Room, sending off deputations to the party leaders. Then, after the House had convened and greeted the stunning news of the invitation to a conference at Munich with an ovation, the meeting convened again at Grosvenor Crescent. Dugdale kept a diary of that grim meeting where Archibald Sinclair, Noel-Baker, and other MPs 'were like men who had been bruised. Violet Bonham Carter, hard as steel, took Archie Sinclair, her leader, to task in front of us all for having said nothing. He and Philip both assured us that it would have been *physically* impossible, but Violet was implacable . . . She would not even join in a very critical resolution, because it began: "While sharing the universal relief . . ."'

Dugdale unfortunately lost track of who said what, but she captured the mood in a series of comments she recorded: 'Musso will expect heavy payment for his intervention and will get it in Spain.' 'Germany's road to the East is now cleared. This is only a first instalment of Danegeld.' 'This is the first time a British House of Commons has acted like a Fascist Parliament.'[63]

The resolution which emerged from this gathering, with the reference Bonham Carter did not like (about sharing 'the relief occasioned by the instant menace of war'), said that Hitler should not be allowed to wring further concessions from the Czechs. It was not much, but it was more than the Executive Committee could agree to when it met on the following day.

The Munich Conference left the Executive almost paralysed with uncertainty. The worst part of the whole situation for believers in the fundamental soundness of public opinion was that Chamberlain had that opinion behind him. Only weeks before, in a resolution urging the maintenance of Czech independence, the LNU used its stock phrase, that it 'believed that that policy has the support of the country'. Now they knew it was not so, Lytton told the Executive that it would be 'suicidal' to take action now, just when a 'universal sense of relief and joy . . . existed throughout the country that the danger of war had been averted'. Nor could they criticize Chamberlain who would, if he succeeded at Munich, be regarded as a hero.[64] The response among LNU members outside of Grosvenor Crescent was the same. In Wales the Council Secretary reported that 'it would be difficult, if not impossible, to describe the effect of the strain, upon the members of our Branches

. . .' They 'face courageously the fact that they have to begin building again almost from the very foundations'.[65]

After Munich the Union kept up a broadside against the Government. Churchill used the pages of *Headway* to attack the Munich agreement and plead for support.[66] The Executive backed the Youth Groups' plans for massive demonstrations on Spain, the need for co-operation with the Soviet Union and the continuation of the Franco–Soviet Pact.[67] The LNU issued its strongest rearmament resolution yet, insisting that 'the strengthening of British armaments is essential to the discharge of our duties under the Covenant, and . . . all defensive precautions should be taken'.[68] Cecil thought increasingly about the need to organize joint opposition to Chamberlain across party lines. If this could not be done, he ruminated on the possibility of joining the Labour Party.[69]

This continuing opposition to appeasement was predictable. But Munich, and the shock of those September days when the LNU lost its audience, turned Grosvenor Crescent in new directions as well. Union leaders had to show that they stood for something more than a tough line against Hitler. It was too easy for opponents to 'type' them; Lothian praised Chamberlain by contrasting him to Cecil, 'the real war mind . . . in Europe today'.[70] The Union's rigid opposition to Covenant revision reinforced this negative image. Conservative appeasers and pacifists both talked about the League's failure to provide for peaceful boundary revisions as the reason why the Covenant could not be enforced.

After Munich, the Executive was ready to call for 'a careful and systematic examination of . . . grievances before they are exploited and embittered to a point where they will either precipitate a war or bring about a hurried settlement which will create new injustices'. Committee members set to work on a new Statement of Policy in October, guided by the assumption that the Versailles Treaty had not made peace secure and looking at the prerequisites for another peace treaty, 'framed by agreement and not dictation'.[71] The December 1938 statement they produced was not quite as ambitious as that might suggest, but it did urge the creation of machinery to remedy grievances.[72]

The search for new approaches led the LNU into a reconsideration of the colonial question. Englishmen could hardly expect to leave their empire out of a discussion of new territorial arrangements which might avert war. For LNU leaders like Lytton, the

son of a Viceroy and himself a former Governor of Bengal, this
not an easy step to take. The report which the Union issued at th
end of 1938, 'The Colonial Problem; Native Welfare the First
Consideration', proposed the establishment of an international
consortium of European powers, including Germany, to determine the broad lines of colonial policy in sub-Saharan Africa. This
was supposed to be an inducement to Germany to co-operate in
the League if she wanted her share of imperial power in Africa.
Individual nations would still administer separate territories held
under the consortium plan, although a kind of multinational civil
service of officials would provide specified services in these territories. The whole arrangement was to be supervised by the
Mandates Commission or some other impartial body of experts.[73]

This plan neatly squared the circle of problems raised by
German grievances, luring Germany back to the League into the
bargain. But it did not impress anti-imperialist opinion in the
peace movement, and it upset pro-imperialists even more. Lord
Lugard, who had often won kudos from *Headway* as member of the
Permanent Mandates Commission, took strong exception to the
plan. He thought international control unworkable and not even
of much value for appeasement's sake; equal commercial opportunity could be established without it.[74] Nevertheless, the idea of
an international trust for the benefit of the inhabitants and offering
an 'open door' to trade remained alive in League circles for years
to come. During the war years, the LNU continued to foster
discussions of its plan, although by then the focus of it was not
German grievances but the long-range needs of the colonized
peoples.

Another new course taken by the Union after Munich was
towards refugee relief and settlement. Rathbone and several other
Executive Committee members urged the Government to accept
responsibility for the plight of refugees from the Sudetenland.
They suggested that financial aid, temporary shelter on imperial
territory, and eventual large-scale settlement in the Dominions
were desirable.[75] In November the Refugee Committee, which
studied the problem of Jewish emigration from Germany as well as
the Sudetenland, called for a liberal attitude towards the admission of refugees into the United Kingdom, and British co-
operation in the work of the Inter-Governmental Committee of
Refugees.[76] Under the tutelage of Dugdale, a leading Zionist and
friend of Chaim Weizman, the General Council prodded the
Government to bend its rigid quotas on Jewish immigration to

o criticized the White Paper of May 1939, which
and urged that it not be implemented.[77] Many a
nch could find in the 'adoption' of a refugee a
tence in these troubled times.[78]

NU now had what was in effect a twofold policy which
stressed the immediate need for co-operation with France and the
Soviet Union to stop aggression and the long-range need for
creative planning in a League framework. This policy kept
members reasonably united in early 1939. Some issues still provoked internal difficulties: the Youth Groups were at odds with the
Executive over conscription. The National Youth Groups Council
opposed National Service while the Executive refused to take a
stand on it.[79] Generally speaking, Grosvenor Crescent felt that it
had succeeded in rallying its remaining members after Munich.

Something had changed, though, more significant than a drop
in membership or a shift in policy. At the heart of the LNU had
been a faith in British public opinion as a force capable of mould-
ing a new world order. A large and influential Union could sway
the Government which in turn could lead the League and the
world. But the first bubble had burst when Britain—despite the
encouragement of the Peace Ballot—had refused to pursue a full
sanctions policy against Italy. After Munich it seemed clear that
Britain's influence on world events was not decisive. As *Headway*
put it, since Munich 'it is by others that the word will be given for
peace—or war'.[80] While the Union's leaders continued to press for
collective security in 1939, their real struggle had already been
lost. That struggle had been to put foreign policy on a new
foundation, to build a world regulated by law and not force.

The LNU applauded the agreements which Britain reached
with France and Poland in March 1939, but such agreements had
little to do with the principles of the Covenant which the Union
was established to uphold. The fundamental objection to British
policy which Cecil and Murray had stated in January remained
that 'recent British policy has not been based on any clear principle. It has consisted of a series of opportunist expedients for
avoiding temporary difficulties as they arise, often with little regard to our international obligations or even our ultimate interests.'[81]

Grosvenor Crescent was divided in its response to Government
initiatives in the last months before war. Halifax's speech before
the Lords on 20 March was taken by most of the Executive to be a
clear sign that the Government had turned to collective security.

Lytton notified the branches that 'the tide seems to be running in our direction . . . It is now not a question of vague mutual obligations in certain hypothetical circumstances, but of specific joint action to resist aggression of a kind that has already threatened.' But was the speech a clear enough indication that the Government had changed its spots? By the following week committee members were dismayed at 'the absence of any statement by the Government as to the action it has taken in order to assure the co-operation of all peace-loving states in the policy announced by Lord Halifax'.[82]

When Chamberlain announced a guarantee of Polish independence on 31 March Union leaders kept some of their misgivings. For one thing, these emergency measures might harden into military alliances, and balance-of-power politics would be back for good. The public might then dismiss the League as a well-intentioned mistake.[83] Another difficulty with guarantees to eastern European states was that they might be seen as an alternative to co-operation with the Soviet Union. The LNU was insistent on the need to create 'a Peace Front too formidable to be challenged'; without the Soviets this was impossible.[84] Cecil remained much more sceptical about Whitehall's good intentions than Murray and other LNU leaders in the summer before the war. He wanted Halifax to be 'quite definite in pressing for a Russian alliance, before the Union should give its blessing.[85]

In its meeting of 27 July 1939, the Executive Committee discussed the fate of the Union in the event of war. Some members took it for granted that its work would be ended and even discussed the dismissal of staff. Some argued for continuing, Noel-Baker referring to the role of League societies during World War One to support his case.[86] That same wartime experience may have weighed on the minds of those who expressed uncertainty, because in the first years of that war the Government had imposed limits on propaganda groups. Extensive public discussion on how to prevent future wars had been restricted before 1918.

The officers of the LNU agreed on a statement for the September *Headway* which expressed the need to work for some world organization. 'The nations of Europe cannot go on existing as separate units, owing no duties to one another; they must have some sort of international control.'[87] At the Executive's 28 August session, they decided to continue working to keep alive public interest in the principles of the Covenant. When peace came, the LNU would 'seek to create an irresistible demand for the application of these principles'.[88] By the time Britain entered the war, then, the issue of the Union's existence had been decided.

That the League should have to share the blame for the war seemed a cruel irony to LNU leaders. To them it was obvious that if the League had failed to provide collective security, it was only because it had not been used properly. The British were, Cecil said, the League's 'chief supporters and we used that position to betray and abandon it . . . from 1931 onwards'.[89] Only a few League movement leaders were ready to bring the blame closer to home. Harold Nicolson, for one, said that 'it is of slight value to blame successive Governments for their hesitation to defend the League since 1931 unless we admit that we who believe firmly in League policy have failed clearly to bring home that such a policy is not one of evasion of difficulties'.[90]

Chapter XII

World War Two

In wartime the LNU was small and feeble compared to what it had been. In 1940 it collected just over 100,000 subscriptions and attracted only 1,861 new members. Its budget of £10,500 for that year forced a cut in staff to seventeen, about one-sixth its former size. The Union dropped its Regional Representatives and reduced *Headway* in size. Headquarters moved from Grosvenor Crescent to more modest quarters at 60 St. Martin's Lane. Most of its records went to the home of Geoffrey Mander, the Liberal MP where they were destroyed by fire during the Blitz.[1]

The Union's leaders were now old. Murray, at seventy-three, appeared to the staff to be more frail than Cecil, who was two years older.[2] Cecil seemed more than willing to plunge into the war. He expressed to Eden his willingness to attend the League Assembly in Geneva, but Eden did not respond.[3] With no official role, Cecil took advantage of his few remaining forums for activity, quickly preparing a note 'War Aims of L.N.U.'[4] Not until late in 1944 did he raise the subject of his resignation seriously. Murray felt unsure even then whether 'the Union had better get rid of all its Methuselahs together' or keep them in office 'as a bridge'.[5]

Others in the LNU leadership had also aged; with Lytton seventy and Angell sixty-seven, Dugdale noted in 1941 that she had spent 'a day of Committees with the L.N.U. ghosts'. In 1945 she briefly observed after an Executive meeting: 'Very rambling, everybody older and deafer than ever!'[6]

The first wartime *Headway* was filled with brave words about how the Union would carry on and build a new world order 'free from the errors and the disturbing influences which wrecked the first'. Murray's specific instructions to branches sounded much less exhilarating: 'Whether there are public meetings or not, there should be conferences in private houses for discussion and study . . . We all find in daily intercourse with friends and acquaintances that talk about the war and matters connected to it is inevitable. This provides each one of us with an opportunity of spreading information about what the Union stands for and enlisting support for it. . . .'[7]

No one could tell what activities would be permitted or whether the public would be at all interested. Major Freshwater, the LNU Secretary, speculated that the main obstacle to public appeals might be an attitude that winning the war was all that mattered. People could be told that you can win the war yet lose the peace, and this 'can be presented as supporting the Government . . .'[8] With Chamberlain at 10 Downing Street, this concern about pleasing the Government was understandable. Once Churchill took over, there was no reason for it. Relations with the Government were good, and the Ministry of Information facilitated the Union's work and asked its co-operation in supplying speakers.

The British public was receptive to the idea that an international authority would be required after the war. In the long run, this helped the LNU; but the Union was pledged to support the existing League and not some ideals to be fulfilled in the future. This caused some immediate problems, since the League was moribund, its Assembly postponed indefinitely. Britain took the trouble to notify the League that she was at war, citing her obligations to Poland rather than to the Covenant as justification. The Executive protested the way this 'seems to acquiesce in the total destruction of the peace-keeping powers of the League'. It was on weak ground here, for it could hardly suggest that an appeal to the League would have any real meaning. In fact it asked Whitehall to make a face-saving gesture, a statement that the League's powers were 'in suspension'. The response was curt, the British note to the League had been a 'frank recognition of an obvious state of affairs from which certain logical conclusions had to be drawn'.[9]

The LNU wanted the League Assembly to meet, if not in Geneva then elsewhere. It could then rule on Hitler's aggression and make Britain's cause its own. Britain might benefit from this by demonstrating to neutrals and the Dominions that it was fighting to defend more than its own national interests. The League could stay active in its non-political work, in the neutral countries and in refugee and prisoner-of-war work.[10] It is, Davies wrote to Churchill, 'a calamity that this conflict is not definitely and universally regarded as a League war—a war in which all its members are under a moral and, to a certain extent, a legal obligation to assist to the limit of their capacities . . . At the conclusion of the struggle the League would then emerge as a federation of States whose solidarity and cohesion would be unassailable.'[11]

The attack on Finland by the Soviet Union on 30 November, 1939, and Finland's subsequent appeal to Geneva revived the League. But the League's expulsion of Russia from the organization embarrassed the LNU. Even Finland had not expected or wanted expulsion. This action undercut the Union's case for involving the League in the war.[12] If the move against the Soviet Union was taken seriously it should lead to new military calculations about what the League would need to stand up to this new enemy, an obvious absurdity. Cecil said that the Soviets had acted in fear and not aggression, and that Germany was the real problem.[13]

The Union tried to use the League's action against the Soviets to prod Whitehall. If the Government wanted to show it was even-handed and that it had not singled out 'red' Russia for punishment, it would try to get League authorization for British action against Germany. Why use the League in one case and not others? The Foreign Office found it easy to turn this argument around: Britain was at war with Germany so how could it ignore the Soviet attack on Finland completely? As to the LNU's request that all acts of aggression be condemned, this might affect the 'delicate topic' of Italian neutrality.[14] The Union was making no progress in its efforts to breath new life into the League.

Blocked in its immediate goals, it turned to the matter of war aims. Cecil presented the Executive with a 'Note on World Settlement After the War' on 14 September. This eleven-point proposal included some specific aims, such as restoring political independence to Poland and Czechoslovakia, with a number of general ones. These amounted to little more than a recital of the LNU's familiar litany: world anarchy was condemned, the supremacy of law recognized, and the League taken as the basis of the new order, armaments should be reduced, economic prosperity restored by the elimination of barriers to international commerce, and so on.[15]

This note launched a process of defining war aims that became one of the Union's major pursuits during the war. Where the Foreign Office had been cool to the LNU's suggestions about current policy, it was sympathetic to this effort. Halifax encouraged Cecil in it in September, telling him that if Hitler made a sudden peace offer Britain should be ready with a general statement of what it wanted.[16] The Executive elaborated on the Cecil note, Dugdale making sure it included a specific reference to the Jewish question ('The protection accorded by the Minorities Treaties to religious, racial and linguistic minorities in certain countries should be extended to all countries and made more effective . . .'). At the December 1939 General Council meeting this statement was approved.[17]

The statement, 'World Settlement After the War', went beyond the original Cecil proposal in several ways. The most important change made at the Council's direction was a section stating that 'economic prosperity and social justice are not less important for world peace than political security'. This reflected a strong concern in the Union rank and file that the war should usher in extensive social change. The Executive, still balanced between parties and concerned about Conservative opinion, was on the defensive on this issue against those who demanded 'a peace worth fighting for'. The statement also proposed an approach to the old problem of the 'gap' in the Covenant, legal war. It specified that all international differences not settled by negotiation be submitted to third party judgement, which could be arbitration, binding mediation or some kind of judicial decision. The use of force, under this proposal, was restricted to action specifically approved by the international authority.[18]

In the debate on war aims, Cecil and the Executive had to pay as much attention to what their over-zealous followers might propose as to the attitude of the public at large. The war had opened the way to far-reaching speculation about the future, accompanied by a widespread tendency to condemn the League. The spate of polemical books on inter-war foreign policy which followed Cato's *Guilty Men* in 1940 kept the debate over past mistakes alive. The Union's leaders insisted time and again that if their advice had been followed, all would have been well. Cecil was particularly opposed to the suggestion that some new and improved international organization could now be created. He remembered the difficulty he had had in getting the Covenant accepted and was not willing to scrap it for something else that might never materialize.[19] When the General Council advocated things which seemed to him too far-reaching, he took the position that the Government should not be asked to declare itself in favour of specific post-war programmes.[20] This alienated many fervent internationalists who felt that the League had failed because it had been too restrictive in its reliance on sovereign states.

Davies, with the support of the Union's Welsh National Council, kept drum-beating for the cause of a restructured

League. The lengthy memorandum he circulated to LNU branches in Wales when the war started restated his case for an Equity Tribunal and international air police force.[21] The *New Commonwealth* magazine was sometimes critical of the LNU, so friction between the two closely linked societies Davies was active in persisted.[22]

The New Commonwealth presented a familiar challenge. The Federal Union movement was, by contrast, newer and more threatening. The initial impetus to this newer drive came from the United States, which almost guaranteed it an audience among British internationalists anxious to foster the 'special relationship'. It originated in the proposals of Clarence Streit, an American journalist, who in 1933 began to elaborate a scheme for uniting the North Atlantic democracies in a common defence system, and a customs, postal, and monetary union. France, Switzerland, and the Scandinavian and Benelux countries would join the United States and the British Commonwealth as the nucleus of this group. They would then encourage the co-operation of other nations and form the nucleus of a world government.

Streit's book *Union Now* was published in the United States in March 1939, where it led to the formation of the Inter-democracy Federal Unionists. It soon appeared in Britain and other 'nuclear' countries where it attracted considerable attention. Lothian encouraged support for it in Liberal circles and urged Lionel Curtis to establish the British Federal Union Society.[23] Streit, who had been a correspondent in Geneva, had a lot to say about the failures of the League, which, he said, was merely an extension of the pre-war system based on national sovereignty. Further 'patching' would not suffice.

Headway ran several articles on *Union Now* in the spring of 1939. Wickham Steed reported on a conference held in London to discuss Streit which had been quite derogatory about the League.[24] The British Federal Union did not base itself entirely on Streit's book, and its members, discouraged by Washington's isolationism, turned gradually towards a European federation. In the early wartime years, before concrete proposals for a United Nations organization emerged, the federalism notion in one form or another beguiled what used to be called 'League opinion'.

Cecil, often sympathetic to New Commonwealth, remained wary of Federal Union. He resisted Murray's suggestion that he include reference to *Union Now* in his 'World Settlement' proposal in September. It was not just the 'fantastic utopianism' of it which put him off; it was also his set strategy in dealing with Americans never to take the lead and risk arousing suspicions across the Atlantic.[25] Murray saw the potential threat to the LNU posed by the Federal Union, this 'toadstool' growing out of the League movement. He tried not to alienate Federal Unionists and allowed them to argue their case at Union study groups. But he discouraged LNU leaders from attending their meetings,[26] and he objected to co-operation with them. Murray agreed with most other Executive Committee members that internationalists (the New Commonwealth, the LNU and the IPC), should share expenses and sponsor joint activities while keeping their separate identities. However, Federal Union, with its 'totally impossible' ideas, should be kept away.[27]

However, popular sympathy for Federal Unionism was apparent at the General Council meeting held at the end of 1939, so LNU leaders pushed through a resolution which they hoped would assuage the rank and file. It said that 'peace and security can only be obtained by international action [and] in advocating the restoration of the League of Nations together with any developments of it in the direction of federalism which may be found practicable'.[28] In December's *Headway* Cecil conceded that Federal Union had its 'good points' although he was not clear that it would work. Another article in the same issue said that the League and Federal Union were not antithetical.[29] In this spirit, the Executive weighed passing a kind of non-aggression pact with the federalists, ruling out joint meetings but stressing the common aims of the two societies.[30]

Cecil was still a bit dubious about the LNU associating itself with 'the kind of nonsense Lionel Curtis and his friends may be talking'. But he saw the need to avoid antagonizing Federal Union supporters, and hoped the LNU could advance its own case and say as little about federalism as possible.[31] The trouble with this was that Federal Union kept saying a good deal about the League's faults, making it difficult for the LNU to restrain itself. *Headway*'s columns turned more openly hostile to federalism. By May 1940 an editorial on 'The Double Challenge' equated the challenge of Federal Union to that posed by nationalist aggression. 'Federation is not a magic word', it warned, and it was most unlikely that it could be achieved in this generation.[32] When *Headway* picked upon union between Britain and the United States the following September, it was with a piece by Arnold Foster which hinted darkly that Streit's plans might serve as a cover for the United States to guarantee that the British fleet would be preserved no matter what happened to Britain.[33]

The discussion about federalism took a new turn early in 1940. Officials of the French League movement proposed a joint discussion on war aims with the LNU. The 'World Settlement After the War' statement had aroused their interest and they suggested through the International Federation of League of Nations Societies that a conference be held on the subject. Co-operation between two wartime allies seemed a much more practical proposition to Union leaders than the legalistic web proposed by Streit's followers. Cecil was anxious to talk about 'a European spearpoint much more closely wrought', with the League retained as a symbol of unity.[34] Lytton raised the only minor objection to this kind of joint planning before the conference was arranged for London in February. He insisted that the LNU make it clear to the French in advance that it would not support a 'Carthaginian Peace'.[35]

This concern about a new 'Diktat' was evident in the statement prepared for the French. It distinguished between armistice and peace terms, of course assuming Allied victory. An armistice would have to guarantee self-determination to Austrians, Poles, and Czechs with German troops withdrawn. But the peace terms must be freely negotiated in a neutral country by equal parties. Such a meeting could work towards re-establishing the League, or some effective international organization with the power to limit armaments and maintain the peace, and perhaps even to abolish national air forces and create an international air force.[36]

The French sent a delegation headed by Émile Borel, the former Minister of Education, to the joint conference held in London on 9 and 10 March 1940. The two societies agreed to a statement calling for a three-stage peace settlement. First, the armistice which would restore Germany's conquered territories. Secondly, a freely negotiated peace treaty between belligerents, which would include Austrian, Polish, and Czech representatives. Then, finally, a General Peace Settlement with all states invited to establish a new world order. The conferees agreed to meet later in Paris and include Polish and Czech League society representatives in their deliberations.[37]

Cecil encouraged plans for a European confederation based on further Anglo-French co-operation. He discussed this possibility in a radio broadcast in March, stealing some thunder from Federal Unionists in the process.[38] The LNU's plans for the next stage of discussions with the French included a suggestion that the Anglo-French entente be used as a basis for developing a group of states as 'guardians of the law' with a common secretariat which could advise on common obligations and defence requirements. This would be the nucleus of a wider grouping of European states aimed at keeping the peace. It was hoped that this would function alongside other regional groupings within the League.[39] The French showed interest in strengthening ties with England, but not much in the broader confederation or the revived League.[40] All these plans were cut short abruptly by the fall of France in any case.

During the first winter of the war, the LNU was faced with a tricky internal problem, as the dispute between the Executive and the Youth Group leaders heated up badly. Union leaders were first angered by the National Youth Campaign's demand for Chamberlain's resignation in the spring of 1939.[41] In August the magazine *Youth* was put under the direct control of the LNU Secretary, not as an editor but as a censor. He checked *Youth*'s editorials and deleted anything he deemed objectionable.[42]

The war divided the National Youth Committee, and spokesmen for both the moderate and leftist factions appeared before the General Council in December 1939. Even the moderates expressed reservations about the Executive's war aims statement, demanding attention to social justice and other desirable post-war goals. Gabriel Carritt, who had been censured by the Executive during the Spanish Civil War, spoke for the extremists. The war, he said, was not being fought to resist aggression or uphold collective security, but 'for domination and for the control of great colonial territories'. He berated the Government for refusing to consider the demands of the Indian Congress for independence and suggested that the real duty of internationalists was not to support the war effort but to build up the peace movement in preparation for the end of the war. The Executive tried not to over-react to this, Arnold Foster suggesting that while the younger generation's views might not be popular, all should listen sympathetically to what it was saying.[43]

This approach did not molify Carritt and his 'stop-the-war' faction. They were in the majority at the National Youth Group Council in March 1940, and used the occasion to push through a series of twenty resolutions. The first and most provocative of these denounced the war as 'imperialist' and called for the installation of a Government which would end it. Other resolutions urged the LNU to work against the involvement of neutrals to widen the war, criticized the restrictions on civil liberties in France and demanded a new democratic constitution for India. It also berated Whitehall for its prejudice against the Soviet Union and advocated better Anglo-Soviet relations.[44] At the end of this Easter meeting, Youth Group leaders agreed that their members could advocate LNU policy 'without compromising Youth Group opinion', and that statements damaging to the Union should be kept private.

This compromise between Youth Group factions broke down quickly amid mutual recriminations. Several of the 'moderates' resigned in April and the whole mess was passed on to the Executive Committee. The Executive sorted through the resolutions, accepted four of the more innocuous ones, and ruled the rest out of order. It then suspended the National Constitution of its Youth Groups on 25 April, allowing individual Youth Groups to function but abolishing the national committees and councils which were supposed to represent them.[45] At the June Council, when these actions were presented for approval, Youth Group leaders could not attend to defend themselves unless a regular branch delegated them to attend. The Executive's case against them ('passing resolutions of a highly controversial character such as might well have been passed by . . . Young Communists'), thus went unanswered. One moderate who had resigned from the National Youth Group Council got the floor as the representative of a Regional Federation, but she attested to the loyalty of most rank-and-file Youth Group members to the LNU.[46]

The Union was indirectly involved in one other effort to purge 'party line' opposition in 1940. The British National Committee of the IPC, headed by A. D. Lindsay, had to reckon with the opposition of an active Communist minority. Although there was no threat of a take-over of the organization from the inside, there was enough dissension to cause the Chairman to suspend the committee's activities in January. The International Executive of the IPC then withdrew recognition from the committee and asked the LNU to reconstitute it.[47] The Executive saw no further need for the IPC as a separate entity, so it recommended that it merge with the International Federation which also had headquarters in Geneva. It also set up a new advisory committee to assume control of the British IPC.[48]

This committee, which included Cecil, Lytton, Murray, Courtney, and other long-time regulars, paved the way for the most noteworthy LNU activity of the war—the London International Assembly. The idea of the Assembly was to involve foreigners, specifically the representatives of the many governments-in-exile based in London, in planning for the post-war world. The Union, with its international contacts, was well situated for this kind of effort, and after the collapse of the Anglo-French talks in mid-1940 it was a logical thing to do. LNU leaders were searching for ways to be useful. Murray lamented to Angell in August that 'there seems to be no work at present for us L.N.U. people; whether there is political prejudice against us in high quarters, I do not know, but our brains do not seem to be wanted. . .'.[49] By providing a forum for foreigners in London, the Union demonstrated that, although the League was dead, it could do more than mark time.

In the fall of 1940 the Executive launched an exchange of views with representatives of the League societies of Belgium, China, Czechoslovakia, France, Holland, Greece, and Poland. The Union's 'World Settlement After the War' statement was the focus of the discussions it proposed. A conference of representatives from the various societies met on 14 November and agreed on the need for closer economic co-operation between their countries and on the need for further meetings.[50] Individual LNU leaders tried to encourage discussions with Americans as well. Murray and Davies both wrote to Nicholas Murray Butler, Davies as an MP trying to contact American legislators interested in an inter-parliamentary link.[51]

The Union explored various schemes for working with foreigners. Its Council for Education in World Citizenship held a conference in January 1941 at Oxford for professors and teachers from Allied countries and representatives from the Ministry of Education. The Executive considered establishing a 'European Centre' in London or a study-research facility on the order of Chatham House.[52] With its library moved to a school near Bristol during the war, the LNU would have had difficulty accommodating this sort of operation. The Executive agreed to co-operate with the New Europe Circle in sponsoring lunches to bring *émigrés* together and in establishing a standing conference of representatives of foreign governments in London, not to advocate policy or pass resolutions, but to exchange views in preparation for the peace settlement.[53] There was a good response to this. President Benes of Czechoslovakia was sceptical about discussing peace aims with Europe so unsettled, and shocked the Executive with a letter reminding them they they had plenty of time for planning ahead, what with a number of wars to be fought out first; he added that 'a little blood-letting would do us no harm!'[54]

The Foreign Office asked the Union to delay its scheme for a study discussion centre until the machinery for operating official Allied meetings had been worked out. But Eden was encouraging and liked the idea of an unofficial meeting-place for foreign representatives.[55] The Union set up the London International Assembly in the summer of 1941, working through a multi-national preparatory committee which included Americans as well as Europeans. It set forth the ground rules for the new organization in a privately circulated leaflet: members of the Assembly were to meet as private individuals rather than as government or party delegates; their discussions would be private so as to promote a free exchange of views; the Assembly would be free to record its agreement on particular proposals although its purpose would not be to pass resolutions on international issues.

The LNU funded the Assembly, and got the help of the Czechoslovak Institute, the Belgian Committee for the Study of Post-War Problems, and the Polish Research Centre in the form of space, secretarial help, and duplicating facilities. These sources were of somewhat questionable independence from their respective governments, but the Assembly described itself as being funded by 'independent' sources as a way of emphasizing its unofficial character. The research facilities for the Assembly were supplied by Chatham House, the Royal Institute for International Affairs, with a liaison officer maintaining contact between the two groups.[56]

The first plenary session of the London International Assembly was held on 15 September 1941. Ten full members participated initially, one from each member state, the exiled governments in London. The Soviet Embassy in London sent observers, although they did not accept membership. The preparatory committee invited many other foreigners resident in London so as to represent different political and religious viewpoints, and after a year the Assembly had 150 such members. René Cassin, Jan Masaryk, and other dignitaries addressed the opening session, but press coverage of the event was restricted. The *Manchester Guardian* mentioned it two days later, but after that there were few public references to the work of the Assembly.[57]

The idea of the London International Assembly, of bringing together representatives of the governments-in-exile and other foreigners, was a good one. It made sense to take advantage of the unique situation of wartime London and to hope to develop a sense of common awareness within the embryonic United Nations located there. Each of the governments-in-exile was studying the possible effects of a post-war settlement on their own country, and there were many ways in which a combination forum and research group could help in this effort, enabling planners to see the relationship of their own plans to others.

In its three-year existence the Assembly thus served the needs of the twenty-one countries eventually associated with it. It produced reports on some immediate issues, such as one on 'Trial and Punishment of War Criminals', and surveyed the long-range needs of the United Nations in the field of education. The Assembly was a disappointment in that some of its members never treated it very seriously or provided adequate representation to the various commissions it spawned. Others—the Czechs especially—took responsibility for the attendance of their nationals and made a great contribution. There was then unevenness in the Assembly's operation and the idea never reached its potential.[58]

From the LNU perspective the Assembly presented other difficulties. Many of its members were not interested in the League, so Cecil, who presided over the Assembly, was cautioned not to push the subject of a reformed League or suggest that all independent bodies should come under its jurisdiction.[59] The relative obscurity in which the Assembly worked, partly at Eden's insistence, was not in keeping with the Union's approach. One motive for sponsoring the venture had been to gain publicity, so this had not worked out well.[60] Even given these drawbacks, some LNU leaders wanted to see it perpetuated after the war to further the Union's international contacts.[61] This did not prove practicable, but when the Assembly was terminated at the end of 1944 the Union rated it a great success.

The planning for reconstruction which went on within the Union itself was a very different matter, less successful by any standard. This sort of planning was exceedingly popular in Britain. One writer surveying the situation in 1942 said that 'groups and societies for the study of problems of the peace sprang up like mushrooms overnight. Pamphlets, broadsheets, "newsletters"... burgeoned from every printing works ...'[62] The LNU suffered from the same weaknesses as other newer groups, for now it did not command a large staff or research facilities, and its

Executive no longer attracted front-rank talent in close touch with Government and party leaders. Moreover, it was unwilling to pool its resources with others in the peace movement or co-operate with other societies in advancing common programmes. Murray was enthusiastic about the war aims statement which the Union of Democratic Control circulated in the summer of 1940, but he said he could 'not well sign it when the L.N.U. is just about to issue a similar statement'. He went along with Cecil's draft proposals out of loyalty, although he feared they 'might almost lay us open to the charge that we have learned nothing and forgotten nothing. . .' [63] The Union did not co-operate with the National Peace Council, which in 1941 proposed a number of regional conferences on peace aims to give peace societies more information about the public's attitudes and needs.[64]

The LNU had some disadvantages which most other groups working on programmes for reconstruction did not have. It was, after all, formed from a broad coalition of members who could agree to support the League while disagreeing about everything else. With no more League to support and the way open for a fundamental reconsideration of domestic and international goals, there was not enough commonality of interest to make the Union work effectively. Cecil, Murray, Lytton, and other top leaders were slow to embrace the ambitious plans for reshaping society which attracted the most vocal section of Union opinion. They justified this by arguing that while leftists were making all the noise, as Murray put it, 'the Conservatives, who may in the end be very important, tend to sulk and say nothing'.[65] There was a point here, that most Englishmen were not at war to fulfil the programme of the Fabian Society.

The debate over peace aims and reconstruction served as the vehicle for a challenge to the LNU leadership, so there was an added layer of confusion surrounding it. The ageing 'liberals' who led the Union seemed out of touch to many members. The most active leader of the wartime opposition on the Executive was Konni Zilliacus. As the LNU kept revising its statements on peace aims during the middle years of the war, Zilliacus led a minority on the Executive in pressing for far-reaching plans for social and economic action and the extension of the authority of any proposed international organization through such devices as a world parliament. Behind Zilliacus's tactical moves in supporting these measures was a deeply rooted feeling that the mistakes of 1919 must not be repeated. At the end of the war he elaborated on his view that the 'peace conference liberals' had not learned that their faith in democracy had been misplaced in 1919, because defence and foreign affairs remained the bastions of plutocracy.[66] Murray and other leaders got the message. 'The essence of the Zilli scheme', Murray wrote to Cecil in December 1943, 'is really a vote of no-confidence in the government of the L.N.U.'[67]

The LNU had declared itself in favour of extensive social reform in the last months before the war, and the war increased that emphasis. The formation of the Churchill Government in May 1940 pushed that tendency even further, perhaps because the presence of Labourities in the Government invited more thoughts about the future, perhaps too because of a lingering suspicion of Churchill on the left. *Headway* tempered its enthusiasm about his leadership and reminded readers that they now had to keep patriotism from degenerating into jingoism and vindictiveness. The Union would have 'great work to do', providing the public with 'a leaven of reason and farsightedness'.[68] Union leaders often returned to this theme, Lytton telling the General Council that someone had to concentrate their thoughts on the future. 'Victory was not enough.'[69]

The Union's long-range planning was in a transitional stage in the summer of 1940. All of the elaborate plans which had been drawn up on the assumption of close Anglo-French co-operation had to be scrapped. There was a lot of talk about an Anglo-American nucleus, but few signs that the Americans would prove willing partners. The Executive set to work on a new policy statement in this interim period. The statement it adopted on 24 October was addressed to economic and social reconstruction as well as maintaining future peace. It said that the League would be needed to solve these problems, but that there should be some changes in the Covenant to facilitate this. Nevertheless, each member would have to be the sole judge of the action it would take in enforcing the Covenant.

This conclusion displeased enthusiastic rank-and file-members who wanted a stronger League to emerge from the war. Above all, they wanted real commitment to social and economic change, and this was lacking in the Executive statement. Their patience wearing thin, members attacked their leaders at the General Council in December. Murray tried to forestall criticism by pointing out that the statement on reconstruction had been brief and tentative because it would be out of place to go into elaborate schemes. Critics were not impressed by this line, one stressing the need to change 'the framework of economic plutocracy', others from the New Commonwealth side pushing for commitment to centralized force. The Council ended on an uncertain note, with no one able to muster enough votes to secure the adoption of significant amendments. The Executive statement on world settlement was provisionally adopted with only minor modifications, but it was clear that nothing had been settled.[69]

Cecil took note of the demands for a policy of social reconstruction but remained uncertain as to how far the LNU should go towards meeting them. He had even less sympathy by early 1941 with the New Commonwealth positions; Davies was 'a fanatic'.[70] He decided to concede just enough to divide and placate the opposition at the next Council in June. He agreed to have the Executive statement on 'World Settlement After the War' go into more detail on the economic side, but he gave nothing substantial away to the New Commonwealth people. This worked. 'World Settlement' was adopted in June, on the understanding 'that further opportunity will be afforded of considering the subjects of Social and Economic Reconstruction, Colonial Policy, peaceful Change, Minorities, and Education in World Citizenship'.[71]

The 'World Settlement' statement was at last issued, but it seemed to be such a patchwork of proposals designed to satisfy one faction or another that it left no one happy. Where the Union espoused an international air force as a gesture to the New Commonwealth, it antagonized others who felt the idea was utopian or that it had not been worked out sufficiently.[72] Where it brought out a colonial report, it aroused the vehement opposition of Conservatives who resented the way it omitted the 'good side' of imperialism or attributed motives of gain or ambition to Britain in Africa.[73] Sir Rowland Evans published an attack on the LNU's 'sloppy internationalism', which said that the various proposals in the 'World Settlement' statement did not fit together. The alternative to an 'inflexible' League statement, Evans suggested, was Anglo-American co-operation.[74]

American co-operation was being touted as an alternative to the League well before Pearl Harbor, and the Union tried to counter it. Lytton argued in a rebuttal to Evans that 'if anyone thinks that the U.S.A. is going to support us in the protection of British interests he is living in a fool's paradise'. Moreover, Anglo-American co-operation would not provide peace to Europe; it was no alternative to a new European alignment.[75] Yet the LNU wanted co-operation with the United States, bringing Americans into the London International Assembly and becoming the British affiliate of the International Free World Association at the urging of Clark Eichelberger of the American League of Nations Association.[76] The Atlantic Charter, and then the Anglo-American Agreement of 23 February 1942, committed the United States to internationalism and made it easier to talk about America as a supporter of world authority rather than as an alternate choice.

The entry of the United States into the war strengthened the resolve of LNU leaders not to get committed to ideas about a future world organization or reconstruction which might frighten Americans away. Cecil agreed with Murray in June 1942 'that a lot of these people are talking great nonsense about all these things that are going to happen after the war, and will mix it up with international affairs'. Cecil even began to wonder if social reform might not lead 'to such violent disputes between different countries as to be more a danger than a support for peace'.[77]

The June 1942 General Council was not to be cheated out of a strong resolution aimed at social reform. It was bolstered by recent statements by members of the Government, and called for action now to realize the aims expressed in those remarks.[78] Cecil did not try to stem this tide at the Council, but at the next Executive session he argued that the Union had no business promoting social reform, and he pushed for the creation of a small committee to determine what was and what was not in the Union's province.[79] Murray tried to head off this manœuvre, regaling Cecil with stories about his own local branch to show that it would be dangerous to ignore rank-and-file sentiment.[80] But Cecil continued to fulminate about the 'strictly international' aims of the LNU.[81] Murray tried again, in his unfailingly diplomatic way. 'Our statement of policy, though very good and careful', was 'a little lacking in power of appeal.' Unfortunately 'our people seem to be intimidated by the left-wing, and keep on talking as if economic distress was the cause, or a principal cause, of war'.[82]

Cecil's diehard positions on reconstruction and on co-operation with other internationalist societies weakened his grip on the Executive Committee, where there was talk about the need to bring in new people able to represent the 'under 30's' age group.[83] The Executive was prodded into action by the initiatives of local LNU organizations. The Tyne District Council, for instance, joined the Tyneside Federal Union in joint meetings and in issuing a joint statement on the need ultimately for a democratic world state. A majority of the Executive, following the lead of Zilliacus and Sir George Young, then agreed to joint discussions with the Federal Union to consider how they might co-operate in the future.[84]

Zilliacus and his faction on the Executive (James MacDonald, Alan Thomas, Young on some issues) proposed a direct way to establish the LNU's right to deal with domestic reconstruction issues. They referred to the Beveridge Report on social security of November 1942, which raised some international questions. The report which Zilliacus and Young prepared for the Executive urged the Government to act as soon as possible to secure a common economic policy between states under an international authority. 'Underlying all our economic policies and commitments is the need for a new social attitude towards economic problems.'[85]

Cecil was reduced to fighting a rearguard action on the Executive, for so long his instrument, to prevent the adoption of this report. He talked about resignation, but this was no longer a very potent threat except perhaps to Murray who came back into line behind him. At times he left the narrower issue of what should properly concern the LNU and confessed to 'an obstinate doubt whether you can rid of poverty by taking from the rich and giving to the poor'.[86] He circulated an amendment of the draft report which insisted that the LNU should stick to its job, the maintenance of peace on the lines of the Covenant, and that 'any teaching which implies the contrary is a grave danger to peace'.[87]

Zilliacus countered with a 'Draft compromise amendment' which maintained that nations would be better at peace-keeping if they organized their common economic interests and pledged themselves to common social purposes. This was not meant to be taken as a substitute for international political organization to prevent aggression.[88] Zilliacus won the point. A final draft of the reconstruction report, with amendments along the lines he suggested, passed the Executive on 1 April 1943. Cecil spoke against it at the June Council, and when that failed to achieve anything, he tried to find consolation in the thought that it was a 'recommendation' and not a 'decision' of the LNU to back the statement.[89] Too many factors had been working against him on the reconstruction issue: popular sentiment (The National Peace Council, after holding its wartime conferences, responded to public pressure with an even stronger 'National Petition for a Constructive Peace')[90] the conjunction of leftist and Federal Unionist interests, and the sentiment of a few members of the

Executive (Lady Hall, for instance) with pacifist leanings that sweeping economic reform might create such binding international ties that aggression would become less possible.[91]

Zilliacus turned next to securing commitment to a draft pact for the future international authority. Here, in championing something approximating the Federal Union programme, he did not have as strong a hand to play as on reconstruction. Zilliacus had enough support to keep Cecil and Murray worried in the autumn of 1943, including the backing of the London Regional Federation (which Murray then said was 'very unrepresentative' and anxious to 'bait' the Executive).[92] Murray speculated as to whether Zilliacus might be preparing to rig a Council meeting as Mosley had tried to do once in the early years.[93] Cecil tried to persuade Noel-Baker to appear before the Council, to persuade his fellow Labourites that the Executive were not 'a set of reactionaries . . . trying to resist enlightenment as typified by Zilly!'[94]

The Moscow Declaration of 30 October 1943, altered the whole context of the discussion about a future international authority. Before it, the way was open for far-reaching proposals about the shape of the post-war world. However, once the Allies, with the tides of war in their favour, issued their 'Declaration of Four Nations on General Security' and foreshadowed the character of a new organization, this changed. It specified in Article 4 the need to establish 'a general international organization based on the principle of the sovereign equality of all peace-loving States, and open to membership by all such States, large and small, for the maintenance of international peace and security'.

Even before the Moscow Conference Zilliacus did not have the votes on the Executive to push through his Draft Pact, with its plans for a world parliament. Murray was willing to give the pact a modified endorsement as a desirable set of goals for the (very) distant future.[95] After Moscow there was no need to worry about placating the Zilliacus faction; the rug had been pulled out from under them.

At Cecil's instigation, the LNU made the Moscow Declaration the basis for all its propaganda. Its new posters and stationery were now headed 'In support of the Moscow Four Power Declaration, Relief and Reconstruction, and the Atlantic Charter'.[96] Cecil could present his version of the Draft Pact for the Future International Authority to the Council in December 1943 as a responsible illustration of what the Moscow Conference had been aiming for. This time he got the Council's support. Zilliacus pleaded his case well, reminding Council members, who still suspected that wartime promises might be broken once peace came, that Cecil's (unlike his own) did not oblige states to co-operate on economic or social policy or other questions. He was able to salvage something. His 'minority' report was to be circulated to interested branches and the Executive was asked to give it further consideration.[97]

Cecil felt vindicated when he led the LNU deputation to the Foreign Office to present his Draft Pact on 13 January 1944. Eden did not assent in detail to the Union's proposals, but he was quite receptive. The only specific criticism he made, reflecting the terms of the Moscow Declaration, was that it had not given sufficient emphasis to the position of the great powers. When Cecil made a point of saying that social and economic reform must follow and not precede political organization, Eden agreed.[98]

The advocates of extensive change could still carp. Davies issued a twenty-six-page set of 'Comments' on the LNU Draft Pact, which criticized it for perpetuating the Covenant system responsible for the war. 'Voluntary societies [should] educate the peoples, not the vested interests' he argued. 'It is no answer to say that the governments . . . would refuse to consider a more radical plan.'[99] But the LNU leadership could take all this in its stride in the spring of 1944 and even initiate new proposals for co-operation with other internationalist groups—in support of the Moscow Declaration, of course. As Noel-Baker said to Cecil in June, 'New Commonwealth will probably be very reasonable now and the Federal Unionists have lost all their momentum already.'[100]

In promoting its Draft Pact, the Union did not try to contradict the critics who said the plan was a rehash of the Covenant. It argued unashamedly that the essentials of the Covenant had been sound. Certain lessons in the 'great experiment' of the League could not be ignored, however. The essential point was that the powers would now have to be ready to stop aggression by force. The Union incorporated plans for a 'Defence Council' in its Draft Pact to emphasize the duty of the powers to maintain collective security. It also tried to eliminate the 'gap' in the Covenant under which Article 15 had allowed for the possibility of a legal war under certain circumstances by setting a standard of complete peace as an ideal.

Union leaders were ready to encourage superficial changes to make the new world body appear distinct from the League. The name 'League of Nations' was an obvious candidate for change; it arouses a feeling of boredom, Courtney told Cecil in 1943.[101] The Draft Pact dropped it in favour of 'international authority' so as to emphasize, especially to Americans, that something more than a revival of the almost-defunct League was envisaged. The term 'United Nations' was already common, but it referred to the wartime Allies rather than to the future world organization. In the same way the LNU talked about a 'Director General' instead of a 'Secretary General' and tried to allow the new post greater powers than the old.[102]

By 1944 debates on the new world authority did not excite much passion. League supporters debated the familar issue of whether to keep the League's unanimity procedure in voting, for instance—the Draft Pact kept it in modified form—but in quite a subdued way. There was none of the anthusiasm of 1918, the LNU *Newsheet* observed. 'Rose-coloured spectacles are out of fashion. We know that the future will not be easy . . .'[103]

The one debate which did heat up the General Council at the end of 1944 hinged on the question of post-war boundaries in eastern Europe. The Union avoided making any pronouncements on particular frontiers, apart from saying that they should be settled by general agreement after the war. When Russian-Polish differences became aggravated early in 1944 Murray prodded the Executive into reminding the Soviet Union of its earlier pledge under the Atlantic Charter not to seek territorial aggrandizement.[104] The resolution also applauded Britain's position that it would not recognize any territorial changes which took place during the war unless they had the free consent of the concerned parties.[105] Cecil was less concerned about Atlantic Charter morality than Soviet good will, and he felt it was reasonable for the Soviets to maintain that they did not 'feel able to plunge into any fresh negotiations until the Poles have got a thoroughly trustworthy government'.[106] He praised Stalin's 'great moderation' in dealing with Poland and aroused enough support from others on the Executive reluctant to commit the Union to any position on territorial changes to get the resolution tabled two weeks later.[107]

This manoeuvre, and the appearance of an anonymous *Headway* article[108] in June 1944, following Cecil's line, aroused strong resentment in the Union. That the LNU should acquiesce in a vindictive policy against Germany seemed to them preposterous, and the implication of Stalin's proposals was that Germany should cede East Prussia and Upper Silesia to Poland while Poland's eastern regions went to the Soviet Union. The Council could not meet in mid-1944 because of wartime travel restrictions, but when it convened in December it was in an angry mood. The Dean of Chichester led the assault on the eastern European settlement, insisting that if the LNU wanted church support it would have to uphold the Atlantic Charter. LNU leaders defended the Cecil position, but to no avail. The Council went on record against territorial changes which violated Article 2 of the Atlantic Charter.[109]

The preparatory work for the new world organization done at Dumbarton Oaks in late 1944 received a cool reception from the LNU. Cecil had been particularly upset by American policy: Roosevelt seemed to him to be 'ridiculous' in his attitude to De Gaulle and losing his grip generally.[110] Murray shared some of this uneasiness about Britain's 'Big Three' partners; he talked about the Soviets as 'a savage unknown quantity' and the Americans as 'out for economic domination'.[111] The refusal of the Soviets to accept third-party judgements in disputes which directly concerned them aggravated concern on the Executive that things were not shaping up well.

On a whole range of questions Dumbarton Oaks seemed to represent a misstep. The phrase 'United Nations' appeared inappropriate because of its links with the wartime alliance, yet it had been adopted. The Dumbarton Oaks proposals did not include any equivalent to Article 10 of the Covenant, which had pledged members 'to respect and preserve as against external aggression the territorial integrity and existing political independence of all members of the League'. The LNU—while agreeing that it was not desirable to freeze the status quo—still wanted something in the Charter to protect small states. It suggested a modified form of Article 10, omitting the word 'preserve' so as to make the article a general directive rather than a specific understanding.[112] Another troubling omission was a rule of publicity which would promote openness in United Nations diplomacy.

The LNU's main concern about the Dumbarton Oaks proposals was that the organization might become too much of a big power club, so in addition to the reintroduction of Article 10, it suggested other measures for righting the balance in the UN. For instance, it asked for greater flexibility in the appointment of members to the Security Council, with provision for the immediate re-election of non-permanent members. It wanted the General Assembly to retain the right of general discussion on security issues, even on matters dealt with by the Security

Council. In order to lessen big power control of military affairs, the LNU even suggested the creation of an international force, recruited by and under the orders of the organization itself. Pending the establishment of such a force, it wanted national contingent forces available for immediate use by the organization without special consent by the country concerned.[113]

The General Council wanted the new organization to include a guarantee of freedom of speech, worship, and other basic freedoms. Cecil doubted the expediency of this kind of international Bill of Rights, which he thought would have to be either meaningless or insincere.[114] The question of civil liberties presented itself in another, more pressing, form. In one country after another liberated by the Allies, governments were being set up without the consent of the governed. The LNU's discussions had always assumed that hostilies would cease, and then that boundaries and other matters could be discussed. Instead, by early 1945, the war still raged but the 'peacetime' decisions were being made. The Executive worried over this, and asked that all changes be considered temporary until the end of the war, when elections could be held and the Atlantic Charter followed.[115]

Whatever doubts the Dumbarton Oaks proposals might have raised, the LNU took it for granted that it would try to win support for the United Nations just as it had for the League. This dictated a change in name, and because the Union operated under a Royal Charter such a change required Government permission. The Lord President of the Council, Clement Attlee, told the Union that he could not grant a supplementary charter in wartime and that it might be better to let the charter lapse and start again with a new name. The name 'United Nations Association' was selected (after some consideration of 'United Nations Union') and the April 1945 General Council approved the plan.[116]

Plans went ahead for the creation of the United Nations Association in the spring of 1945 without much enthusiasm. However, as news trickled in from the San Francisco Conference, which met from April to June, the situation improved somewhat. The agreement at San Francisco to preface the Charter with a statement of general principles was in line with a recommendation the LNU had sent to Whitehall. The Union felt it deserved some credit not only for this improvement, but also for the extension of the Economic and Social Council's authority and the provisions made for a Trusteeship Council to replace the Permanent Mandates Commission.[117]

There was some hyperbole in these claims of influence although they were not without substance. C. K. Webster, the eminent historian working at the Foreign Office complimented the Union because 'so many of its recommendations had been adopted at San Francisco'.[118] However, neither the LNU nor any other non-governmental group was given much consideration in policy formation by Whitehall at this stage;[119] Cecil, Drummond (now Lord Perth), and others resented this.[120] The reports Courtney sent back to the LNU from San Francisco made it clear that Britain itself was moving further from the centre of the world stage. 'In the League of Nations', she wrote, 'the European countries played a predominant part and France was always a leader. In San Francisco many European countries were not represented at all . . . The emergence of [an] American bloc . . . coincides oddly with the end of the legendary belief in the bloc of the British Commonwealth.'[121] If Britain was to play a lesser role in the UN, then the potential power of British public opinion was diminished accordingly.

The changes made in the Dumbarton Oaks draft at San Francisco were well received at the Union. The modification of the veto right in the Security Council which the smaller powers were able to push through helped overcome the fears which had been aroused about domination by the permanent Council members. Courtney's favourable coverage of the conference's work in *Headway* encouraged a positive Union response. 'The Charter', she wrote, 'is a great document, and if it is loyally supported and honourably worked it may mark the beginning of new developments in human welfare and human freedom.'[122]

The Union did its best to gain support for the Charter in the General Elections of July 1945. However, the collapse of branch organizations in many areas meant that any polling efforts would be more or less token. The questionnaire which the LNU prepared was issued to candidates in 204 English constituencies and to all Welsh and Scottish candidates.[123] It asked:

1. Do you believe that the greatest interest of our country and the world is the preservation of a lasting peace based on freedom, justice and good faith, and that a world organization for peace and security and for the promotion of the social and economic welfare of the peoples is essential for that purpose?
2. In the event of such a world organization being established and H.M. Government becoming a member of it, would you be prepared to support it?
3. Would you also support the International Labor Organization, whether it is incorporated in the world organization or not, in promoting the highest standard of living conditions for all?

4. Do you agree that loyalty to the world organization by this country as a
   Member State is essential to its success and quite consistent with the highest
   national patriotism?[124]

The questionnaire, and Cecil's widely printed letter to the electorate, helped arouse interest in the Charter. If the British public
showed little enthusiasm for it, it also showed almost no hostility.
Only one candidate gave negative answers to the Union's
questions on this 'motherhood' issue.[125]

During July the Foreign Office initiated talks with the Union
to encourage the formation of a society to promote the United
Nations. Gladwyn Jebb, Head of the Reconstruction Department,
had not been in touch with the LNU and did not know that an
effort in this direction was already under way when he launched
this initiative. Professor Webster, who had co-operated with the
Union for years, worked from within the Foreign Office to make
sure that his old colleagues were in charge of the effort to start
the new society. 'Unless the LNU got hold of the name United
Nations' he feared, 'some group of publicists would seize upon it
and in no time have half the Bench of Bishops and other notabilities on their notepaper.' Webster introduced the Union's
Secretary to Jebb, who promised the LNU his full support. He
instructed the Ministry of Information to allow the Union as much
paper as it needed, suggested the publication of popular
pamphlets on the Charters and discussed details of the organization of the UNA.[126]

The plans called for the 50,000 members of the LNU to become
members of the successor organization unless they specifically
declined to join. The entire organizational structure of the Union,
from branches up to officers, would be transferred to the United
Nations Association. Most officers would take over equivalent
positions, although Cecil finally submitted his resignation in July.
The General Council meeting on 6 and 7 September would, as its
last act, approve the arrangements. It was originally expected that
the LNU and UNA would be merged under a new Royal Charter.
However, it was eventually decided to perpetuate the LNU's
existence under its charter to facilitate the handling of bequests
and payments of pensions to former employees.[127]

For all practical purposes the LNU ended its existence on 10
October 1945, when the UNA was launched. It was done with
appropriate fanfare at a meeting in the Royal Albert Hall in
London. The Prime Minister, Eden, Secretary of State Edward
Stettinius, Noel-Baker (then a Minister of State), Cecil and Lytton

were the speakers. Lytton became a Joint President and Acting Chairman of the UNA.[128]

The sequel to this meeting came on 8 April 1946, when the Assembly of the League met for the last time. Cecil was there to proclaim 'The League is dead, Long live the United Nations.'[129] If events had bypassed them, Union leaders could find consolation in the establishment of this new world organization. It confirmed their feeling that things would not have been so bad if their advice had been followed.

Conclusion

LNU leaders often speculated on how history would judge them. They thought that the failure of appeasement and the onset of war demonstrated that their policies had been sound. The establishment of the United Nations confirmed their conviction that a world organization was indispensable. Philip Noel-Baker wrote in 1958 of Cecil and other League supporters that 'history has proved that they were right'.[1]

Historians did not agree. Far from lauding the League movement, they ignored or attacked it. A popular view emerged of pre-war British foreign policy which combined staunch Churchillianism with a condemnation of the League which Churchill did not share. According to this view internationalists were unrealistic, Utopian. Cecil had 'taken Wilsonism seriously to the point of imagining that national policies ought at times to be subservient to the needs of the League'.[2]

The LNU was mentioned in accounts of the inter-war period, but usually in connection with the Peace Ballot and in the context of popular pacifism. Because it advocated disarmament it was sometimes blamed for the state of Britain's defences. Confusion of this kind stemmed from the unwillingness of many writers to distinguish between pacifist unilateralism, the controlled arms limitation which the LNU proposed, and the budget-cutting policies which actually prevailed.

The British Government was occasionally depicted as a prisoner of disarmament doctrine, moving only 'with very profound reluctance' from 'the chimera of total disarmament'. Whitehall's faith was taken to be obvious, proved by falling defence expenditures.[3] Indeed, Corelli Barnett wrote that the collapse of British power was the work of 'a constellation of moralising internationalist cliques' who 'successfully imposed on governments their pretension to represent public opinion at large'. It was the counsel of these leaders (Cecil, Murray, Lothian, Allen, and others), 'intimate, insidious, bigotedly certain, that prevailed', and Britain was disarmed 'materially and spiritually' as a result.[4]

Denunciations of this sort did not normally figure in the scholarly re-evaluations of the pre-war era which appeared in the 1960s and 1970s. Writers reacting against what Donald Watt called the 'sin theory of international relations' were as careful as the anti-appeasers had been cocksure. On the subject of the League, however, there was little to choose between the two schools. F. H. Hinsley, in *Power and the Pursuit of Peace*, dismissed the argument that the League might have succeeded if not for various misfortunes by maintaining. that 'if these particular obstacles to success had not existed, others would have taken their place . . .' The League could not have worked because 'its basic conception is impracticable at any time'.[5] F. S. Northedge was equally emphatic in *The Troubled Giant*. 'The League Council,' he explained, 'had it disposed of its own forces in the conditions of the 1920s, would probably have been either as deadlocked as the UN Security Council after 1945, or would have acted as the policeman of the *status quo*.' British determination to assign real power to the League would presumably have backfired on internationalists because 'the old world', which they repudiated, 'would have been confirmed'.[6] The League could not or at least should not have succeeded, and its supporters were fortunate not to have had their way.

Leonard Woolf tried to rebut many of these arguments when they were first advanced by E. H. Carr in 1940. It was not accurate, Woolf said, to imply that the League could not have dealt with conflict. The essence of the League idea was a recognition that the interests of states do conflict. Nor was it convincing to argue that a policy was Utopian simply because it failed, and that the League's failure proved that it was Utopian.[7] Woolf's comments still apply to those who later discovered in inter-war history a conclusive demonstration that a sanctions policy can never work.

We can grant that collective security was no panacea, yet recognize its value in certain situations. It does not follow that because the League could not do everything its supporters wanted, it could not do anything at all. Moreover, the Union never relied on sanctions as a cure-all. In the 1920s particularly, it also emphasized conciliation.

Britain's consistent foreign policy aim of preventing the emergence of an all-powerful state on the continent accorded well with the League ideal in the 1930s. If a sanctions policy against Italy had been followed resolutely, Geneva might have become a rallying point. Churchill, at odds with the LNU over Ethiopia and other things, came round to the view that the 'war could easily have been prevented if the League of Nations had been used with courage and loyalty by the associated nations. Even in 1933 and 1936 there was a chance, by making an armed Grand Alliance under the aegis of the League, to hold in subjection the rising furies in Germany or at the very least to enter into armed conflict on terms more favourable than those eventually forced upon us'.[8]

Could a collective security policy have worked then? Perhaps, but despite the LNU's campaigning it was not tried. The impact of League opinion on Whitehall was sometimes significant: in 1926, for instance, in shaping policy towards German admission to the League; in 1933, with Britain's arms embargo in the Far Eastern crisis; and in 1935 in leading to British sanctions against Italy. At other times the Government considered the Union's views. But the LNU rarely had its way.

We should remind ourselves that while Cecil and Murray may have been, as A. J. P. Taylor wrote, 'men of the Establishment, not Dissenters',[9] they were not in the foreign policy-making establishment that mattered. Their cause, the League, was dimly regarded by Hankey and other leading figures in power.

The hostility was most obvious in the service departments. Initially military leaders objected because they assumed that the adoption of the Covenant would force disarmament on them while requiring extensive commitments. Even though the Ten-Year Rule, which restricted their budgets from 1919 to 1932, and the Washington naval treaties of 1922, were not the work of the League, service opposition persisted. It undermined the internationalist case when the Draft Treaty of Mutual Assistance was considered for adoption in 1923,[10] and again during the Ethiopian conflict in 1935.

When the Foreign Secretary tried to impose sanctions against Italy he had to contend with service chiefs who were, he found, 'the worst pacifists and defeatists in the country'.[11] One reason for their foot-dragging emerged in a letter which Admiral Chatfield, the First Sea Lord, wrote during the crisis. Confessing his 'mixed feelings' about fighting a 'bumptious' Italy, Chatfield hoped 'the Geneva Pacifists will fail to get unanimity and the League will break up'.[12]

With this kind of opposition the League remained a peripheral factor in British policy-making. One scholar concluded after a study of the archives for the early 1920s that British Governments made no sacrifices for the League. 'Doubting whether sanctions could ever be enforced, they refused to undertake any more general obligations; but they did not share their doubts with the electorate until the attempt had been made.'[13] Neville Chamberlain expressed those doubts, but apart from that the conclusion is sound for the thirties as well as the twenties. Foreign policy was, as Maurice Cowling noted, usually 'presented in terms which the League of Nations Union would approve'.[14] It was not, however, a policy based on collective security.

The results of saying one thing and doing another were unfortunate. British prestige was tied to the League and when sanctions against Italy failed, it was a defeat for Britain. Sir Warren Fisher observed that the 'parade of force in the eastern Mediterranean, so far from impressing others, has merely made a laughing-stock of ourselves'.[15]

The League of Nations Union cannot be held accountable for the failures of the 1930s, then, but it can be faulted for the notions the public had about the League. Cecil admitted that he should have emphasized in the early days that if you want peace, you must be prepared to fight for it. The LNU did not offer the kind of rigorous critique of the League mechanism or of the principle of collective security that might have equipped the British public to face the challenges of the 1930s with a sober, realistic perspective.

Union leaders failed, not only in the sense that the organization they supported collapsed or the war they sought to prevent came. Their failure was in a sense complete, for they had been determined to achieve broad political appeal and influence, even if other things remained undone. They glossed over the League's inadequacies and submerged all other considerations to building mass support. This tactic could only be justified by results, and these never came.

Notes

Introduction

1. *League of Nations Journal*, Aug. 1919, 275.
2. E. H. Carr, *The Twenty Years' Crisis* (New York, 1939, 1964), 38.
3. HW, Oct. 1945, 3.
4. Murray to Henderson, 18 May 1931, GM.
5. HW Nov. 1930, 215.
6. John Eppstein interview with author, 18 Aug. 1969.
7. Freshwater to Regional Representatives and County Secretaries, 31 Jan. 1934, D.S. 1624, National Council Papers of the LNU NLW 193.
8. A. J. P. Taylor, *The Troublemakers* (Bloomington, 1958), 171.
9. R. B. McCallum, *Public Opinion and the Last Peace* (London, 1944), 146.
10. Iain Macleod, *Neville Chamberlain* (New York, 1962), 181.
11. Stephen Roskill, *Hankey, Man of Secrets*, iii (New York, 1974), 382.
12. Daniel Waley, *British Public Opinion and the Abyssinian War 1935–6* (London, 1975), 94. Waley describes Cecil as one who 'never feared to come forward to press the Union's views', for example. This may have been accurate for the period of the Peace Ballot, but it obscures an important point about Cecil's over-all role in the League movement.

Chapter 1   A New Departure

1. Henry R. Winkler, *The League of Nations Movement in Great Britain 1914–1918* (New Brunwick, N.J., 1952).
2. Martin David Dubin, 'Towards the Concept of Collective Security: the Bryce Group's "Proposals for the Avoidance of War"', *International Organization*, xxiv 1970, 288–318, 289.
3. Bryce.was an eminent historian and the former Ambassador to the United States. Others in the group were Willoughby Dickinson, the Liberal MP who became head of the League of Nations Society, J. A. Hobson, the economist, Graham Wallas, the sociologist, Arthur Ponsonby, Liberal MP, E. Richard Cross.
4. Bryce to C. Eliot, 9 Feb. 1915, Copy, fo. 12, USA 2, Bryce Papers, Bodleian Library, Oxford.
5. Dubin, 'Towards the Concept . . .', 298.
6. Marvin Swartz, *The Union of Democratic Control in British Politics During the First World War* (Oxford, 1971), 97. Ponsonby, Norman Angell, the journalist, and Hobson were in both groups.
7. Bryce to C. Elliot, 9 Feb. 1915, loc. cit.
8. Swartz, *The Union. . .*, 97.
9. Circular letter, F. N. Keen to Graham Wallas, 19 May 1915, Box 5, Wallas Papers, British Library of Political and Economic Science.
10. G. Lowes Dickinson to Murray, 20 December 1916, as in Keith Robbins, 'Lord Bryce and the First World War', *The Historical Journal*, x, 2, 1967, 225–77, 270.
11. Ibid. 271.
12. Harold Owen, *Disloyalty: the Blight of Pacifism* (London, 1918).

13. Ronald Burrows to Graham Wallas, 5 Oct. 1917, Box 6, Wallas Papers. Others involved in New Europe were Ramsey Muir, Ernest Barker, Wickham Steed, and A. E. Zimmern.

14. League of Free Nations Association Organization Committee, 12 July 1918, iii, 1. Papers of the LNU.

15. W. Dickinson to Arthur Steel-Maitland, 4 July 1918; A. Williams to Steel-Maitland, 5 Sept. 1918, 90 (1), Sir Arthur Steel-Maitland Papers, Scottish Record Office, Edinburgh.

16. G. L. Dickinson to W. H. Dickinson, 4 June 1918, c.403, W. H. Dickinson Papers, Bodleian Library, Oxford.

17. Dickinson to Mrs R. C. Trevelyan, 12 Oct. 1918, as in E. M. Forster, *Goldsworthy Lowes Dickinson* (New York, 1934), 170.

18. 21YR i. 28.

19. League of Free Nations Association Executive Committee, 16 July, 1918, ii, 1, LNU.

20. In her *Return Passage* (London, 1953), Violet Markham says she could not remember any meeting 'where the atmosphere was more full of emotion'. (165).

21. 'Joint Meeting of Representatives of the League of Nations Society and the League of Free Nations Association to Consider Amalgamation, Held at National Liberal Club', 10 Oct. 1918, GM.

22. EC, 9 Nov. 1918, ii. 2, LNU.

23. LNU Pamphlet, *The League of Nations Union* (London, 1919), 3.

24. Winkler, *League Movement . . .*, 77.

25. W. Dickinson to Judge Wadhams, 13 Aug. 1918, Box 12, League to Enforce Peace Papers, Houghton Library, Cambridge, Massachusetts.

26. Percy to Steel-Maitland, 4 Mar. 1919, 90(1), Steel-Maitland Papers.

27. Maxwell Garnett, 'The Psychology of Patriotism and the Aims of the League of Nations Associations', *The Problems of Peace* (London, 1927), 326–51, 351.

28. Sheele to Steel-Maitland, 26 Nov. 1918, 90(1), Steel-Maitland Papers.

29. W. Dickinson, 'Report to LNU, Conference of Associated Societies at Brussels', 1–3 Dec. 1919, Box 13, League to Enforce Peace Papers.

30. Wilson to T. Marburg, copy, 6 May 1918, fo. 320, USA 8, Bryce Papers.

31. G. Murray, 'Notes about Lord Grey', 30 Aug. 1935, GM.

32. 21YR iii. 5–6.

33. Ibid. 7.

34. EC 13 Jan. 1919, ii. 2, LNU; Cecil to Murray, 4 Jan. 1919, GM.

35. 'Notes by Sir Eyre Crowe on Lord R. Cecil's Proposals for the Maintenance of Future Peace', 12 Oct. 1916, Cabinet Paper GT 404a, CAB 24/10; Discussed by Winkler, *League Movement . . .*, 231–2, and by George Egerton, 'The Lloyd George Government and the Creation of the League of Nations', *American Historical Review*, lxxix. 2, April. 1974, 419–44, 424–5.

36. Egerton, 'Lloyd George . . .', 443.

37. Ibid. 438–42, for a discussion of these events. Egerton concludes that 31 Jan. 1919, marked a point of no return for Britain's League plans and that the Government 'found itself in fundamental disagreement with the type of organization that emerged from the Paris Peace Conference'.

38. 37A CAB 27/626, FP(36) 2, 23 Dec. 1918, PRO.

39. Cecil to Balfour, 5 Dec. 1924, 51071, RC. C. P. Scott Diary, 21–22 Feb. 1919, 50905 C. P. Scott Papers, British Library.

40. Douglas Goldring, *Pacifists in Peace and War* (London, 1932), 46.

41. *The League*, Dec. 1919, 76–8.

42. There were forty signatories to the letter which appeared in several newspapers. *League of Nations Journal*, June 1919, 199–200.

43. Hobhouse to Scott, 12 May 1919, in Trevor Wilson, ed., *The Political Diaries of C. P. Scott 1911–1928* (London, 1970), 374.

44. Bryce to Scott, ibid. 380.

45. H. G. Wells, *Experiment in Autobiography* (New York, 1934), 611.

46. Forster, *Goldsworthy . . .*, 172.
47. *League of Nations Journal*, July 1919, 263.
48. Ibid. 234.
49. The Executive followed Cecil's advice. EC 13 June 1919, 90(1) Steel-Maitland Papers.
50. 'Report of the Special Committee on Reorganization', 24 July 1919, c.404, 3, W. Dickinson Papers.
51. *The Covenant*, May 1919, 45–57, 10–13.
52. *League of Nations Journal*, Sept. 1919, 317.
53. Ibid., July 1919, 235.
54. Ponsonby to Murray, 21 and 25 Nov. 1922, Folder 'L of N after 1921 to 1925', GM.
55. Drummond to Balfour, 29 June 1921, P33, Dossier 3, 21, Drummond Papers, United Nations Library, Geneva.
56. *League of Nations Journal*, Aug. 1919, 274–6.
57. Gilbert Murray, *The Foreign Policy of Sir Edward Grey* (Oxford, 1915).
58. Bertrand Russell, *The Policy of the Entente* (London, 1916), 2.
59. The *New York Times* article appeared on 7 Feb. 1918. Murray to Balfour, 25 Mar. 1918; Ian Malcolm to Murray, 23 Mar. 1918, GM.
60. H. Wilson Harris, *Life So Far* (London, 1954), 201.
61. Murray to Lady Gladstone, 21 Dec. 1923, copy; Gladstone to Murray, 27 Dec. 1923, GM.
62. S. de Madariaga, 'Gilbert Murray and the League', 176–97 in Gilbert Murray, *An Unfinished Autobiography* (London, 1960).
63. Murray to Cecil, 29 Apr. 1938, 51133 RC.
64. *The League*, Oct. 1919, 10–11.
65. LNU offices were at 22 Buckingham Gate until early 1920, when they were moved to 15 Grosvenor Crescent. EC 9 Apr. 1919, c.404, W. Dickinson Papers.
66. W. Dickinson to Murray, 7 Mar. 1919, c.403, ibid.
67. Murray to W. Dickinson, 24 Mar. 1919, c.403, ibid.
68. W. Dickinson to Murray, 2 Apr. 1919, c.403, ibid.
69. Fisher to Davies, 15 May 1919, Folder 'LNU from Inception', GM.
70. P. Comert to Drummond, 7 May 1920, League Secretariat Papers, United Nations Library, Geneva, 22/4404/357.
71. Drummond to Cecil, 19 May 1920, ibid.
72. *The League*, Jan. 1920, 135–6.
73. LNU *Newsheet*, Spring 1925, 2.
74. LNU, *Today and Tomorrow*, Apr.–May 1920, 5–6.
75. EC 26 Feb. 1919, ii, 2, LNU; Lt.-Col. Fisher to Sir John Taverner, 31 Mar. 1919; Taverner to Fisher, 6 June 1919, Folder 'LNU from Inception', GM; P. Munch, ed., *Les origines et l'oeuvre de la Societé des Nations* (Copenhagen, 1923), 197. Fisher, who arranged the deal, was soon ousted as LNU General Secretary.
76. Kingsley Martin, *Harold Laski* (New York, 1953), 41.
77. LNU *Newsheet*, 'Xmas, 1922', 3.
78. A. C. F. Beales, *The History of Peace* (London, 1931), 318.
79. Charles Chatfield discusses the changing definition of pacifism in *For Peace and Justice* (Knoxville, 1971), 4. Chamberlain letter, 22 May 1938, in Keith Middlemas and John Barnes, *Baldwin* (London, 1969), 239.
80. Bryce to Lowell, 24 Jan. 1921, fo. 217, Bryce Papers.
81. Cecil to Col. Heaton-Ellis, Apr. 1922, 7, 51075 RC.

Chapter II The Early 1920s

1. Cecil to Bryce, 19 July 1920, UB 58, Bryce Papers; *Today and Tomorrow*, Nov.–Dec. 1920, 297.
2. Lloyd George to Chamberlain, 10 Aug. 1921, F/7/4/22, David Lloyd George Papers, Beaverbrook Library, London.

3. Michael G. Fry, *Illusions of Security* (Toronto, 1972), 8.
4. Lord Shaw of Dumfermline was President of the League of Nations Society during the war. These comments of his were in the *League of Nations Journal*, Jan. 1919, 1.
5. Cecil to the Prime Minister, 4 Apr. 1919, F/6/6/25; 10 Apr. 1919, F/6/6/33, Lloyd George Papers. G. M. Trevelyan, *Grey of Falloden* (London, 1937), 351.
6. Grey to Murray, 24 Feb. 1919, GM; Lowell to Garnett, 18 Nov. 1920, Box 13, League to Enforce Peace Papers.
7. *Today and Tomorrow*, Apr.–May 1920, 9.
8. Ibid. Dec. 1920, 339.
9. HW June 1923, 345.
10. T. Wilson, *Scott Diaries . . .*, 370.
11. Bryce to Henry White, 30 Sept. 1919, fo. 182; Bryce to Rhodes, 2 Oct. 1919, fol. 184 USA 23, Bryce Papers.
12. Sondra Herman, *Eleven Against War* (Stanford, 1969), 48.
13. Richard Ullman, *The Anglo-Soviet Accord* (Princeton, 1972), iii. 54. The consignment which stevedores refused to load on to the *Jolly George* was scheduled to be the last in a series of shipments.
14. Ibid. 57–8; EC 13 May 1920, ii. 2, LNU.
15. House of Commons, Debates, cols. 1701–3, as in ibid. 58–9.
16. Duff Cooper, *Old Men Forget* (New York, 1954), 157.
17. *Today and Tomorrow*, June–July 1920, 87.
18. HW Jan. 1921, 1.
19. LNU *Newsheet*, 'Xmas, 1922', 2.
20. *Today and Tomorrow*, May–June 1920, 49; June–July 1920, 119. The Council of Ambassadors was an informal mechanism for consultation by the Ambassadors of the four major Allied powers in Paris.
21. Ibid. Dec. 1920, 348.
22. Robert Vogel, *A Breviate of Diplomatic Blue Books* (Montreal, 1963), xvi–xvii.
23. Murray to Wallas, 30 Nov. 1931, Box 7, Wallas Papers.
24. HW Feb. 1921, 17.
25. Gerda Richards Crosby, *Disarmament and Peace in British Politics* (Cambridge, Mass., 1957), 41, 87, 96.
26. Viscount Esher, *The Captains and the Kings Depart*, ii. (New York, 1938), 244.
27. EC 22 Mar. 1921, ii. 3, LNU.
28. Committee on Limitation of Armaments, 14 June 1921, iv. 43, LNU.
29. Murray to Balfour, 13 July 1922, GM.
30. HW Nov. 1921, 21–2.
31. HW Dec. 1921, 52.
32. LNU Pamphlet No. 76, 'A Speech by Lord Robert Cecil on a League of Nations Policy', (London, 1922), 8.
33. Management Committee, 12 Jan. 1922, iii. LNU.
34. HW May 1922, 84.
35. LNU Pamphlet No. 76 . . ., 10.
36. Balfour to Cecil, 4 June 1923, 51071 RC.
37. Balfour to Fisher, 23 July 1923, H. A. L. Fisher Papers, Bodleian Library, Oxford.
38. Fisher-Williams to Murray, 12 Aug. 1920, Box 'XX', GM.
39. Bonham Carter to Garnett, 10 Aug. 1923, GM.
40. Murray wrote that Cecil 'with difficulty dragged the whole Executive' to take this step. Murray to Wallas, 15 Apr. 1922, Box 7, Wallas Papers: EC 2 Mar. 1922, ii. 4, LNU.
41. EC Feb. 1922, ii. 4, LNU.
42. 'Report of the Basis Sub-committee to the Executive Committee', 28 Feb. 1919, 90(1) Steel-Maitland Papers.
43. League of Nations. Temporary Mixed Commission on Armaments. *Report*, 7 Sept. 1922.
44. Cecil to Baker, 22 Mar. 1924, 51106 RC.

45. EC 16 Mar. 1922, Annex A, 'Draft Skeleton Disarmament Treaty', ii. 4, LNU.
46. Cecil to Hankey, 15 Dec. 1922, 51088 RC.
47. The Chanak crisis, when Britain almost blundered into a war between Greece and Turkey, was doubly irritating to Leaguers because its solution was entrusted to an *ad hoc* conference of the powers and not to the League.
48. Anne Orde, *Great Britain and International Security, 1920–1926* (London, 1978), 39, on service opposition to the Draft Treaty.
49. Helen M. Swanwick, *Builders of Peace* (London, 1924) on UDC opposition to the treaty. HW July 1924, 133.
50. EC 11 and 18 Jan. 1923, ii. 4–5, LNU.
51. HW Feb. 1923, 267.
52. EC Jan. 1923, 'Reparations and the League of Nations,' ii. 5, LNU.
53. EC 15 Feb. 1923, ii. 5, LNU.
54. Murray to Cecil, 7 Feb. 1923, 51132 RC.
55. EC 22 Feb.–1 Mar. 1923, ii. 5, LNU.
56. HW Mar. 1923, 282.
57. EC 20 Mar. 1923, ii. 5, LNU.
58. EC 3 May 1923, ii. 5, LNU.
59. HW Mar. 1923, 284; July 1923, 365.
60. Baker to Murray, 31 Oct. 1923, GM.
61. Murray to Cecil, 13 Nov. 1923; Cecil to Murray, 16 and 18 Nov. 1925, Murray to Cecil, 17 Nov. 1925; Murray to Cecil, 14 Aug. 1927, 51132 RC.
62. Cecil to Curzon, 21 May 1923, 51077 RC.
63. Curzon to Cecil, 14 and 18 June 1923, 51077 RC.
64. Viscount Cecil of Chelwood, *All the Way* (London, 1949), 180.
65. Cecil to Baldwin, 1 Sept. 1923, 51080 RC.
66. HW Oct. 1923, 427.
67. Cecil to Curzon, Telegram 'R'. 5 Sept. 1923, 51104; Cecil to Baldwin, 7 Sept. 1923, 51080 RC.
68. Oswald Mosley, *My Life* (London 1968), 141.
69. Davidson to Cecil, 1 Oct. 1923, 51080 RC.
70. EC 25 Oct. 1923, ii. 5, LNU.
71. LNU Pamphlet No. 125, 'Did the League Fail?' (London, 1923), 6, 11.
72. Management Committee, 11 Dec. 1923, iii. LNU.
73. Murray to Carruthers, 7 June 1931, as in Christopher Thorne, *The Limits of Foreign Policy* (London, 1972), 107 n. 1.
74. Cecil to Murray 30 June 1936, 51132 RC.
75. HW Oct. 1921, 7. This 'committee' was an amorphous group, rather than a regular LNU committee reporting to the Executive. It did have a nine person sub-committee which kept the Executive informed.
76. *National Review*, Mar. 1924, as in Joe Allen Thompson, 'British Conservatives and Collective Security 1918–1928' (Ph.D. dissertation, Stanford U., 1966), 13.

Chapter III   Suggestion is not Opposition: the Mid-1920s

1. HW Jan. 1924, 1.
2. MacDonald to Murray, 9 July 1923, GM.
3. HW Dec. 1923, 472.
4. Murray to Cecil, 21 June 1924, 51132 RC; Rosenberg to Murray, 23 June 1924, GM.
5. Cecil to Harris, 15 Jan. 1923, 51164 RC.
6. Murray to Cecil, 21 June 1924, 51132 RC.
7. Munch, *Les origines . . .*, 204.

8. Garnett to Davies, 9 Oct. 1922, 6, NLW; HW Feb. 1924, 32.
9. HW Aug. 1921, 118.
10. Hugh Cecil to Cecil, 20 Mar. 1922, 51157 RC.
11. HW July 1921, 95.
12. G. N. Barnes proposed the resolution. HW Jan. 1926, 12.
13. HW June 1926, 106.
14. Management Committee, 31 Jan. 1927, SG 1588, iii. LNU.
15. General Council, 22–24 June 1927, i. 2, LNU.
16. Management Committee, 11 Dec. 1923, iii. LNU.
17. LNU *Newsheet*, Winter, 1925, 3.
18. HW July 1924 131.
19. HW May 1926, 83.
20. HW Feb. 1926, 29.
21. LNU *Newsheet*, Aug. 1927, 2.
22. EC 1 Dec. 1926, SG 1505, ii. 8, LNU.
23. EC 13 Dec. 1928, ii. 9, LNU.
24. MacDonald to Cecil, 22 Feb. 1923, 51081 RC.
25. LNU Pamphlet No. 142, 'Draft Treaty of Mutual Assistance' (London, Mar. 1924); Cecil to MacDonald, 26 Feb. 1924, 51081 RC.
26. Hankey to Smuts, 1 Apr. 1924, 4/16, Hankey Papers, Churchill College, Cambridge.
27. Cecil to Prime Minister, 23 June 1924, 51081 RC.
28. Cecil comment on British note to League of Nations on the Treaty of Mutual Assistance, 24 July 1924, GD 193, Box 106, fo. 1, Steel-Maitland Papers.
29. HW Sept. 1924, 164.
30. Cecil to Murray, 15 July 1924, 51132 RC.
31. Murray to Cecil, 5 Sept. 1924, 51132 RC.
32. Hankey to Haldane, 9 Sept. 1924, MS 5916, Haldane Papers, Scottish National Library, Edinburgh.
33. Murray to Cecil, 19 Sept. 1924, 51132 RC.
34. General Council, 18 Nov. 1924, c.13 NLW.
35. HW Nov. 1924, 201.
36. Drummond to Cecil, 27 June 1924, 51110 RC. Drummond was worried about MacDonald's rejection of a proposal for a League Financial Committee to investigate defaults on reparations and about Parmoor's willingness to increase the size of the Council to gain German admission.
37. Cecil to Bridgeman, 22 July 1924, 51164; Cecil to Drummond, 30 June 1924, 51100 RC.
38. HW Dec. 1924, 227.
39. A. Chamberlain to his wife, 5 Nov. 1924, as in Thompson, 'British Conservative . . .', 92.
40. A. Chamberlain to Hills, 5 Aug. 1925, GM; A. Chamberlain to J.E.M., 2 Jan. 1925, Chamberlain Papers FO 800/257 PRO.
41. Cecil to Chamberlain, 17 Nov. 1924, AC 51/41; Cecil to Chamberlain, 21 Nov. 1924, AC 51/45, Chamberlain Papers, Birmingham University Library.
42. EC 20 Nov. 1924, ii. 6, LNU; Murray to Cecil, 20 Nov. 1924, 51132 RC.
43. Chamberlain to Cecil, 19 Nov. 1924, AC 51/42, Chamberlain Papers.
44. Lampson Memo, 6 Jan. 1925, FO 800/257 PRO.
45. Cecil assured Baldwin of his support for the Franco-German pact proposal. Cecil to Baldwin, 16 Mar. 1925, 51080 RC.
46. HW Apr. 1925, 65.
47. HW May 1925, 91.
48. Drummond to Cecil, 16 Apr. 1925, 51110 RC.
49. See, for instance, J. Ramsay MacDonald, 'Protocol and Pact', *Labour Magazine*, iii. 12, Apr. 1925, 531–4.
50. Murray to Cecil, 28 May 1925, 51132 RC.
51. Management Committee, Garnett letter, 15 May 1925, DS 535, iii. LNU.

52. Cecil to Murray, 9 June 1925, 10 June 1925, GM.
53. CAB 23/50, 35 (25), 7 July 1925 PRO.
54. Wilson to Bell, 20 June 1925, AC 52/93, Chamberlain Papers.
55. Cecil to Chamberlain, 23 June 1925, 51078 RC; Chamberlain to Murray, 29 July 1925; Murray and Hills to Chamberlain, 30 July 1925, FO 800/258 PRO.
56. Cecil to Murray, 16 Nov. 1925; Murray to Cecil, 17 Nov. 1925, 51132 RC.
57. Murray to *The Times*, 12 Sept. 1925, 13.
58. Baker to Murray, 30 Oct. 1925, GM.
59. EC 22 Oct. 1925, ii. 7, LNU.
60. Selby to Chamberlain, 4 Feb. 1926, FO 800/259 PRO.
61. Murray to Chamberlain, 11 Feb. 1926, AC 53/495 Chamberlain Papers.
62. EC 2 Feb. 1922, ii. 3, LNU.
63. Churchill to Chamberlain, 6 Feb. 1922. FO 800/259 PRO.
64. Cecil to Chamberlain, 11 Feb. 1926, FO 800/259 PRO.
65. HW June 1926, 111.
66. The comments were by Harold Nicolson, who was perhaps bending over backwards to show that his own early interest in the League was safely over. Central Department Memo, 6 Jan. 1925, FO 800/257, PRO.
67. HW Mar. 1926, 48.
68. Tyrrell to Chamberlain, 11 and 15 Mar. 1926, FO 800/259 PRO.
69. HW Apr. 1926, 71.
70. Ibid.
71. Cecil to Murray, 16 Nov. 1926, 51132 RC.
72. Chamberlain to Buxton, 20 Mar. 1926, FO 800/259 PRO.
73. Chamberlain to Crewe, 31 Dec. 1926, FO 800/259 PRO.
74. Chamberlain's penned reply at foot of memo, Selby to Chamberlain, 4 Feb. 1926, FO 800/259, p. 2, PRO.
75. HW Aug. 1927, 154.
76. HW July 1927, 123.
77. HW Oct. 1927, 191.
78. HW Aug. 1926, 146.
79. Ibid. General Seeley dissented on the last point on regulating war.
80. Cecil to Prime Minister, 'Naval Disarmament', 17 Dec. 1929, 51081 RC.
81. Tom Jones, Whitehall Diary, ii. (London, 1969), 110 n. 1.
82. Cecil to the Prime Minister, 1 Apr. 1927, 51104 RC.
83. David Carlton, 'Great Britain and the Coolidge Naval Disarmament Conference of 1927', *Political Science Quarterly*, Dec. 1968, quotes Cecil to Baker, 29 Aug. 1927, in support of the doctrine of requirements.
84. Cecil to Chamberlain, 24 July 1927, FO 800/261 PRO.
85. Cecil to Baldwin, 9 Aug. 1927, 51080 RC.
86. Chamberlain to Cecil, 14 Aug. 1927, FO 800/261 PRO.
87. Copy of memo on Cecil resignation from Baldwin Papers, vol. 130, 41–5, 26–28/27, for Balfour's comments to this effect. Cambridge University Library. Memo on Cecil's resignation, 8 Aug. 1927, 8/25, Hankey Papers.
88. Cecil to Murray, 2 Sept. 1927, 51132 RC.
89. Murray to Samuel, 3 Sept. 1927, Item 3, A/70, Samuel Papers, House of Lords Record Office.
90. Duff Cooper to Murray, n.d. (Sept. 1927) GM.
91. Murray to Brown, 22 Sept. 1927, GM.
92. Murray to Cecil, 14 Aug. 1927, 51132 RC.
93. There was some uncertainty in the Foreign Office over this letter. Selby wondered if it would help if the private meetings were not held in Geneva! Selby to Grey, 3 Sept. 1927, FO 800/261, PRO.
94. Chamberlain to Tyrrell, 15 Sept. 1927, FO 800/261 PRO.
95. Selby to Grey, 3 Sept. 1927, FO 800/261 PRO.

96. Grey to Selby, 8 Sept. 1927, FO 800/261 PRO.
97. Murray to Samuel, 3 Sept. 1927, Item 3, A/70, Samuel Papers.
98. Murray to Samuel, 12 Sept. 1927, loc. cit.
99. Murray to Samuel, 5 Oct. 1927, Hobhouse to Samuel, 6 Oct. 1927, loc. cit.
100. Samuel to Murray, 7 Oct. 1927, GM; Cecil to Murray, 17 Sept. 1927, GM.
101. Baker to Murray, 6 Sept. 1927, GM. Enclosed 'Memorandum on the Present Need for Propaganda Concerning Disarmament'.
102. Baker to Murray, 21 Sept. 1927, GM. Here Baker hesitated because of his differences with the *New Statesman*.
103. Scott meeting with Cecil, 8 Sept. 1927, 50907, Scott Papers.
104. For the Foreign Office responses to these letters, see W. N. Medlicott, Douglas Dakin, and M. E. Lambert, *Documents on British Foreign Policy 1919–1939*, Ser. Ia, iv. no. 211, (London, 1971), 374–7.
105. General Council, 21 Oct. 1927, i. 2, LNU.
106. Finance Committee, 20 Oct. 1927, c.11, iii. LNU.
107. Cecil to Murray, 9 Nov. 1927, 51132 RC.
108. Cecil to Murray, ? Nov. 1927, GM.
109. Management Committee, 27 Oct. 1927, iii. LNU.
110. HW Jan. 1928, 2.
111. HW Jan. 1928, Supp. i.
112. HW July 1927, 123.
113. Murray to Chamberlain, 13 Jan. 1928, FO 800/262, PRO.
114. Cecil to Murray, 3 Mar. 1928, GM.
115. Cecil memo, 'The League of Nations Union and Disarmament', 23 Mar. 1928, SG 2160a, iv. 37, LNU.
116. HW May 1928, 91.

Chapter IV   The Late 1920s to the Early 1930s

1. HW Oct. 1928, Supp. ii.
2. Murray to Cecil, 5 Oct. 1928, 51132 RC.
3. Penman to Murray, 27 May 1927, GM.
4. General Council, 7 Dec. 1928, i. 2, LNU.
5. Regional Representatives were salaried LNU employees based in the country. There were seven in the 1930s, with none in London or the south-eastern region. SG 2454 'Decentralization', 29 Oct. 1928, Administration Committee, iii. LNU.
6. Some of them—the Earl of Birkenhead, an Honorary Vice-President in 1924, for instance—were not at all restrained in their criticism of the League while in 'office'.
7. Reorganization Sub-committee, 16 Jan. 1930, EC ii. 9, LNU.
8. EC 4 Dec. 1930, ii. 10, LNU.
9. Lieut.-Gen. Sir Alexander Gordon *et al.*, 'The League of Nations Union', 1 Jan. 1931, K9:25–26; Burn memo on LNU, 8, K90:21, NA.
10. Branches Committee, 26 Feb. 1931, iv. 3, LNU.
11. 'Composition of the Executive', EC ii. 17, LNU. Courtney Murray, 3 Nov. 1931, GM.
12. Cecil to Murray, 20 Nov. 1934, 51132 RC.
13. Finance Committee, 22 Apr. 1931, 22 July 1931, iii. LNU.
14. Barry G. Buzan, 'The British Peace Movement from 1919 to 1939' (Ph.D. thesis, University of London, 1973), 40, 41.
15. LNU membership dues were on a sliding scale, with the minimum 6*d*. fee providing no benefit to the organization. The average subscription in 1924, for instance, was just over 2*s*. of which the branches got 40 per cent, literature to the member 40 per cent and Grosvenor Crescent 20 per cent. Finance Committee, 12 Oct. 1924, iii. LNU.
16. Fisher Report, Appeals Committee, iv. 2, LNU. Fisher had some success with this

tactic, but his successor, W. J. Hawkey, did less well in the late 1930s in his efforts to block the International Peace Campaign. However, in 1938 the LNU contributions were still unbalanced, with five sources accounting for £9,000 of the Union's £46,749 income. In fact the contribution to headquarters from the branches fell from 52.5 per cent in 1930 to 46 per cent in 1938, so the need for wealthy outside supporters was greater than ever.

17. Drummond to Cecil, 24 Apr. 1928, 51111 RC.
18. HW July 1928, 123.
19. Bartlett to Cecil, 9 Aug. 1923, 51096 RC.
20. Cecil to Drummond, 27 Apr. 1928, 51111 RC.
21. Murray to Henderson, 20 June 1930, Henderson Papers, FO 800/284 PRO.
22. Madariaga, *Gilbert Murray . . .*, 184.
23. HW Oct. 1928, 1919.
24. Chamberlain to Murray, 17 Aug. 1935, GM.
25. Robert Ferrell, *Peace in their Time* (New Haven, 1952), 125.
26. Cecil to Balfour of Burleigh, 2 Jan. 1928, 51166 RC.
27. EC 5 Nov. 1928, SG 2462, ii. 9, LNU.
28. Lord Robert Cecil, *The Moral Basis of the League of Nations* (London, 1923), 26.
29. Revision of the Covenant Committee, 15 June 1927, iv. 66, LNU.
30. Ibid., 13 July 1927.
31. Murray to Lloyd George, 8 Mar. 1928, G/4/1/1; Lloyd George to Murray, 13 Mar. 1928, G/4/1/2; Cecil to Lloyd George, 21 Mar. 1928, G/41/4, Lloyd George Papers.
32. Garnett to Kerr, 29 Mar. 1928, 228, Lothian Papers, Scottish Record Office, Edinburgh.
33. 'The Kellogg Proposals', DS 910A, 25 May 1928, 124, NLW.
34. R. Cecil, 'The American Peace Proposals and the British Reply', 7 July 1928, as in J. G. Thayer, *Selected Articles on the Pact of Paris* (New York, 1929), 223.
35. HW June 1928, 111.
36. Noel-Buxton to Cecil, 6 July 1928; Cecil to Noel-Buxton, 9 July 1928, 51140 RC.
37. HW Aug. 1928, 151.
38. General Council, 7 Dec. 1928, i. 2, LNU.
39. Kerr to Cecil, 22 Jan. 1929, Lothian Papers 229; P. Kerr and Noel-Baker, 'Amendments to the Covenant which are necessary to bring it into harmony with the Pact of Paris for the Renunciation of War', 21 Feb. 1929, Lothian Papers 117, 69.
40. EC, 14 Mar. 1929, ii. 9, LNU. Memorandum 'The Pact of Paris', 12 Mar. 1929, 47–8, Lothian Papers 118. Revision of the Covenant Committee, 7 Mar. 1929, iv. 66, LNU.
41. Kerr to Cecil, 8 Mar. 1929, Lothian Papers 239.
42. Cecil to Kerr, 27 Feb. 1930, 51107 RC.
43. Fisher Williams to Murray, 4 June, 1930, GM.
44. EC, 22 May 1930, SG 2439, 124, NLW.
45. Jones, *Whitehall . . .*, 11 Dec. 1928, 162.
46. Keith Robbins, *Sir Edward Grey* (London, 1971), 360.
47. Robert Rhodes James, *Churchill, A Study in Failure* (New York, 1970), 203.
48. Snowden to MacDonald, 27 Sept. 1930, as in David Carlton, *MacDonald versus Henderson* (London, 1970), 19.
49. Hugh Dalton, *Call Back Yesterday* (London, 1953), 222.
50. Baker to Cecil, 1 Aug. 1929; Cecil to Baker, 9 May 1930, 51107 RC.
51. Hankey to Halifax, 22 Jan. 1940, FO 800/321, Halifax Private Papers, PRO.
52. Cecil to Baker, 9 May 1930, 51107 RC.
53. Thorne, *Limits . . .*, 109 n. 2.
54. Murray to Cecil, 5 Dec. 1933, 51132 RC.
55. William MacDougall, *Janus: the Conquest of War* (London, 1927), 122ff.
56. HW Aug. 1929, 12.
57. General Council, 27–29, June 1929, i. 2, LNU.
58. HW Nov. 1929, 211.
59. EC 6 Mar. 1930, ii. 10, LNU.

60. General Council, 'Statement upon International Policy', 27 June 1930, i. 2, LNU.
61. HW Aug. 1930, 145–6.
62. MacDonald to Cecil, 13 Aug. 1930, 51080 RC.
63. Cecil to MacDonald, 18 Aug. 1930, 51080 RC.
64. Murray to Cecil, 11 and 17 Oct. 1930, 51132 RC.
65. Cecil to Murray, 30 Mar. 1931, GM.
66. 21YR chap. 3, 26; 'Policy of the LNU for a Disarmament Campaign', 1931, 124, NLW.
67. In his memoirs Liddell Hart mentions that he tried out his ideas on an LNU meeting. *The Memoirs of Captain Liddell Hart* (London, 1965), i. 184.
68. HW Apr. 1931, Supp. ii.
69. 'International Disarmament: Activity of the League of Nations Union with a view to assuring success of the World Disarmament Conference March 1–31, 1931', 41, International Federation of League of Nations Societies Papers, United Nations Library, Geneva.
70. Cecil to Butler, 17 Mar. 1931, 80627, Carnegie Endowment Papers; Butler to Cecil, 8 May 1931, Carnegie Endowment Papers, Columbia University, New York.
71. HW June, 1931, 102.
72. HW Aug. 1931, 146.
73. HW Oct. 1931, 183.
74. 'Comments on Sir Norman Angell's Paper', Nov. 1931, K8:17, NA.
75. Louis R. Bisceglia, 'Norman Angell: Knighthood to Nobel Prize, 1931 to 1935' (Ph.D. dissertation, Ball State University, 1967), 134.
76. Murray to Baldwin, 29 June 1930, GM.
77. Murray to Bartlett, 18 Aug. 1930, GM; Murray to Cecil, 11 Oct. 1930, 51132 RC.
78. Cecil to Murrary, 15 Oct. 1930, 51132 RC.
79. EC 24 Sept. 1931, ii. 10, LNU.
80. HW Oct. 1931, 194.

Chapter V   The Manchurian Crisis

1. Churchill to Chamberlain, 6 Feb. 1926, FO 800/259 PRO.
2. 21YR chap. iii. 29–30.
3. R. Bassett, *Democracy and Foreign Policy* (London, 1952) and Thorne, *Limits . . .*, devote considerable attention to the LNU.
4. A. L. Rowse, *The End of an Epoch* (London, 1948), 50.
5. HW Apr. 1930, 72.
6. HW Jan. 1930, 9.
7. HW Feb. 1931, 27.
8. Viscount Cecil, *A Great Experiment* (New York, 1941), 225–6.
9. Bassett, *Democracy . . .*, says that 'it is possible that there might have been greater and more severe criticism of the British Government had it not been for the fact that Lord Cecil was the Government's representative on the League Council throughout the first phase'. 15.
10. C. G. Thorne, 'Viscount Cecil, The Government and the Far Eastern Crisis of 1931', *Historical Journal*, xiv. 4, 1971, 812–13.
11. Bisceglia, 'Norman Angell . . .', 4, discusses this.
12. EC 24 Sept. 1931, ii. 11, LNU.
13. HW Nov. 1931, 217.
14. HW Nov. 1932, 204. A year later Lytton said that Japanese and Chinese society members might have tried 'to keep in touch with each other and sought to understand each other's case'.

15. EC 15 Oct. 1931, ii. 11, LNU.
16. Cecil to Murray, 13 Nov. 1931, GM.
17. Thorne points out that Cecil had already explored the idea of using British and other neutral troops in the Far East but that Simon and others had discouraged him. 'Viscount Cecil. . .', 813. Cecil to Murray, 28 Nov. 1931, GM. Cecil to Simon, 23 Nov. 1931, FO 800/285 PRO.
18. Drury-Lowe to Murray, 26 Nov. 1931, Murray to Drury-Lowe, 28 Nov. 1931, GM. Cecil Note, 19 Nov. 1931, FO 800/285 PRO.
19. Bassett, *Democracy . . .*, 26–7.
20. EC 24 Nov. 1931, SG 4476, ii. 11, LNU.
21. Baker to Murray, 10 Nov. 1931, GM.
22. Zimmern to G. Davies, 19 Dec. 1931, v. 2, 73, Reverend Gwilym Davies Papers, National Library of Wales, Aberyswyth.
23. Murray to Cecil, 25 Nov. 1931, 51132 RC.
24. HW Jan. 1932, 1.
25. Harris to Murray, 21 Dec. 1931, GM.
26. Cecil to Drummond, 18 Dec. 1931; Drummond to Cecil, 29 Dec. 1931, 51112 RC.
27. HW Jan. 1932, 11.
28. Zimmern to G. Davies, 6 Jan. 1932, v. 2, 74, Davies Papers. HW Jan. 1932, 7.
29. EC 'The Far East', DS 1325, 30 Jan. 1932, 124, NLW.
30. EC 28 Jan. 1932, ii. 11, LNU.
31. EC 12 Feb. 1932, ii. 11, LNU.
32. Bassett, *Democracy . . .*, 164.
33. 'Murray Suggestions', 16 Feb. 1932, FO 800/286 PRO.
34. Cecil to Simon, 26 Feb. 1932, FO 800/286 PRO.
35. EC 18 Feb. 1932, ii. 11, LNU.
36. HW Mar. 1932, 50.
37. Bassett, *Democracy . . .*, 164.
38. Cecil to Baker, 7 Mar. 1932, 51107 RC.
39. Baker to Cecil, 3 Feb. 1932, 51107 RC.
40. Carruthers to Murray, 27 Feb. 1932; Murray to Carruthers, 29 Feb. 1932, GM.
41. HW Apr. 1932, 76. Bassett, *Democracy . . .*, 166–7.
42. HW Mar. 1932, Supp. i.
43. Cecil to Baker, 7 Mar. 1932, 51107 RC.
44. Bassett, *Democracy . . .*, 168–9; Thorne, *Limits . . .*, 220; Trevelyan, *Grey . . .*, 353–4.
45. Murray to Drummond, 16 Mar. 1932, GM.
46. 'Conclusions of the Meeting of March 21, 1932', Proceedings of Cabinet Committee on Disarmament Conference, 1932, Ministerial Committee, CAB 11, 13, PRO.
47. Baker to Murray, 17 Mar. 1932, GM.
48. Zimmern to G. Davies, 15 Mar. 1932, 75, Davies Papers.
49. Cecil to Baker, 29 Apr. 1932, 51107 RC.
50. Staff (Freshwater, Eppstein, Mills, and Thomas) to Murray, n.d. Probably late March 1932, GM.
51. General Council, 28 June 1932, i. 2, LNU.
52. Thorne, *Limits . . .*, 141, in reference to the 1931 phase.
53. 'The United Kingdom and Europe', C.P. 4(32), 1 Jan. 1932, CAB 27/476, PRO.
54. Simon to Hoare, 15 Sept. 1932, FO 800/287, PRO.
55. EC 15 Sept. 1932, ii. 11, LNU.
56. Murray to Baker, 7 Oct. 1932, GM.
57. HW Oct. 1932, 191.
58. EC 27 Oct. 1932, ii. 11. LNU.
59. HW Nov. 1932, 204.
60. Ibid. 211.
61. EC 12 Jan. 1933, ii. 11, LNU.
62. Cecil to Baldwin, 12 Dec. 1932, 51080 RC.
63. *The Times*, 11 Jan. 1933, 13.

64. Thorne, *Limits*. . ., 338.
65. Murray to Simon, 14 Dec. 1932, FO 800/287, PRO.
66. Simon to Murray, 29 Dec. 1932, GM. Thorne, *Limits* . . ., 338–9.
67. Far East Committee, 24 Jan. 1933, iv. 7, LNU.
68. EC 2 Feb. 1933, ii. 12; Far East Committee, 2 Feb. 1933, iv. 7, LNU.
69. Bassett, *Democracy* . . ., 469.
70. Murray to Cecil, 7 Mar. 1933, 51132 RC.
71. Cecil to Murray, 9 Mar. 1933, 51132 RC.
72. EC 21 Mar. 1933, ii. 12, LNU.
73. Murray to Cecil, 17 Mar. 1933, 51132 RC.
74. Chamberlain to Murray, 24 Mar. 1933, GM.
75. Cecil to Murray, 23 Mar. 1933, 51132 RC.
76. Murray to Cecil, 31 Mar. 1933; Murray to Hills, 31 Mar. 1933, 51132 RC.
77. EC 11 May 1933, ii. 12, LNU.
78. Chamberlain to Garnett, 2 Jan. 1934, AC 40/6/8, and 17 May 1933, AC 40/5/67, Chamberlain Papers.
79. Vyvyan Adams, Conservative M.P. and member of the Executive, used this phrase. HW Jan. 1934, 10–11.
80. EC 31 Jan. 1935, ii. 13, LNU. Cecil to Cranborne, 17 Oct. 1935, Cranborne Papers FO 800/296, PRO. 'A Boycott of Goods from Japan . . .', LNU Circular, n.d., 109 NLW. 'Boycott of Japanese Goods', 23 Dec. 1937, 51146 RC.
81. Murray to Lady Gladstone, 28 Jan. 1938, GM.
82. Cecil to the Prime Minister, 13 Jan. 1938, PREM 1/280, PRO.
83. EC 27 July 1939, ii. 17, LNU.
84. Thorne, *Limits* . . ., describes Murray as 'an example of the common phenomenon of an unofficial lobbyist being made use of by his official contact as much as, if not more than, the other way round', 342.
85. Cecil to Murray, 29 Aug. 1934, 51132 RC.
86. Cecil to Halifax, 4 Jan. 1939, 51141 RC.
87. HW May 1934, 84.
88. HW Feb. 1935, 23, and June 1936, 1. In the same way the LNU used the slogan 'The Union may save the League' during the Ethiopian War.
89. HW Dec. 1923, 464. Noel-Baker's 1922 memo, 'The Failure of the League and its Causes', elaborates on this view that for the League to succeed one member government would have to make it the keystone of its action in international affairs, 51106 RC.

Chapter VI   The Early 1930s

1. Louis R. Bisceglia, 'Norman Angell and the "Pacifist Muddle"', *Bulletin of the Institute of Historical Research*, xlv. (1972), 104–21, 106, says that 'an examination of the minutes of the No More War Movement, Fellowship of Reconciliation, and National Peace Council reveals that these groups were fraught with disagreement' on this issue.
2. HW Nov. 1934, 217.
3. Cecil to Butler, 17 Mar. 1931, 80627, Carnegie Endowment Papers.
4. Cecil to Butler, 18 Sept. 1931, 80633, Carnegie Endowment Papers.
5. Cecil to Chamberlain, 13 Jan. 1932, 51079 RC. Industrial Advisory Committee, 12 Mar. 1932, SG 5012, iv. 33, LNU.
6. Cecil to Simon, 30 Nov. 1931, FO 800/285, PRO.
7. Henderson to MacDonald, 6 May 1931, FO 800/285, PRO.
8. Simon to the Prime Minister, 1 Dec. 1931, FO 800/285, PRO.
9. Cecil to Drummond, 31 Dec. 1931, 51112 RC.
10. Murray to Lloyd George, 8 Jan. 1932, G/33/2/7, Lloyd George Papers, Murray to Simon, 9 Jan. 1932, FO 800/286, PRO.

11. Chamberlain to Cecil, 11 Jan. 1932, Cecil to Chamberlain, 13 Jan. 1932, 51079 RC. Foster to Murray, 18 Jan. 1932, GM.
12. Cecil to Murray, 22 Mar. 1932, GM.
13. Murray to Cecil, 24 May 1932, 51132 RC.
14. Cecil speech, 18 May 1932, P41, International Federation of League of Nations Societies Papers.
15. Cecil to Baldwin, 9 Mar. 1933, 51080 RC.
16. General Council, 28–30 June, 1932, i. 2, LNU. Cecil to Simon, 24 June 1932, FO 800/287, PRO.
17. LNU *Newsheet*, July 1932, 2.
18. Wright to Murray, 27 July 1932, GM.
19. EC 29 July 1932, SG 5380, ii. 11, LNU.
20. See Bisceglia, 'Norman Angell . . .', 192, for more on this. EC 28 July 1932, ii. 11, LNU. Arnold Foster to Angell, 7 Aug. 1932, K 94:8, NA.
21. HW Sept. 1932, 164.
22. Hankey said of this that the Government 'have "got their wind up" badly owing to the threats of the pacifists, Bishops and the Free Churches over the coming failure of the Disarmament Conference, which has been certain from the first'. Roskill, *Hankey . . .*, iii. 60.
23. 'The Disarmament Campaign', 1 Nov. 1932, SG 5525, iv. 43, LNU.
24. Cecil to Baker, 16 Nov. 1932, 51107 RC.
25. F. P. Walters, *A History of the League of Nations* (London, 1952, 1960), 543.
26. LNU *Newsheet*, Aug. 1933, 3.
27. EC 19 Oct. 1933, ii. 12, LNU.
28. HW Dec. 1933, 238–9.
29. Lord Allen of Hurtwood, 'Public Opinion and the Idea of International Government', *International Affairs*, xiii, Mar. 1934, 186–207, 193.
30. Murray to Cecil, 3 Oct. 1933, 51132 RC.
31. Cecil to Murray, 17 Sept. 1927, GM. Cecil to MacDonald, 23 Sept. 1929, 51081 RC.
32. HW July 1930, 132.
33. EC 2 and 30 Nov. 1933, ii. 12, LNU.
34. Hills to Murray, 4 Feb. 1934, GM.
35. EC 1 Feb. 1934, ii. 12, LNU.
36. EC 12 July 1934, ii. 13, LNU.
37. Jones, *Whitehall . . .*, ii. 124.
38. HW July 1934, 122.
39. Courtney to Cecil, 9 June 1934; Cecil to Courtney, 11 June 1934, 51141 RC,
40. EC 30 July 1934, ii. 13, LNU.
41. Buzan, 'The British . . .', 22, 23, 29.
42. HW Nov. 1932, 201–2.
43. EC 26 May 1932, 2 June 1932, ii.11, LNU.
44. General Council, June 1932, i. 2, LNU.
45. Chamberlain to Cecil, 3 Apr. 1933, 51079 RC. Chamberlain to Murray, 15 Apr. 1933, GM.
46. Cecil to Murray, 3 Apr. 1933, 51132 RC.
47. Cecil to Davies, 3 Mar. 1934, 51138 RC.
48. Cecil to Davies, 4 Dec. 1934, 51138 RC.
49. EC, 8 Nov. 1934, ii. 13, LNU. Davies to Murray, 23 Nov. 1934, GM.
50. Courtenay to Murray, 21 Nov. 1934, GM. Murray to Cecil, 16 Nov. 1934, 51132 RC.
51. HW May 1935, 90–1.
52. LNU *Yearbook*, 1936, 57.
53. Industrial Advisory Committee, 12 Mar. 1932, SG 5012, iv. 33, LNU.
54. Arthur Marwick, 'Middle Opinion in the Thirties: Planning, Progress and Political "Agreement" ', *English Historical Review*, lxxix, 1964, 285–98.
55. C. R. Attlee, 'The Socialist View of Peace', *Problems of Peace*, 9th ser. (Geneva, 1935), 114.

56. General Council, 5 Feb. 1920, i. 1, LNU.
57. LNU *Newsheet*, Oct. 1931, 2.
58. HW Sept. 1933, 172.
59. Lothian to Cecil, 1 May 1939, 51183 RC; Garnett to Lothian, 9 July 1934, Lothian to Wright, 1 Aug. 1934, 283 Lothian Papers. Lothian to Cecil, 5 Mar. 1937, 51175 RC.
60. HW Feb. 1935, 24.
61. EC 28 Jan. 1935, SG 7204, ii. 13, LNU.
62. Ibid.
63. EC 28 Feb. 1935, 11 Apr. 1935, ii. 13, LNU.
64. HW Oct. 1934, 196.
65. HW Feb. 1936, 30–1.
66. HW Feb. 1937, 51.

Chapter VII   Educating for Peace: LNU Propaganda Methods

1. Higham had made similar suggestions during the 1920s, but aroused more interest in them in the early 1930s. HW May 1925, 83; HW Mar. 1931, 42.
2. HW May 1935, 88–9.
3. HW Jan. 1926, 3.
4. In *Nine Troubled Years* (London, 1954), 113, Viscount Templewood said that 'the meetings held by the (LNU) became semi-religious services. I attended many of them. They began and ended with prayers and hymns, and were throughout inspired by a spirit of emotional revivalism'.
5. Thorne, *Limits . . .*, 338, describes Murray using it with Simon during the Far Eastern crisis.
5. Cecil to Branch Secretaries, Sept. 1935, 51171 RC.
7. HW Aug. 1921, 118.
8. Management Committee, 26 Oct. 1922, iii. LNU.
9. HW Dec. 1922, 221.
10. HW Dec. 1930, 233.
11. *The League*, Nov. 1919, 21–2. Woolf to Bryce, 17 Mar. 1919, UB 58 Bryce Papers.
12. Murray to Garnett, 12 Apr. 1934, GM.
13. Alfred A. Hero, *Voluntary Organizations in World Affairs Communication* (Boston, 1960) relates the size of such groups to level of activity in the American context.
14. HW May 1922, 86.
15. Bonham Carter to Garnett, 10 Aug. 1923, GM.
16. HW Aug. 1926, 145.
17. LNU, 'Study Circles', 1 Apr. 1921, League to Enforce Peace Papers. HW Nov. 1919, 23.
18. 80 meetings in 1918; 300 in 1919; over 1,000 in 1920. By 1921 the Union could boast of holding 'more than ten meetings on every weekday'. HW Dec. 1921, 58.
19. HW Feb. 1926, 32.
20. Official Speakers Reports. Ab 155(2) NLW.
21. HW May 1925, 98.
22. HW Feb. 1936, 27.
23. Freshwater to Regional Representatives and County Secretaries, 31 Jan. 1934, Ab l93 NLW.
24. LNU, 'About Organizing Meetings' (1938–9), Ab l09 NLW.
25. Administration Committee, 27 June 1938, iii. LNU.
26. For instance, see 'Sketch of a Campaign around the League Assembly Meeting on September 5, 1938', SG 9932, Administration Committee, 8 June 1938, iii. LNU.

27. General Council, Dec. 1929, i. 2, LNU.
28. HW Sept. 1922, 165.
29. Management Committee, 26 Jan, 27 July 1922, iii. LNU.
30. Dawson to Murray, 30 July 1923, GM.
31. Cecil to Murray, 4 Apr. 1939, 51133 RC.
32. Eppstein memo, 'Reorganizing the Press Section', Sept. 1931, K6:38 NA.
33. Management Committee, 24 June 1931, SG 5273, iii. LNU.
34. *The League*, Dec. 1919, 51.
35. HW Feb. 1930, 25–6.
36. H. Wilson Harris, *Life So Far* (London, 1954), 202.
37. Management Committee, 9 Dec. 1926, 1 Jan. 1927, iii. LNU.
38. EC 17 Feb. 1927, ii. 8, LNU.
39. Basil Murray, 'Report on Publicity', 13 July 1932, GM. Murray to Angell, 26 Sept. 1932, K89 NA.
40. Administration Committee, Angell Preface to Report, n.d., 1932, iii. LNU.
41. Angell memo, 4 Apr. 1932, K52:7 NA. Bisceglia, 'Norman Angell . . .', 214.
42. Eppstein to Angell, 8 Aug. 1932, K94:3 NA. Bisceglia, ibid. 211.
43. Committee to Investigate the Income and Expense of the Whole Union, iv, 39, LNU. This body was set up to examine LNU finances in 1935. It estimated that each branch spent an average of almost £37 in that year and then arrived at a total LNU expenditure of £86,750. Of this, Grosvenor Crescent accounted for £38,396 and the District Councils for £9,000.
44. Maxwell Garnett, *A Lasting Peace* (London, 1940), 111.
45. The heading of a funds appeal by the Welsh National Council in Dec. 1924, Ab 62 NLW.
46. Bryce to Lowell, 18 July 1919, fo. 164, Bryce Papers.
47. HW Oct. 1922, 187.
48. LNU Pamphlet No. 143, Sept. 1926.
49. Proposed by Lady Selborne to the Dec. 1928, General Council and adopted by the Executive in June 1929.
50. Murray to Archbishop of Canterbury, 16 Aug. 1930, GM. LNU *Newsheet*, Oct. 1930, 3.
51. Eppstein interview, . . .
52. EC 12 Oct. 1922, ii. 4, LNU.
53. Evans to Angell, 16 Mar. 1934, 056:18 NA.
54. HW July, 1923, 372.
55. Harris to Murray, 4 June 1937, GM.
56. HW Jan. 1931, 12.
57. Willis, 'Education for the Great Society', *League of Nations Educational Survey*, Jan. 1931, 48.
58. Ibid., July 1929, 12–64.
59. Ibid., Mar. 1932, 79–100, 83, 86, 90–2.
60. 'League of Nations Pioneers', 9 Mar. 1936, 109 NLW; HW Oct. 1934, 186–7.
61. Lyon to Murray, 10 Nov. 1938, GM.
62. Murray to Henderson, 27 Nov. 1938, GM.
63. 'Draft Articles for an Agreement between the Executive and the Education Committee', 27 Apr. 1939, Carnegie Endowment Papers, 80647.

Chapter VIII   The Peace Ballot

1. LNU *Yearbook*, 134, 20.
2. HW June 1941, 9.
3. G. M. Young, *Stanley Baldwin* (London, 1952), 129. C. T. Stannage, 'The East Fulham

By-Election 25 October 1933', *Historical Journal*, xiv. 1, 1971, 165–200, discusses the League issue in the by-election and disputes the contention that the policies of the National Government changed as a result of the election. On the broader issue of the role of pacifism and its influence on Government policy, see University Group on Defence Policy, *The Role of the Peace Movement in the 1930's*, Pamphlet No. 1 (London, 1959).

4. Buzan, 'The British . . .', 122, discusses the eight major inter-war petitions.
5. HW Feb. 1934, 22.
6. Garnett to Samways, 6 Mar. 1934, 62(2) NLW. P. J. Noel-Baker, *Challenge to Death* (London, 1934), 56.
7. Leslie Aldous interview with author, 7 Aug. 1969.
8. Cecil, *All . . .*, 187. Dame Adelaide Livingstone, *The Peace Ballot* (London, 1935), 7, for the Ilford poll totals.
9. HW Apr. 1934, 74–5.
10. EC 1 and 8 Mar. 1934, ii. 12, LNU.
11. Livingstone, *Peace . . .*, 9.
12. EC 17 May 1934, ii. 13, LNU. The total cost of the ballot was £12,000, some of it from outside organizations and two direct public appeals by Cecil.
13. EC 7 June 1934, ii. 13, LNU.
14. Herbert to Livingstone, 19 June 1934, vol. 133, Baldwin Papers. Fry memo of conversation with Lord Cranborne, 14 May 1934, ibid.
15. EC 19 July 1934, ii. 13, LNU.
16. Ibid.
17. Chamberlain to Garnett, 14 July 1934, AC 40/6/43, Chamberlain Papers.
18. Cranborne to Chamberlain, n.d., AC 40/6/50; Murray to Chamberlain, 21 July 1934, AC 40/6/47, Chamberlain Papers.
19. EC 30 July 1934, ii. 13, Livingstone, *Peace . . .*, 12.
20. LNU, 'Plans for a National Declaration on the League of Nations and Armaments', 5 June 1934, SG 6820, 109(2), NLW.
21. The total of those over 18 who voted was 11,640,066. 21YR, chap. iii. 43. Livingstone, *Peace . . .*, 15, 16.
22. HW July 1935, 131.
23. Livingstone, *Peace . . .*, 19.
24. Barbour to Murray, 1 Sept. 1934, GM. Murray to Paton, 23 Sept. 1936, GM. The West of Scotland District Council aggravated matters more by condemning the 'militant and aggressive attitude' of Grosvenor Crescent.
25. HW Sept. 1934, 164.
26. EC 4 Oct. 1934, ii. 13, LNU.
27. Murray to Syrett, 16 Nov. 1934, GM. Murray to Cecil, 16 Nov. 1934, 51132 RC.
28. Cecil to Murray, 20 Nov. 1934, 51132 RC.
29. Cranborne to Cecil, 12 Nov. 1934; Cecil to Cranborne, 12 Nov. 1934, 51087 RC.
30. Cranborne to Cecil, 18 Nov. 1934, 51087 RC.
31. Chamberlain to Murray, 19 Nov. 1934, GM.
32. Topping to Fry, 9 Nov. 1934, vol. 133, Baldwin Papers.
33. *The Times*, 24 Nov. 1934, 7.
34. Cecil to Baldwin, 26 Nov. 1934; Cecil memo of interview with Baldwin, 26 Nov. 1934, 51080 RC. EC, 27 Nov. 1934, ii. 13, LNU.
35. L. M. Weir, *The Tragedy of Ramsay MacDonald* (London, n.d.), 493.
36. Ibid.
37. Syrett to Murray, 28 Nov. 1934, GM.
38. John F. Naylor, *Labour's International Policy* (Boston, 1969), 65, discusses the *Daily Herald* commentary of 25 Mar. 1935. Middlemas and Barnes, *Baldwin*, 792, mentions the use of the ballot in this way in Lambeth North and succeeding by-elections.
39. John Cornford to *Cambridge Review*, Feb. 1935, as in Peter Stansky and William Abrahams, *Journey to the Frontier* (London, 1966), 229–30.
40. Livingstone, *Peace . . .*, 25.

41. Ibid. 61–2.
42. Templewood, *Nine* . . ., 128.
43. Hoesch to Foreign Ministry, 2 July 1935, no. 188, *Documents on German Foreign Policy 1918–1945*, ser. c, iv. 393–4.
44. Hoesch to Foreign Ministry, 17 Oct. 1935, no. 355, ibid. 733.
45. Note taken by Treasury reporter, 23 July 1935, PREM1/178, PRO.
46. Earl of Avon, *Facing the Dictators* (Boston, 1962), 265.
47. Harold Nicolson, 'British Public Opinion and Foreign Policy', *Public Opinion Quarterly*, Jan. 1937, 53–63, 58–9.
48. Nevile Butler memorandum, 'Peace Ballot Deputation', 20 July 1935, PREM 1/178, PRO.
49. Templewood, *Nine* . . ., 128.
50. Murray to Dean of Chichester, 19 May 1936, GM.
51. HW Jan. 1936, 8.
52. Gertrude Bussey and Margaret Tims, *Women's International League for Peace and Freedom* (London, 1965), 97.
53. Bertrand Russell, *Which Way to Peace?* (London, 1936), 198.
54. Zilliacus to Angell, 'For What will you Fight?' 14 Oct. 1936, N1:8 NA.
55. Baker to Cecil, 3 Jan. 1938, 51108 RC.
56. Murray to Baker, 4 Jan. 1938, GM. Cecil to Baker, 6 Jan. 1938, 51108 RC.
57. Waley, *British* . . ., 39.
58. James C. Robertson, 'The British General Election of 1935', *Journal of Contemporary History*, ix. 1, Jan. 1974, 149–64, 159. Waley, *British* . . ., 138. Waley's observation, that League opinion's effect 'on government pronouncements was strong, that on government policy much less so' is just. His further comment that 'the Abyssinian affair can certainly be read as an encouraging story for pressure groups' (139) is not.

Chapter IX   The Ethiopian Crisis

1. Baldwin's friend Tyrell referrred to it as such in a letter to the Prime Minister. Middlemas and Barnes, *Baldwin*, 860.
2. F. S. Northedge, *The Troubled Giant* (New York, 1966), 416.
3. HW July 1933. 125.
4. Northedge, *Troubled* . . ., 416.
5. Drummond to Hoare, 27 Aug. 1935, Hoare Papers FO 800/295, PRO. Murray memo of interview with Prime Minister, 13 Dec. 1935, 51132 RC.
6. Hoare memo of interview with Churchill, 21 Aug. 1935, 118, 119, FO 800/295; James, *Churchill* . . ., 285.
7. LNU leaders had opposed Avenol's appointment and had long been critical of his conduct in office. HW Oct. 1932, 181–2; James Barros, *Betrayal from Within* (New Haven, 1969), 53, 146; HW Nov. 1936, 206.
8. HW Feb. 1924, 25.
9. HW Feb. 1933, 32–3.
10. HW Feb. 1935, 11; June 1935, 102.
11. For instance, his secretary indicated in April that 'the Prime Minister is anxious, not only in this particular respect, but in any other way, to enable the League of Nations Union to have all the facts . . . in order that the great influence of the Union may be used at this time to ensure that public opinion is united in supporting the Government in the effort to maintain peace . . .' Glyn to Murray, 11 Apr. 1935, GM.
12. EC 20 June 1935, ii. 14, LNU.
13. EC 27 June 1935, ii. 14, LNU.
14. Hoare memo, 26 June 1935, 19, 20, FO 800/295, PRO.
15. EC 12 July 1935, ii. LNU.

16. Keith Feiling, *The Life of Neville Chamberlain* (London, 1947), 265.
17. Murray to Cecil, 9 July 1935, 51132 RC.
18. Cecil to Murray, 12 July 1935, 51132 RC.
19. EC 25 July 1935, ii. 14, LNU.
20. EC 12 Aug. 1935, ii. 14, LNU.
21. Walters to Cecil, 14 Aug. 1935; Cecil to Walters, 19 Aug. 1935, 51114 RC.
22. Hoare memo of interview with Cecil, 21 Aug. 1935, 116, 117, FO 800/295, PRO.
23. Hoare memo of interview with Lloyd George, 21 Aug. 1935, ibid.
24. Cecil to Murray, 21 Aug. 1935, encloses memo of interview with Eden by Cecil on that date, GM.
25. Cecil to Hoare, 22 Aug. 1935, GM.
26. EC 29 Aug. 1935, ii. 14, LNU.
27. Angell, 'Sanctions', 2 Sept. 1935, SG 7685, NA.
28. EC 10 Sept. 1935, ii. 14, LNU.
29. HW Sept. 1935, 162, 164.
30. H. V. Seymour note of call from Eppstein of LNU, 13 Sept. 1935, FO 800/295, PRO.
31. HW Oct. 1935, 184.
32. Cecil to Syrett, 20 Sept. 1935, 51137 RC,
33. Cecil to Cranborne, 3 Oct. 1935, 51087 RC.
34. EC 3 Oct. 1935, ii. 14, LNU.
35. EC 10 Oct. 1935, ii. 14, LNU.
36. Syrett to Murray, 25 Oct. 1935, GM. EC 24 Oct. 1935, ii. 14, LNU. The results, garnered from an analysis of speeches as well as by direct replies from MPs, showed that in the new House 550 members were in favour of maintaining League pressure on Italy until her aggression was halted, with 52 for this short of any step involving the use of armed force by the League and 299 in favour of fresh efforts to secure disarmament once the crisis ended. LNU *Year Book*, 1936, 36–7.
37. Cecil to Cranborne, 17 Oct. 1935, 51087 RC.
38. EC 31 Oct. 1935, ii. 14, LNU.
39. HW Nov. 1935, 204.
40. Walters, *A History . . .*, 668, says that Italian oil purchases from the United States had risen sharply but that Washington was using 'moral pressure' to stop the increase.
41. EC 14 Nov. 1935, ii. 14, LNU.
42. EC 21 Nov. 1935, ii. 14, LNU.
43. EC 28 Nov. 1935, ii. 14, LNU.
44. HW Dec. 1935, 224, 222.
45. Cecil to Cranborne, 14 Jan. 1936, 'Sanctions', 51087 RC.
46. EC 12 Dec. 1935, ii. 14, LNU.
47. A. J. P. Taylor, *English History 1914–1945* (Oxford, 1965), 385.
48. Cecil to Hazelrigg, 26 Aug. 1936, 51173 RC.
49. LNU deputation to the Prime Minister, 13 Dec. 1935, PREM 1/195, PRO; Draft memo by Murray on interview with the Prime Minister, 13 Dec. 1935, 51132 RC.
50. Cecil to Murray, 16 Dec. 1935; Murray to Cecil, 14 Dec. 1935, 51132 RC.
51. Murray to *The Times*, copy, 18 Dec. 1935, 51132 RC.
52. HW Jan. 1936, 2.
53. James, *Churchill . . .*, 286–7.
54. Halifax to Chamberlain, 26 Dec. 1935, as in Feiling, *Neville . . .*, 275.
55. Tom Jones, *A Diary with Letters* (London, 1954), 160.
56. Sinclair to Garnett, 3 Feb. 1936; Murray to Sinclair, 4 Feb. 1936, 159/73 Thurso Papers, Churchill College, Cambridge.
57. Davies to Cecil, 28 Jan. 1936, petition enclosed; Cecil to Davies, 29 Jan. 1936; Davies to Cecil, 6 Feb. 1936, 51138 RC.
58. EC 5 Mar. 1936, ii. 124, LNU.
59. EC 26 Mar. 1936, ii. 14, LNU.
60. HW Apr. 1936. *Crisis* ceased to appear after May 1936.
61. Garnett to Secretaries, 27 Mar. 1936, 58, NLW.

62. Chamberlain to Cecil, 16 Dec. 1935, 51079 RC. Chamberlain to Murray, 5 May 1936, GM.
63. Chamberlain to Murray, 23 June 1936, GM.
64. EC 16 July 1936, ii. 15, LNU.
65. EC 9 Sept. 1937, ii. 16, LNU.
66. HW Jan. 1938, 9.
67. Cecil to Murray, n.d. (early May 1937), GM.
68. LNU *Newsheet*, June 1936, 1.
69. EC 18 June 1936, ii, 15, LNU.
70. HW July 1936, 124.
71. G. M. Gathorne-Hardy, 'The League at the Cross-Roads', *International Affairs*, xv, July–Aug. 1936, 485–505. This includes a rejoinder by Maxwell Garnett generally sympathetic to Gathorne-Hardy's arguments for retrenchment, although shying away from agreement on the main point, the limitation of collective security to Europe.
72. White to Cecil, 20 June, 1936; Cecil to White, 25 June 1936, 51142 RC.

Chapter X The International Peace Campaign and Rearmament

1. Cecil to Murray, 30 July 1936, 51132 RC.
2. Ibid.
3. HW Mar. 1936, 42.
4. HW Aug. 1936, 144.
5. Ibid.
6. EC 29 Oct. 1936, ii. 15, LNU.
7. *The Advocate*, Magazine of the St. Helens' League of Nations Youth Group, I, 5–6 Aug.–Sept. 1936, 2.
8. 'British Armaments', SG8910, 22 Mar. 1937, 51146 RC.
9. Cecil to Murray, 21 Dec. 1936, GM.
10. Ashby to Lytton, 23 Dec. 1936, GM.
11. Lytton to Courtney, 30 Dec. 1936, 51139.
12. Murray to Allen, 1 Jan. 1937, fo. 'LNU 1937', GM.
13. 'British Armaments', SG8941a, 6 Apr. 1937, 51146 RC.
14. Murray to Henderson, 31 Dec. 1938, GM.
15. *New Commonwealth*, x. 5 July 1937, 160.
16. James, *Churchill . . .*, 254.
17. D. C. Watt, *Personalities and Powers* (London, 1965), 125–6, describes the Anglo-German group. While Cecil was not involved, he was strongly opposed to an anti-German alliance in 1934, arguing that proposals to that end would only create more pro-German opinion in England. Cecil to Stanford, 23 July 1934, 51139 RC.
18. Keith Middlemas, *Diplomacy of Illusion* (London, 1972), 97.
19. Murray to Churchill, 26 Sept. 1936, GM.
20. EC 19 Nov. 1936, ii. 15, LNU.
21. Eugen Spier, *Focus* (London, 1936), 78.
22. Mary D. Stocks, *Eleanor Rathbone* (London, 1949), 235.
23. Murray to Henderson, 13 Dec. 1938, GM.
24. Churchill to Cecil, 2 Dec. 1936, 51073 RC.
25. Murray to Cecil, 6 Apr. 1938, 51133 RC.
26. Cecil to Baker, 9 Nov. 1936, 51108 RC.
27. 'The Growth and Importance of the International Peace Campaign', G/4/1/20, Lloyd George Papers.
28. EC 15 Oct. 1936, NLW.

29. Cecil note of interview with the Prime Minister, 19 Oct. 1937, 51087 RC.
30. Hinsley to Cecil, 13 Dec. 1938, 51182 RC.
31. Cecil to Lady Mary Murray, 22 Mar. 1937, 51132 RC.
32. Garnett to Cecil, 6 Sept. 1936, SG8478, Appeals Committee, iii. LNU.
33. Lansbury Speech, 3 Nov. 1935, fo. 361; Lansbury to *The Times*, 19 Aug. 1935, copy, fo. 353–4, vol. 15, Lansbury Papers, British Library of Political and Economic Science, London.
34. Stafford Cripps, *The Struggle for Peace* (London, 1936), 61–2.
35. Michael Foot, *Aneurin Bevan*, i (New York, 1936), 211.
36. Naylor, *Labour'* . . ., 174.
37. Kingsley Martin, *Editor* (London, 1968), 220.
38. Finance and Joint Appeals Committee, Bevin to LNU, n.d. (Feb. 1937), iii. LNU.
39. Buzan, 'The British . . .', 30.
40. Garnett to Sinclair, 17 Mar. 1937, 159/74 Thurso Papers. Bailey to Murray, 15 Nov. 1937, GM.
41. Bisceglia, 'Norman Angell and the Pacifist . . .', 106.
42. *Peace News*, 27 June 1937, 4.
43. Murray to Carter, 24 Apr. 1937, GM.
44. Helen M. Swanwick, *Collective Insecurity* (London, 1937), 279–80.
45. Aldous Huxley, *Means and Ends* (New York, 1937), 126.
46. Russell, *Which* . . ., 139.
47. 'The Reform and Development of the League of Nations', July 1936, 'The League and the Crisis', Sept. 1936.
48. HW Dec. 1936, 230–1.
49. HW Dec. 1937, 224.
50. HW Jan. 1938, 10–11.
51. Baker to Editor, n.d. (June 1937), PI:4, NA.
52. HW July 1937, 140.
53. Cecil, *A Great* . . ., 287. Castlerosse remarks in *Peace News*, 31 Oct. 1936, 6.
54. Murray to Henderson, 28 Jan. 1938, GM.
55. Administration Committee, 25 Nov. 1937, iii. LNU.
56. Angell to Murray, 29 Dec. 1937, GM.
57. Cecil to Murray, 30 Dec. 1937, 51132 RC.
58. Cecil to Murray, 17 Dec. 1937, 51132 RC.
59. Murray to Cecil, 27 Dec. 1937, 51132 RC.
60. Cecil to Murray, 30 Dec. 1937, 51132 RC.
61. Glazebrook to Murray, 7 Jan. 1938, GM.
62. Livingstone to Murray, 3 Jan. 1938, GM. Arnold Foster to Cecil, 11 Jan. 1938, 51140 RC. Baker to Cecil, 3 Jan. 1938, 51108 RC.
63. Murray to Cecil, 31 Dec. 1937, 51132 RC. Murray to Cecil, 9 Jan. 1938, 51132 RC.
64. Murray to Lytton, 21 Jan. 1938, GM. Murray to Cecil, 19 Jan. 1938, 51132 RC.
65. Murray to Cecil, 28 Apr. 1938, 51132 RC. Murray to Allen, 7 May 1938, GM.
66. Davies to Samways, 10 July 1938, Ab 21 Davies Papers. Smith to Lytton, 16 July 1938, 51139 RC.
67. Murray to Cecil, 22 July 1938, 51133 RC.
68. Garnett to Murray, 25 July 1938, 51133 RC.

Chapter XI   A Spirited Foreign Policy: The Late 1930s

1. Murray to Cecil, 27 Dec. 1937, 51132 RC.
2. Murray to Executive Committee, 29 Dec. 1937, GM.
3. Administration Committee, 24 and 27 Jan. 1938, iii. LNU.
4. Murray to Cazalet, 27 June 1936, GM.

5. Murray to Cecil, 19 Jan. 1938, 51132 RC.
6. In a reply to the National Liberal League on 30 Mar. 1922, Lytton explained that while his political viewpoint was liberal, he had never found the Liberal Party any more liberal than the Conservative, and on women's suffrage he found it too illiberal. *Lord Lytton in Bengal* (Calcutta, 1929), 26.
7. Murray to Lytton, 2 July 1938, GM.
8. Mosley to Murray, 25 July, 1923, GM.
9. Eleanor Rathbone, *War Can Be Averted* (London, 1938), 160. Rathbone to Murray, 19 Feb. 1938, GM.
10. Harold Macmillan discussed a '1931 in reverse' with Hugh Dalton, Dalton Diary, 12 Oct. 1938, Dalton Papers, British Library of Political and Economic Science, London. Macmillan had been on the Executive off and on since 1929 but rarely attended and was not active in the LNU.
11. K. W. Watkins, *Britain Divided* (London, 1963), 86–7. Noel-Baker interview with author, 20 Nov. 1973.
12. Cecil to Murray, 12 Aug. 1936, GM.
13. Gauntlett to Murray, 7 Aug. 1936, GM.
14. EC 27 Aug. 1936, ii. 15, LNU.
15. EC 17 Sept. 1936, ii. 15, LNU.
16. Churchill to Adams, 7 Aug. 1936, File 2, Vyvyan Adams Papers, British Library of Political and Economic Science, London.
17. HW Oct. 1936, 196.
18. EC 1 and 6 Oct. 1936, ii. 15, LNU.
19. Murray to Eden, 7 Nov. 1936, GM.
20. EC 7 Jan. 1937, ii. 15, LNU.
21. National Youth Committee, 6 Feb. 1937, iii. LNU.
22. Cecil to Cranborne, 15 Feb. 1937, 51087 RC.
23. J. Pole Note 1/1, Labour Spain Committee Papers, Churchill College, Cambridge.
24. EC 29 Apr., 6 and 20 May 1937, ii. 15, LNU.
25. EC 9 Sept. 1937, ii. 16, LNU.
26. Murray to Eden, 10 Sept. 1937, GM. HW, Oct. 1937, 185.
27. EC 14 Oct. 1937, ii. 16, LNU. HW, Nov. 1937, 3.
28. The National Youth Committee objected to the Executive's call for an armistice in Spain and wanted to restore the Spanish Government's right to buy arms. Gauntlett to Cecil, 18 June, 1938, 51180 RC.
29. HW July 1938, 130–2.
30. EC 28 Oct. 1938, S177a, ii. 17, LNU.
31. Eppstein to Murray, 8 Oct. 1936, GM. HW Oct. 1936, 196.
32. Hinsley to Cecil, 13 Apr. 1938, 51179 RC.
33. HW Mar. 1938, 41.
34. Ibid. 42, 44.
35. HW Dec. 1937, 240.
36. Giles to Cecil, 14 Mar. 1938, 51136 RC.
37. Murray to Cecil, 4 Mar. 1938, GM.
38. Cecil to Murray, 7 Mar. 1938, ii. 16, LNU.
39. EC 3 Mar. 1938, ii. 16, LNU.
40. Corbett Ashby to Adams, 21 Feb. 1938, File 7, Adams Papers.
41. Murray to Eden, 28 Feb. 1938, GM.
42. Murray to Clift, 11 and 16 Mar. 1938, GM. EC 10 Mar. 1938, ii. 16, LNU.
43. Duchess of Atholl, *Working Partnership* (London, 1958), 228–9.
44. EC 7 Nov. 1939, ii. 17, LNU.
45. Cecil to Murray, 25 Oct. 1938, GM.
46. HW Nov. 1936, 205.
47. Cecil to Allen, 22 Mar. 1938, Allen Papers, University of South Carolina.
48. D. C. Watt, 'Christian Essay in Appeasement', *Wiener Library Bulletin*, xiv. 2, 1960.
49. Murray to Lothian, 18 Feb. 1938, 356, Lothian Papers.

50. EC 20 Jan. 1938, ii. 16, LNU.
51. Cecil to Garnett, 31 May 1937, 51136 RC.
52. 'The Austrian Crisis', SG9688, 23 Feb. 1938, NLW.
53. Halifax's reply of 24 Mar. said that the Covenant could not be applied in all cases, However, he did not rule out action to apply the Covenant. HW Apr. 1938, 62.
54. EC 10 Mar. 1938, ii. 16, LNU.
55. EC 15 Mar. 1938, ii. 16, LNU. Carr in *Twenty* . . . cites Cecil's comment (from the *Daily Telegraph*) as evidence of Cecil's abandonment of his earlier 'utopiansim' and says that Chamberlain could have replied that if he did hold this view he might have learned it from Cecil's earlier utterances!, 37.
56. HW Apr. 1938, 70–1.
57. EC 25 Nov. 1937, ii. 16, LNU.
58. Cecil to Allen, 22 Mar. 1938, Allen Papers.
59. Cecil to Murray, 31 Aug. 1938, with enclosure, 'Draft Proposals', 51132 RC.
60. Lytton to Halifax, 8 Sept. 1938, EC, ii. 16, LNU.
61. EC 23 Sept. 1938, ii. 16, LNU.
62. EC 26 Sept. 1938, ii. 16, LNU.
63. N. A. Rose, ed., *Baffy. The Diaries of Blanche Dugdale* (London, 1973), 107. Liddell Hart, *Memoirs* . . ., ii. 169–70.
64. EC, 29 Sept. 1938, ii. 16, LNU. It sent a letter to the *News Chronicle* correcting a report that the previous day's meeting had been acting on behalf of the LNU.
65. Welsh National Council Secretary's Report. Summary Report, 4 June–11 Nov. 1938, 195, NLW.
66. HW Nov. 1938, 10, 18–19.
67. EC 4 Oct. 1938, ii. 16, LNU.
68. EC 13 Oct. 1938, ii.'16, LNU.
69. Cecil to Murray, 1 Nov. 1938, 51133. In his *All the Way*, Cecil said that if he had voted in 1945 it would have been for Labour.
70. Lothian to Astor, 30 Sept. 1938, as in J. R. M. Butler, *Lord Lothian* (London, 1960), 226.
71. EC 10 Oct. 1938, S147, ii. 16, LNU.
72. Statement of Policy by General Council, Dec. 1938, 109, NLW.
73. EC 20 Oct., 8 Dec. 1938, 12 Jan. 1939, ii. 17, LNU.
74. HW Jan. 1939, 6.
75. EC 13 Oct. 1938, S156, ii. 16, LNU.
76. EC 17 Nov. 1938, ii. 17, LNU.
77. General Council, July 1939, i. 4, LNU. Cecil, although a Zionist, did not actively support Dugdale's efforts.
78. See, for instance, Wadebridge Branch, Minutes. 30 Jan. 1939, County Record Office, Truro, Cornwall.
79. EC 27 Apr. 1939, ii, 17, LNU.
80. HW Feb. 1939, 3.
81. Cecil to Murray, 'The Rome Meeting and After', 24 Jan. 1939.
82. EC 23 and 30 Mar. 1939, ii. 17, LNU.
83. Murray to Cecil, 3 Apr. 1939, 51133 RC.
84. EC 6 July 1939, ii. 17, LNU.
85. Cecil to Murray, 4 July 1939, 51133 RC.
86. EC 27 July 1939, ii. 17, LNU.
87. HW Sept. 1939, 2.
88. EC 28 Aug. 1939, ii. 17, LNU.
89. Cecil to *Manchester Guardian*, 22 Feb. 1939, 51182 RC.
90. HW Aug. 1939, 3.

Chapter XII   World War Two

1. EC 28 Aug. 1939, ii. 17, LNU.
2. Eppstein and Aldous interviews with author.
3. Cecil, *All the Way*, 218.
4. Cecil, 'Notes of War Aims of LNU', 51148 RC.
5. Murray to Cecil, 20 Mar. 1945, 51134 RC.
6. Rose, *Baffy . . .*, 154, 224.
7. HW Oct. 1939, 3.
8. Freshwater to Cecil, 3 Oct. 1939, 51136 RC.
9. Cecil to Cadogan, 10 Oct. 1939; Cadogan to Cecil, 23 Oct. 1939, 51089 RC.
10. HW Oct. 1939, 2.
11. Davies to Churchill, 4 Sept. 1939, copy, G/5/13/12, Lloyd George Papers.
12. EC 14 Dec. 1939, ii, 17, LNU.
13. Cecil to Murray, 3 Feb. 1940, GM.
14. Cecil to Butler, 7 Dec. 1939; Cadogan to Cecil, 11 Dec. 1939, EC ii. 17, LNU.
15. EC Re-draft of Lord Cecil's Note on World Settlement After the War, 14 Sept. 1939, 51146 RC.
16. Cecil note of interview with Halifax, 26 Sept. 1939, EC ii. 17, LNU.
17. EC 5 Oct. 1939, ii, 17, LNU.
18. HW Dec. 1939, 7.
19. Cecil to Figgures, 14 Sept. 1939, 51184 RC.
20. Cecil to Murray, 28 May 1940, GM.
21. Davies memorandum, 15 Sept. 1939, 51138 RC.
22. Cecil threatened resignation after a critical article appeared in *New Commonwealth*. Cecil to Davies, 28 Jan. 1941, 51138 RC.
23. Lothian to Streit, 11 May 1939; Lothian to Curtis, 28 Mar. 1939, 386, Lothian Papers.
24. HW June 1939, 14–15.
25. Cecil to Murray, 13 Sept. 1939, 51133 RC.
26. Murray to Garnett, 18 Sept. 1939, GM.
27. Murray to Lytton, 3 Nov. 1939; Murray to Cecil, 23 Oct. 1939, 51133 RC.
28. General Council, Nov.–Dec. 1939, i. 5, LNU.
29. HW Dec. 1939, i. 5.
30. EC 11 Jan. 1940, ii. 17, LNU.
31. Cecil to Murray, 9 Jan. 1940, 51133 RC.
32. HW May, 1940, 3.
33. HW Sept. 1940, 67.
34. Cecil to Murray, 15 Jan. 1940, 51133 RC.
35. EC 11 Jan. 1940, ii. 17, LNU.
36. EC 12 Feb. 1940, S693b, ii. 18, LNU.
37. HW Apr. 1940, 1, 5.
38. Murray to Courtney, 20 Mar. 1940, GM.
39. 'Suggested Foundations for the Organization of the Peace', 16 May 1940, 51148 RC.
40. Cecil to Courtney, 23 Apr. 1940, 51141 RC.
41. EC 30 Mar. 1939, ii. 17, LNU.
42. EC 3 Aug. 1939, ii. 17. LNU.
43. General Council, Nov.–Dec. 1939, i. 5, LNU.
44. National Youth Groups Council, 23 Mar. 1940, Resolutions, 51146 RC.
45. EC 25 Apr. 1940, ii, 18, LNU.
46. General Council, June 1940, i. 6, LNU.
47. EC 3 July 1940, S758, ii, 18, LNU.
48. EC 1 Aug., 19 Sept. 1940, ii. 18, LNU.
49. Murray to Angell, 5 Aug. 1940, GM.
50. 'Report of an Exchange of Views between Members of the Executive Committee and Representative League-Minded Foreigners', 14 Nov. 1940, iv. 1, LNU.

51. Murray to Butler, 2 Aug. 1940; Davies to Butler, 2 Jan. 1941, Butler Papers.
52. HW Mar. 1941, 11.
53. Advisory International Committee, 13 Mar. 1941, iv. 1; EC 20 Mar. 1941, ii, 18, LNU. Murray to Lytton, 12 July 1941, GM.
54. Beneš spoke to Judd on these lines in April. Advisory International Committee, 21 Apr. 1941, S486, iv, 1, LNU. The letter is paraphrased by Dugdale in her diary for 15 May 1941, Rose, *Baffy . . .*, 184.
55. Eden to Cecil, 24 June 1941, EC ii. 18, LNU.
56. Ethel John Lindgren, 'Reconstruction Research Conducted in Britain by the European Allies', *Agenda*, i. 3, July 1942, 255–72, 255. Viscount Cecil, 'The London International Assembly', *Contemporary Review*, 928, Apr. 1943, 193–7.
57. Lindgren, 'Reconstruction. . .', 255.
58. Ibid. 258.
59. Courtney to Cecil, 29 Apr. 1942, 21 July 1943, 51141 RC.
60. EC 18 June, 16 July 1942, ii, 19, LNU.
61. LNU *Newsheet*, Oct. 1944, 3.
62. Heather J. Harvey, 'War-time Research in Great Britain on International Problems of Reconstruction', *Agenda*, i. 2, Apr. 1942, 164–73, 164.
63. Murray to Courtney, 14 Aug. 1940, GM.
64. EC 3 Apr. 1941, ii. 18, LNU.
65. Murray to Cecil, 25 July 1941, 51133 RC.
66. K. Zilliacus, *Mirror of the Past* (New York, 1946), 309–10.
67. Murray to Cecil, 6 Dec. 1943, 51134 RC.
68. HW May 1940.
69. General Council, Dec. 1940, i. 7, LNU.
70. Cecil to Syrett, 29 Jan. 1941, 51137 RC.
71. General Council, June 1941, i. 8, LNU.
72. HW Apr. 1941, 3–4.
73. General Council, Dec. 1941, i. 9, LNU.
74. Sir Rowland Evans, *Let it Roll. Britain and America can Safeguard Freedom* (London, 1941), 32, 33.
75. HW Aug. 1941, 8.
76. HW Oct. 1941, 4.
77. Cecil to Murray, 3 June 1942, GM.
78. General Council, June 1942, i. 10a, LNU.
79. EC 2 July 1942, ii. 19, LNU.
80. Murray to Cecil, 8 July 1942, 51134 RC.
81. Cecil, 'Attitude of LNU towards Social Reform in this Country', 14 July 1942, 51148 RC.
82. Murray to Cecil, 24 July 1942, 51134 RC.
83. EC 3 Sept. 1942, ii. 19, LNU.
84. EC 1 and 15 Oct. 1942, ii. 19, LNU.
85. EC 10 Dec. 1942, ii. 19, LNU.
86. Cecil to Courtney, 24 Feb. 1943, 51141 RC.
87. 'Social and Economic Reconstruction', 15 Mar. 1943, 51146 RC.
88. 'Social and Economic Reconstruction', Draft compromise amendment for Lord Cecil's consideration by Mr Zilliacus, 51146 RC.
89. EC 1 Apr. 1943, ii. 19, LNU. Cecil to Drummond, 30 July 1943, 51141 RC.
90. The LNU opposed this as 'raising false hopes', HW Nov. 1944, 3.
91. Cecil to Courtney, 24 Feb. 1943, 51141 RC.
92. Murray to Cecil, 19 Nov. 1943, 51134 RC.
93. Murray to Cecil, 8 Oct. 1943, 51143 RC.
94. Cecil to Murray, 3 Nov. 1943, GM.
95. Cecil to Murray, 21 Nov. 1943, 51134 RC.
96. EC 16 Dec. 1943, ii. 20, LNU.
97. General Council, Dec. 1943, i. 11, LNU.

97. Cecil memo of interview with Eden, 13 Jan. 1944, EC, ii. 20, LNU.
99. Davies, 'Comments upon the Draft Pact for the Future International Authority', Mar. 1944, copy, 51149 RC.
100. Baker to Cecil, 9 June 1944, 51109 RC.
101. Courtney to Cecil, 24 Nov. 1943, 51141 RC.
102. Cecil to Buxton, 4 Dec. 1943, 51113 RC.
103. LNU *Newsheet*, Sept. 1945, 1.
104. Murray to Cecil, 24 Jan. 1944, 51134 RC.
105. EC 3 Feb. 1944, ii. 20, LNU.
106. Cecil to Murray, 1 Feb. 1944, 51134 RC.
107. Cecil to Duchess of Atholl, 25 Aug. 1944, 51134 RC.
108. HW June 1944, 4.
109. HW Jan. 1945, 15.
110. Cecil to Murray, 7 June 1944, GM.
111. Murray to Cecil, 3 Nov. 1944, 51134 RC.
112. Lytton memo. S1186, 10 Jan. 1945, 'Reconsiderations by the General Council of the LNU, December 1944', 199, 51149 RC.
113. Ibid.
114. Cecil, 'Note on Dumbarton Oaks Amendments', Dec. 1944, 51149 RC.
115. EC 19 Feb. 145, S1214a, ii. 21, LNU.
116. EC LNU to Nash, copy, July 145; Attlee to LNU, 27 Feb. 1945, ii. 21, LNU.
117. HW June 1945, 4–5.
118. EC Judd memo, 14 July 1945, S1263, ii. 21, LNU.
119. Geoffrey Godwin, *Britain and the United Nations* (New York, 1957), 14.
120. Perth to Cecil, 15 June 1945, 51112 RC.
121. HW Aug. 1945, 4–8.
122. HW Aug. 1945, 2–3.
123. EC 6 June, 19 July 1945, ii. 21, LNU.
124. EC 7 June 1945, ii. 21, LNU.
125. HW Aug. 1945, 2.
126. Judd memo, S1263, ii. 21, LNU.
127. The LNU continues to function with a directorate which includes Maxwell Garnett's son managing its limited affairs.
128. EC 17 Aug. 1945, ii. 21, LNU. Courtney took an active role in the UNA, later becoming its President. Courtney interview with author, 30 Apr. 1974.
129. Walters, *A History . . .* , 815.

Conclusion

1. Philip Noel-Baker, *The Arms race* (London, 1958), xvi.
2. Elmer Bendiner, *A Time for Angels* (New York, 1975), 166.
3. Robert Rhodes James, *The British Revolution*, ii (London, 1977), 255.
4. Corelli Barnett, *The Collapse of British Power* (New York, 1972), 240, 298.
5. D. C. Watt, 'The Historiography of Appeasement', in A. Sked and C. Cook, eds., *Crisis and Controversy* (London, 1976), 110–29, 111; F. H. Hinsley, *Power and the Pursuit of Peace* (Cambridge, 1963), 311, 321, 335.
6. F. S. Northedge, *Troubled . . .*, 123.
7. Leonard Woolf, *The War for Peace* (London, 1940), 127, 166. Woolf was commenting on E. H. Carr's *The Twenty Years' Crisis*.
8. Churchill to Cecil, 1 Sept. 1944, as in Cecil, *All the Way*, 234.
9. Taylor, *Troublemakers . . .*, 171.
10. Anne Orde, *Great Britain and International Security, 1920–1926* (London, 1978), 39–41.
11. Hoare to Eden, 17 Sept. 1935, FO 800/295, 234–7.

12. Chatfield to Fisher, 25 Aug. 1935, Chatfield Papers. Telford Taylor discusses this message in *Munich, The Price of Peace* (New York, 1979), 999.
13. Orde, *Great Britain . . .*, 209.
14. Maurice Cowling, *The Impact of Hitler* (London, 1975), 7.
15. Lawrence Pratt, *East of Malta, West of Suez* (Cambridge, 1975), 34–5.

Bibliography

The sources for the study of the League of Nations Union are almost overwhelmingly full, but also incomplete, because some of the group's papers were lost during World War Two. The collection of LNU papers which I consulted first at the United Nations Association is now at the British Library of Political and Economic Science. This material is supplemented by the Welsh National Council Papers at the National Library of Wales, and by copies of committee reports in various collections of private papers, notably those of Angell, Cecil, and Murray. Another valuable record of the organization's work is the manuscript history, '21 Years; LNU 1918/1939', which was originally prepared for publication by the Union staff. I am indebted to Audrey Davies, formerly an employee of the LNU, for allowing me to see it.

UNPUBLISHED DOCUMENTS AND PRIVATE PAPERS
Adams, S. Vyvyan, Papers, British Library of Political and Economic Science, London School of Economics.
Allen, Clifford, Papers, University of South Carolina.
Angell, Norman, Papers, Ball State University Library, Muncie, Indiana.
——, Memoir of Oral History, Columbia University.
Asquith, H. H., Papers, Bodleian Library, Oxford.
Baldwin, Earl Baldwin of Bewdley Papers, Cambridge University Library.
Balfour, A. J., Papers, British Museum.
Bonar Law, A., Papers, Beaverbrook Library, London.
Bryce, James, Papers, Bodleian Library, Oxford.
Butler, Nicholas Murray, Papers, Columbia University.
Cabinet Office Papers, Public Record Office, London.
Cadogan, Sir Alexander, Papers, Public Record Office, London.
Carnegie Endowment for International Peace, Archives, Columbia University.
Cecil, Lord Robert, Papers, British Museum.
Chamberlain, Austen, Papers, Birmingham University Library.
——, Public Record Office, London.
Cranborne, Lord, Papers, Public Record Office, London.
Dalton, Hugh, Papers, British Library of Political and Economic Science, London School of Economics.
Davies, the Revd Gwilym, Papers, National Library of Wales, Aberyswyth.
Dickinson, Willoughby H., Papers, Bodleian Library, Oxford.
Drummond, Eric, Papers, United Nations Library, Geneva.

Fisher, H. A. L., Papers, Bodleian Library, Oxford.
Haldane, Viscount of Cloan, Papers, Scottish National Library, Edinburgh.
Halifax, Viscount, Papers, Public Record Office, London.
Hankey, Lord, Papers, Churchill College, Cambridge.
Henderson, Arthur, Papers, Public Record Office, London.
Hoare, Samuel, Papers, Public Record Office, London.
International Federation of League of Nations Societies Papers, United Nations Library, Geneva.
Lansbury, George, Papers, British Library of Political and Economic Science, London School of Economics.
League of Nations Archives. Secretariat Archive Group, United Nations Library, Geneva.
League of Nations Union, Papers, British Library of Political and Economic Science, London School of Economics.
League of Nations Union, Wadebridge Branch, Papers, County Record Office, Truro, Cornwall.
League of Nations Union, Welsh National Council, Papers, National Library of Wales, Aberyswyth.
League to Enforce Peace, Paper, Houghton Library, Cambridge, Massachusetts.
Lloyd George, David, Papers, Beaverbrook Library, London.
Lothian, Marquis of, Papers, Scottish Record Office, Edinburgh.
Murray, Gilbert, Papers, Bodleian Library, Oxford.
Prime Minister's Office, Papers, Public Record Office, London.
Samuel, Lord, Papers, House of Lords Record Office.
Scott, C. P., Papers, British Museum.
Simon, John, Papers, Public Record Office, London.
Steel-Maitland, Arthur, Papers, Scottish Record Office, Edinburgh.
Thurso, Lord, Papers, Churchill College, Cambridge.
Wallas, Graham, Papers, British Library of Political and Economic Science, London School of Economics.

PUBLISHED DIPLOMATIC PAPERS
Documents on British Foreign Policy 1918–1939, W. N. Medlicott, Douglas Dakin and M. E. Lambert, eds., Ser. Ia, iv (1971).
Documents on German Foreign Policy 1918–1945, Ser. C, iv (1962).
Vogel, Robert, ed., *A Breviate of British Diplomatic Blue Books* (Montreal, 1963).

BOOKS
Adam, Colin Forbes, *Life of Lord Lloyd* (London, 1948).
Angell, Norman, *After All* (New York, 1951).
Atholl, Katherine, Duchess of, *Working Partnership* (London, 1958).
Attlee, C. R., *As it Happened* (New York, 1954).
Avon, The Earl of, *Facing the Dictators* (Boston, 1962).
Bachofen, Maja, *Lord Robert Cecil und der Volkerbund* (Zurich, 1959).
Barros, James, *Betrayal from Within* (New Haven, 1969).
——, *The League of Nations and the Great Powers. The Greek Bulgarian Incident, 1925* (Oxford, 1970).
Bassett, R., *Democracy and Foreign Policy* (London, 1952).
Beales, A. C. F., *The History of Peace* (London, 1931).
Birkenhead, The Earl of, *Halifax* (London, 1965).

Brailsford, Henry Noel, *After the Peace* (London, 1920).
——, *The Covenant of Peace* (New York, 1919).
——, *If We Want Peace* (London, 1932).
Brett, Oliver, ed., *The First Assembly* (London, 1921).
Brock, Peter, *Twentieth Century Pacifism* (New York, 1970).
Bussey, Gertrude and Margaret Tims, *Women's International League for Peace and Freedom* (London, 1965).
Butler, J. R. M., *Lord Lothian* (London, 1960).
Carlton, David, *MacDonald versus Henderson* (London, 1970).
Carr, Edward Hallett, *The Twenty Years' Crisis* (New York, 1939, 1964).
Cecil, Viscount, *A Great Experiment* (New York, 1941).
——, *All the Way* (London, 1949).
——, *The Moral Basis of the League of Nations* (London, 1923).
——, *Peace and Pacifism* (Oxford, 1938).
Charvet, Jean-Félix, *L'Influence Britannique dans la S.D.N.* (Paris, 1938).
Churchill, Winston, *Arms and the Covenant* (London, 1938).
Colvin, Ian, *Vansittart in Office* (London, 1965).
Cooper, Duff, *Old Men Forget* (New York, 1954).
Cowling, Maurice, *The Impact of Hitler* (Cambridge, 1975).
Cripps, Stafford, *The Struggle for Peace* (London, 1936).
Crosby, Gerda R., *Disarmament and Peace in British Politics 1914–1919* (Cambridge, Mass., 1957).
Dalton, Hugh, *Call Back Yesterday* (London, 1953).
Davies, Lord, *The Problem of the Twentieth Century* (London, 1930).
DeConde, Alexander, ed., *Isolation and Security* (Durham, N.C., 1957).
Dickinson, G. Lowes, *The Autobiography of G. Lowes Dickinson*, Dennis Proctor, ed. (London, 1973).
Eppstein, John, ed., *Ten Years Life of the League of Nations* (London, 1929).
Esher, Reginald, Viscount, *The Captains and the Kings Depart*, ii (New York, 1938).
Estorick, Eric, *Stafford Cripps, Master Statesman* (New York, 1949).
Evans, Sir Rowland, *Let it Roll: Britain and America Can Safeguard Freedom* (London, 1941).
Feiling, Keith, *The Life of Neville Chamberlain* (London, 1947).
Ferrell, Robert H. *Peace in their Time* (New Haven, 1952).
Fisher, H. A. L., *et. al.*, *Essays in Honor of Gilbert Murray* (London, 1936).
Forster, E. M., *Goldsworthy Lowes Dickinson* (New York, 1934).
Garnett, Maxwell, *A Lasting Peace* (London, 1940).
——, *The Organization of Peace* (London, 1933).
——, *World Loyalty; A Study of the Spiritual Pilgrimage Towards World Order* (London, 1928).
——, *The World We Mean to Make* (London, 1943).
Gilbert, Martin, *Plough My Own Furrow* (London, 1965).
Goodwin, Geoffrey L. *Britain and the United Nations* (New York, 1957).
Hamilton, Mary Agnes, *Arthur Henderson* (London, 1938).
Harris, H. Wilson, *The League of Nations* (New York, 1929).
——, *Life So Far* (London, 1954).
Herman, Sondra R., *Eleven Against War* (Stanford, 1969).
Hero, Alfred O., *Voluntary Organizations in World-Affairs Communications* (Boston, 1960).
Huxley, Aldous, *Ends and Means* (New York, 1937).

James, Robert Rhodes, *Churchill, A Study in Failure* (New York, 1970).
Jones, Tom, *A Diary with Letters* (London, 1954).
——, *Whitehall Diary*, Keith Middlemas, ed., ii (London, 1969).
Liddell Hart, Basil, *The Memoirs of Captain Liddell Hart* (London, 1965).
Livingstone, Dame Adelaide and Marjorie Scott Johnston, *The Peace Ballot, the Official History* (London, 1935).
Lytton, Lord, *Lord Lytton in Bengal* (Calcutta, 1929).
Macartny, C. A., *Refugees: the Work of the League* (London, 1931).
MacDougall, William, *Janus, the Conquest of War* (New York, 1927).
Macleod, Iain, *Neville Chamberlain* (New York, 1962).
Mander, Geoffrey, *We Were Not all Wrong* (London, 1941).
Marburg, Theodore, *Development of the League of Nations Idea* (New York, 1932).
Markham, Violet, *Return Passage* (London, 1953).
Martin, David A., *Pacifism* (London, 1965).
Martin, Kingsley, *Editor* (London, 1968).
Martin, Laurence W., *Peace Without Victory; Woodrow Wilson and the British Liberals* (New Haven, 1958).
Marvin, F. S. ed., *The Evolution of World Peace* (London, 1921).
McCallum, R. B., *Public Opinion and the Last Peace* (London, 1944).
Middlemas, Keith and John Barnes, *Baldwin* (London, 1969).
Middlemas, Keith, *Diplomacy of Illusion* (London, 1972).
Mosley, Sir Oswald, *My Life* (London, 1968).
Munch, P., ed., *Les origines et l'oeuvre de la Societé des Nations* (Copenhagen, 1923).
Murray, Gilbert, *The Foreign Policy of Sir Edward Grey* (Oxford, 1915).
——, *From the League to U.N.* (London, 1948).
——, *The Future of the British Empire in Relation to the League of Nations* (Sheffield, 1928).
——, *The League of Nations Movement* (London, 1955).
——, *The Ordeal of this Generation* (London, 1929).
——, *An Unfinished Autobiography*, Jean Smith and Arnold Toynbee, eds. (London, 1960).
Naylor, John F., *Labour's International Policy* (Boston, 1969).
Noel-Baker, Phillip, *Challenge to Death* (London, 1934).
——, *The Arms Race* (London, 1958).
——, *The Private Manufacture of Armaments* (New York, 1937).
Northedge F. S., *The Troubled Giant* (New York, 1966).
Owen, Harold, *Disloyalty; the Blight of Pacifism* (London, 1918).
Percy, Eustace, *Some Memories* (London, 1958).
Petrie, Sir Charles, *The Life and Letters of the Rt. Hon. Sir Austen Chamberlain*, ii (London, 1940).
Rathbone, Eleanor, *War Can Be Averted* (London, 1938).
Robbins, Keith, *Sir Edward Grey* (London, 1971).
Rose, Kenneth, *The Later Cecils* (London, 1975).
Rose, N. A., ed., *Baffy, The Diaries of Blanche Dugdale 1936–1947* (London, 1973).
Roskill, Stephen, *Hankey. Man of Secrets*, iii (New York, 1974).
Royal Institute of International Affairs, *The Future of the League of Nations* (London, 1936).
Rowse, A. L., *The End of an Epoch* (London, 1948).
Russell, Bertrand, *The Policy of the Entente* (London, 1916).
——, *Which Way to Peace?* (London, 1936).

Salter, Sir Arthur, *Security: Can We Retrieve it?* (New York, 1939).

Simon, Viscount, *Retrospect* (London, 1952).

Spier, Eugen, *Focus* (London, 1963).

Stocks, Mary D. *Eleanor Rathbone* (London, 1949).

Swanwick, H. M., *Builders of Peace* (London, 1924).

——, *Collective Insecurity* (London, 1937).

Swarz, Marvin, *The Union of Democratic Control in British Politics During the First World War* (Oxford, 1971).

Taylor, A. J. P., *English History 1914–1945* (Oxford, 1965).

——, *The Troublemakers* (Bloomington, 1958).

Templewood, Viscount, *Nine Troubled Years* (London, 1954).

Thompson, Neville, *The Anti-Appeasers* (Oxford, 1971).

Thorne, Christopher, *The Limits of Foreign Policy* (London, 1972).

Trevelyan, G. M., *Grey of Falloden* (London, 1937).

Ullman, Richard H. *The Anglo-Soviet Accord*, iii (Princeton, 1972).

Vaucher, Paul and Paul-Henri Siriex, *L'opinion britannique, la Société des Nations et la guerre Italo-Ethiopienne* (Paris, 1936).

Waley, Daniel, *British Public Opinion and the Abyssinian War 1935–6* (London, 1975).

Walters, F. P., *A History of the League of Nations* (London, 1952).

Watkins, K. W., *Britain Divided: the Effects of the Spanish Civil War on British Political Opinion* (London, 1963).

Watt, D. C., *Personalities and Powers* (London, 1965).

Weir, L. Macneill, *The Tragedy of Ramsay MacDonald* (London n.d.).

Wells H. G., *Experiment in Autobiography* (New York, 1934).

Wilson, Trevor, ed., *The Political Diaries of C. P. Scott 1911–1928* (London, 1970).

Windrich, Elaine, *British Labour's Foreign Policy* (Stanford, 1952).

Winkler, Henry R., 'Arthur Henderson', in Gordon A. Craig and Felix Gilbert, *The Diplomats 1919–1939*, ii, 311–43 (New York, 1965).

——, *The League of Nations Movement in Great Britain 1914–1919* (New Brunswick, N.J., 1952).

Wolfers, Arnold, *Britain and France Between Two Wars* (New York, 1940).

Woolf, Leonard, *Beginning Again* (London, 1964).

——, ed., *The Framework of a Lasting Peace* (London, 1917).

Young, G. M., *Stanley Baldwin* (London, 1952).

Zilliacus, K., *Mirror of the Past* (New York, 1946).

LEAGUE OF NATIONS UNION PERIODICALS

Advocate, Magazine of the St. Helen's League of Nations Youth Group.

Annual Report.

The Covenant.

Headway.

Kent Quarterly, Magazine of the Kent Federal Council. Later called the *Quarterly News.*

The League.

League of Nations Journal.

Newsheet.

Speaker's Notes.

Today and Tomorrow.

Year Book. Replaces Annual Report from 1933 to 1938.

Youth. Bulletin of the LNU Youth Group.

Youth Bulletin. London Regional Federation.

OTHER PERIODICALS CITED
Bulletin of League of Nations Teaching.
Educational Survey.
New Commonwealth.
Peace News.
The Times (London).

ARTICLES
Allen of Hurtwood, Lord, 'Public Opinion and the Idea of International Government', *International Affairs*, xiii. Mar. 1934, 186–207.

Angell, Sir Norman, 'Current Criticisms of the Peace Front', *Problems of Peace* 12th Ser., 1937.

Bassett, R., 'Telling the Truth to the People', *Cambridge Journal*, Nov. 1948, 84–95.

Birn, Donald S., 'The History Teacher as Propagandist', *The History Teacher*, v. 4, May 1972, 17–22.

——, 'The League of Nations Union and Collective Security', *Journal of Contemporary History*, ix. 3, July 1974, 131–59.

——, 'A Peace Movement Divided: Pacifism and Internationalism in Interwar Britain,' *The Journal of Peace and Change*, ii. 1, Spring 1973, 20–4.

Bisceglia, Louis R., 'Norman Angell and the "Pacifist Muddle"', *Bulletin of the Institute of Historical Research*, xlv. 1972, 104–21.

Carlton, David, 'Disarmament with Guarantees: Lord Cecil 1922–1927', *Disarmament and Arms Control*, iii. 2, 1965, 143–64.

Carr, E. H., 'Public Opinion as a Safeguard of Peace', *International Affairs*, xv. Nov.–Dec., 1936, 846–62.

Cecil, Viscount, 'The London International Assembly', *Contemporary Review*, 928, Apr. 1943, 193–7.

Courtney, K. D., 'A World-wide Effort to Stem the Drift Towards War', *Pax International*, Nov. 1936, 6.

Crewe, Marquess of, 'Lord Cecil and the League', *The Fortnightly*, cxlix. 1941, 209–18.

Dubin, Martin David, 'Towards the Concept of Collective Security: the Bryce Group's "Proposals for the Avoidance of War" 1914–1917,' *International Organization*, xxiv. 1970, 288–318.

Eatwell, R., 'Munich, Public Opinion and the Popular Front,' *Journal of Contemporary History*, vi. 4, 1971, 122–39.

Egerton, George, 'The Lloyd George Government and the Creation of the League of Nations', *American Historical Review*, lxix. 2, Apr. 1974, 419–44.

Garnett, Maxwell, 'The Psychology of Patriotism and the Aims of the League of Nations Associations', *Problems of Peace*, 1927, 326–51.

Gathorne-Hardy, G. M., 'The League at the Cross-roads', *International Affairs*, xv. July–Aug. 1936, 485–505.

Harvey, Heather J. 'War-time Research in Great Britain on International Problems of Reconstruction', *Agenda*, i. 2, Apr. 1942, 164–73.

Hitchner, Dell, 'The Failure of the League: Lesson in Public Relations', *Public Opinion Quarterly*, viii. 1, Spring 1944, 61–71.

Lindgren, Ethel John, 'Reconstruction Research Conducted in Britain by the

European Allies', *Agenda*, i. 3, July 1942, 255–72.

Lukowitz, David C., 'British Pacifists and Appeasement: the Peace Pledge Union', *Journal of Contemporary History*, ix. 1, Jan. 1974, 115–27.

MacDonald, J. Ramsay, 'Protocol and Pact', *The Labour Magazine*, iii. 12, Apr. 1925, 531–4.

Manning, C. A. W., 'The "Failure" of the League of Nations', *Agenda*, i. 1, Jan. 1942, 59–72.

Marwick, Arthur, 'Middle Opinion in the Thirties: Planning, Progress and Political Agreement', *English Historical Review*, lxxix. 1964, 285–98.

Massingham, H. W., 'Two Men', *The Nation and Atheneum*, xxx. 25, Mar. 1922, 934–5.

Murray, Gilbert, 'The Inevitable League', *Agenda*, i. 3, July 1942, 193–204.

Nicolson, Harold, 'British Public Opinion and Foreign Policy', *Public Opinion Quarterly*, i. 1, Jan. 1937, 53–63.

Parker, R. A. C., 'Great Britain, France and the Ethiopian Crisis, 1935–1936', *English Historical Review*, lxxxix. 351, Apr. 1974, 293–332.

Raffo, Peter, 'The Anglo-American Preliminary Negotiations for a League of Nations', *Journal of Contemporary History*, ix. 4, Oct. 1974, 153–76.

——, 'The League of Nations Philosophy of Lord Robert Cecil', *Australian Journal of Politics and History*, xx. 2, Aug. 1974, 186–96.

Robbins, Keith, 'Lord Bryce and the First World War', *The Historical Journal*, x. 2, 1967, 255–77.

Scott, James Brown, 'Public Opinion in Relation to War and Peace', *Problems of Peace*, 1927.

Sharp, Alan J., 'The Foreign Office in Eclipse, 1919–1922', *History*, lxi. 202, June 1976, 198–218.

Stromberg, Roland, 'The Idea of Collective Security', *Journal of the History of Ideas*, xvii. 2, 1956, 250–63.

——, 'Uncertainties and Obscurities about the League of Nations', *Journal of the History of Ideas*, xxxii. 1972, 139–54.

Thompson, J. A., 'The League of Nations Union and Promotion of the League Idea in Great Britain', *Australian Journal of Politics and History*, xviii, 1, Apr. 1972, 52–61.

Thorne, Christopher, 'The Quest for Arms Embargoes: Failure in 1933', *Journal of Contemporary History*, v. 4, 1970, 129–50.

——, 'Viscount Cecil, the Government and the Far Eastern Crisis of 1931', *The Historical Journal*, xiv. 4, 1971, 805–26.

University Group on Defence Policy, 'The Role of the Peace Movements in the 1930's', Pamphlet Series, 1, 1959.

Watt, D. C., 'Christian Essay in Appeasement', *Wiener Library Bulletin*, xiv. 2, 1960,   30–1.

Younger, Kenneth, 'Public Opinion and Foreign Policy', *British Journal of Sociology*, iv. June 1955, 169–75.

INTERVIEWS WITH THE AUTHOR

Aldous, Leslie, 7 Aug. 1969.

Courtney, Dame Kathleen, 30 Apr. 1974.

Davies, Audrey, 18 Dec. 1973.

Eppstein, John, 18 Aug. 1969.

Noel-Baker, Philip, 20 Nov. 1973.

OTHER UNPUBLISHED MATERIAL

Birn, Donald S., 'Pacifism in Britain After World War I', MA thesis, Columbia University, 1960.

Bisceglia, Louis R., 'Norman Angell: Knighthood to Nobel Prize, 1931–1935', Ph.D. dissertation, Ball State University, 1967.

Buzan, Barry Gordon, 'The British Peace Movement from 1919 to 1939', Ph.D. dissertation, University of London, 1973.

League of Nations Union, '21 Years; LNU 1918/1939', MS loaned to the author by Audrey Davies.

Raffo, P. S., 'Lord Robert Cecil and the League of Nations', Ph.D. dissertation, University of Liverpool, 1967.

Thompson, Joe Allen, 'British Conservatives and Collective Security 1918–1928', Ph.D. dissertation Stanford University, 1966.

Wilson, Francesca, 'Dame Kathleen Courtney: A Memoir', MS loaned to the author by Francesca Wilson.

Yearwood, Peter J., 'Robert Cecil and the League of Nations in British Politics: 1919–1925'', Seminar Paper, Sussex University, loaned to the author by Peter Yearwood.

INDEX

Abyssinia, *see* Ethiopia
Acland, Sir Richard, 190
Adams, Vyvyan, 118
Aldous, Leslie, 143
Allen, Lord, of Hurtwood, 114, 118–19, 123, 177–9, 192, 226
Amery, Leopold, 59
Angell, Sir Norman, 91; and Manchuria, 96, 130–2; and LNU publicity 134–5; 143; and Ethiopia, 159; and the IPC, 173; appeals to pacifists, 177; and *Headway*, 190, 201, 210
Arbitration, 58, 61, 70, 81, 120, 183
Arnold-Forster, William, 86, 181, 206, 208
Asquith, Herbert, 14, 57
Astor, Lady Nancy, 54
Atholl, Duchess of, 186, 191
Attlee, Clement, 120, 222
Austria, 120, 192–3, 207
Avenol, Joseph, 156

Bailey, Gerald, 177
Baldwin, Stanley, 5; and Cecil, 47, 49, 58, 61, 66; and the LNU, 73, 85–6, 92; Cecil's reaction to, 107, 119; personal misfortunes, 142; and Peace Ballot, 148, 151, 154; and Italy, 156–7, 162–3; message by, 170; collective security pledges, 189
Balfour, Arthur, 19, 21, 29, 40, 67, 76
Barnes, George, 34–5, 117
Bartlett, Vernon, 143, 191
Beaverbrook, Lord, 24, 68, 105
Benes, Eduard, 210
Bevin, Ernest, 175–6
Birkenhead, Earl of, 55, 59, 68
Bonham Carter, Lady Violet, 41, 130, 142, 160, 172, 190, 195
Boorman, C. J. A., 143
Bourgeois, Léon, 12
Bourne, Cardinal, 137
Brailsford, Henry, 7
Briand, Aristide, 61, 80, 83
Bridgeman, Lord, 71
Bromley, John, 110

Bryce, Lord, and Bryce Group, 6–8, 17, 27, 30, 136
Bulgaria, 63
Burns, C. Delisle, 89
Butler, Nevile, 152
Butler, Nicholas Murray, 31

Cachin, Marcel, 176
Cadogan, Sir Alexander, 166
Cannes Conference (1922), 39
Canterbury, Archbishop of, 136
Carr, E. H., 2, 227
Carritt, Gabriel, 185, 208
Castlerosse, Lord, 180
Cecil, Lord Robert, 2–3, 20–1; first governmental supporter of the League, 8; head of International Federation of League of Nations Societies, 14; and peace settlement, 15–17; Chairman of LNU, 18; and open diplomacy, 34; and the Draft Treaty of Mutual Assistance, 41–4, 46–7; in Baldwin government, 59; resignation from government, 66–9; and disarmament, 71–2; and the Pact of Paris, 83–5; and Manchuria, 96–7; and New Commonwealth, 118; Nobel Peace Prize, 128; heads IPC, 173; and Spain, 185; and Federal Union, 205; and the UN, 223; verdict on, 226; *and passim*
Chamberlain, Sir Austen, supported League, 29; advocated pact with France 43; imperialist, 55; and Geneva Protocol, 59–64; and Cecil, 67–8, 81; and Pact of Paris, 83; at Foreign Office, 85; letter to, 94; and Manchuria, 104–6; in LNU, 118–19, 128; and Peace Ballot, 146–7; and Ethiopia, 160–2, 164–5; effect of resignation from LNU, 184
Chamberlain, Neville, 4, 26, 158, 166, 189, 194–6, 202, 229
Chatfield, Lord, 228
Chichester, Dean of, 221
China, Chapter V, 154
Churchill, Winston, opposed recognition of USSR, 39; opposed treaty with France,